Learning from experience: cooperative learning and global education

A World Studies Sourcebook

Learning from experience: cooperative learning and global education

World Studies in the Primary Curriculum

A World Studies Sourcebook

Miriam Steiner
National Coordinator
World Studies 8-13

tb

Trentham Books

First published in 1993 by Trentham Books Limited

Trentham Books Limited
Westview House
734 London Road
Oakhill
Stoke-on-Trent
Staffordshire
England ST4 5NP

British Library Cataloguing Publication Data
A catalogue record for this book is available from the British Library.

ISBN: 0 948080 89 2

Designed and typeset by Trentham Print Design Limited
and printed by Bemrose Shafron Limited, Chester.

World Studies 8-13

The work of this Project is overseen by the World Studies Trust. At the time this book was written the Trust was funded by Oxfam, Christian Aid and the Rowntree Charitable Foundation.

Acknowledgements

I would like to thank the World Studies Trust for support and encouragement and all the colleagues in global education who have shared ideas so generously and have allowed me to use their activities. I also want to thank the following for help along the way: the staff of the Research Centre and Library of the School of Education at the Manchester Metropolitan University; Sarah Sheldon and Josh Steiner for illustrations; Helen Beetham for clerical and editorial assistance, as well as for intellectual and moral support; Gillian Klein for advice and encouragement; Georgeanne for faith and love; and Bob, my partner, for all his practical help and for just being there.

This book is dedicated to all the teachers, advisers, inspectors and workers in global education who have developed and promoted world studies, and particularly to that group of teachers and children who took part in classroom research to evaluate active learning methodologies in 1991-2.

Contents

Preface

This book is about ways of bringing the wider world into the classroom. It is about the 'whats', the 'whys' and the 'hows' of this global dimension. The subjects of the National Curriculum provide extensive opportunities to do this, as does planning in a cross-curricular way through topics.

This book is also about assessment and evaluation. It discusses how teachers might recognise that children are developing the skills of cooperation, communication and critical thinking, and the attitudes of self-worth, valuing others, open-mindedness and concern for the environment. A wide selection of classroom activities are described. They both help to promote moral and intellectual growth and also contribute to learning about the fundamental concepts, skills and information contained in the National Curriculum.

This book is a mixture of the old and the new. The majority of the core processes and activities described here already have a proven track record — they have been successfully used in primary school for over a decade. They have been reorientated towards specific subjects in order to demonstrate the many opportunities that genuinely exist to widen the curriculum with a global perspective.

What is innovative in this book is the discussion about evaluation and assessment in the context of world studies as well as the National Curriculum. The skills, attitudes and understanding which are the foundation of a 'world aware' person, alongside the relevant knowledge that flows from the Curriculum, are described in terms of both the principles of global education and Attainment Targets. This analysis is grounded in recent extensive classroom research and feedback from teachers in schools throughout England. Their experiences, reflections and comments underlie much of this book.

Some questions about world studies and this book

Q. *Is this something else I have to fit into the curriculum?! What is world studies and why should I take it on? Given everything I have to do already, how do I get 'global issues' into the curriculum?*

A. No, it's not something else you have to fit in. Can we really keep the world out of the classroom? Our children bring it in with them every day and they have a right to find out how interesting it is!

Part I explains what world studies stands for and why it's a relevant and vital feature of education today. It is a way of organising some of your teaching through a variety of *discussion-based activities* that help children explore the immediate world around them as well as the one they see reflected in the media. There are several activities in this section which invite you to relate global education to your own ideas and concerns.

There are lots of practical suggestions in **Part II**, where a core repertoire of active learning and planning processes are described. There are also lots of examples from recent classroom work throughout the text. Global education is also about relationships in the classroom (and the school).

Q. *Oh, you mean it's a 'dimension' like* Equal Opportunities *and* PSE?

A. Global education has a lot in common with Equal Opportunities and PSE. It combines elements of both and, in addition, suggests ways of teaching about events in the wider world. And you can easily, and appropriately, bring it into your everyday work.

It's a question of the kinds of activities you plan for when the children are working on any topic or subject area, and the kinds of resources you use. **Parts II and III** describe some of these activities and how they can be related to the programmes of study. There's also an outline of the benefits of *co-operative groupwork* and of *self-esteem* along with *affirmation activities* to support these. The bibliography will inform you about useful resources.

Q. *O.K., I understand that it's not another subject. But how will I know that the children are learning what I need to teach them? How does a world studies approach help me with the* National Curriculum? *Can it contribute to the assessment I have to do? How can I actually judge if my children are becoming more mature and having a less prejudiced outlook? I'd like some way of feeling more confident that my efforts in this direction are helping my class develop.*

A. This is discussed in **Parts II and III** which outline some exemplar activities which demonstrate how to bring a global perspective into your work as well as suggesting some criteria for evaluating this and assessing the children's uptake.

You'll also find a **Chapter (Seven)** about organising *groupwork* and observing how individual children get on in groups. There are examples throughout the book of recent classroom work, and evaluations of their progress from both teachers and children.

Q. *What about attitudes and values? The head, the parents and the governors will want to know that the children are getting the best possible education and that no one is trying unduly to influence their thinking and attitudes.*

A. As far as *assessing* how the children's social *skills* and ability to understand different *attitudes* are coming on, **Chapter Four in Part I** discusses this from a variety of perspectives.

This chapter is based predominantly on recent research in classes throughout England, designed to investigate how global education activities contribute to children's interest in and understanding of a wide range of issues. A group of forty teachers looked at their classes over a period of two and a half terms to see if skills like communication (speaking and listening), enquiry, cooperation, and clear thinking were being enhanced through these approaches.

World studies has been used successfully in classrooms throughout the UK since the 1970s. **Part I** describes this background and the key concerns which underpin it. Those of us involved in world studies are clear about the values we support. They are to be found in the Universal Declaration of Human Rights and the European Convention on Human Rights, both endorsed by successive British governments.

Throughout the book you'll find the opinions of a wide range of people involved in education — teachers, heads, governors, parents, advisers, inspectors (and also children!) about how this approach contributes to the development of independent-minded, concerned and co-operative youngsters. In the more recent investigation, colleagues found that working in this way helps children ask the kinds of questions about the world that move them on in their understanding in *all areas of the curriculum*. They are also developing those skills that will help them operate more effectively as learners and, one day, as citizens.

Finally, a quick word about terminology. You will find that *world studies* and *global education* are used interchangeably throughout this book.

The Learner's Entitlement: the world studies objectives

World studies aims to develop the knowledge, attitudes and skills which young people need in order to practise social and environmental responsibility in a culturally, 'racially' and linguistically diverse society and an interdependent world.

- To learn how interesting the world is.

- To be willing to listen to others' points of view.

- To be able to negotiate.

- To know the basic geography of the world.

- To be able to imagine the feelings and beliefs of others.

- To be able to make decisions.

- To know about their own society and culture.

- To know about other cultures and countries.

- To be curious to find out more about issues and people.

- To be able to find out and record information.

- To be aware of the causes of poverty and inequality.

- To have a sense of their own worth.

- To be able to express ideas and opinions clearly.

- To recognise bias.

- To recognise that change is a constant part of life and that we can all work to try and make this change for the better.

- To know about major inequalities of power and wealth in the world.

- To care about and for the environment.

- To know that others' decisions and our own can have both helpful and harmful effects for ourselves, others and the environment.

- To be able to change our ideas as we learn more.

- To be aware that we can influence the kind of future we will have, personally and globally.

- To be aware that while conflicts arise between people and groups, it is possible to talk them through.

- To be willing to take part in events around us and farther afield.

- To be aware of how we are all connected and interdependent.

- To be willing to work for a more just society and world.

PART ONE
World Studies in the Primary Curriculum:
Learning from experience

1

Why Global Education Now?

World studies is...

World studies teaches you that you should think what you want to think, not what other people want you to think.
[Year 6 child, Moss Side, Manchester]

It's great — the discussion, the interest, the images, the ability to travel without going anywhere! The knowledge/sharing of human life.
[Teacher, Year 5, Milton Keynes]

Finding out about the world — what's happening now, what has happened in the past, what might come to be in the future — is what world studies is all about. As the teacher quoted above says, a curriculum that deals with global issues cannot fail to be exciting for both children and teachers.

'Global Issues' is not just another way of saying 'world problems'. They are real enough and face us all, children and adults, on the television screen daily. A 'problem' seems to call for a fix, a handy solution (usually arrived at by experts) which as individuals we may feel powerless to achieve. An 'issue', on the other hand, according to *Chambers Twentieth Century Dictionary*, is 'a question awaiting decision or ripe for decision', which suggests more readily that we can and should play a part in making whatever decisions are needed to change things. Asking what the state of the world is and how it arrived at its present condition implies also that this has come about as a result of human actions and consequently that we too can act to change it.

Children may not be able to fully understand what's going on in the world, but at least we can help them become aware. World studies is the best thing we have and, against all odds, it works.
[Staff interview, junior school, Manchester]

World studies is not a subject but a dimension that runs through the curriculum, an extra filter to help children make sense of all the information and opinion the world is throwing at them. It combines a **methodology** — active and experiential discussion-based activities; an **outlook** on the classroom experience — caring, co-operative and open; and **core concerns** — finding out about all the **cultures** of the UK and of other countries and groups, about the causes of poverty and inequality (here as well as in other countries) and about the environment. World studies starts from a **global perspective** — an interest in social and environmental matters and an open-mindedness to listen to different voices, especially those of the disadvantaged and oppressed. Not only is this entirely consistent with the National Curriculum, it is, as one Manchester headteacher put it, 'the relevant cement that binds the curriculum together'.

Children cannot stop famine or floods or abuses of human rights but they can begin 'to think globally and act locally'. They can care for their own environment: playground, parks and streets; they can contribute to creating classrooms free of prejudice and playgrounds without bullying or conflict.

Children in world studies classrooms still need to learn to read, to spell and to become numerate. Indeed, in a happy and stimulating learning environment, this is all the more possible. There is no conflict between sound learning and interesting content that engages children's curiosity and stretches their awareness. Nor should teachers shy away from bringing the complexities of the world into their classrooms. They enter daily into children's homes on the television. The 'world studies classroom' will be based on balance and democratic discussion.

Learning about the world in this co-operative and active way helps them go beyond the feelings of helplessness that individuals have in the face of problems. A world studies child will change the world... later.
[Teacher, year 5 class, West Midlands]

This chapter outlines two of the major reasons for using global education: that is, exploring global issues and the moral dimensions of education. Teachers and schools will find coherent ways to help children make of the forces that shape all our lives. You support in the process of furthering ch development.

1. Global Issues

Democracy and human rights

The changes taking place now in Europe and throughout the world vividly highlight questions of nationalism, racism, democracy and social and environmental rights and responsibilities. Virtually all the children in our schools, from Key Stages One through Four, are aware of these events and issues through the media: for their own immediate futures, they need the skills and understanding that will help them become politically literate.

> Democracy is best learned in a democratic setting where participation is encouraged, where views can be expressed openly and discussed, where there is freedom of expression for pupils and teachers and where there is fairness and justice. An appropriate climate is, therefore, an essential complement to reflective learning about human rights
> [Council of Europe (1985) *Teaching and Learning About Human Rights in Schools*].

Power, Justice and Fairness

Complaints

The teachers all sit in the staffroom,
The teachers all drink tea,
The teachers all smoke cigarettes
As cosy as can be.

We have to play out at playtime
Unless we bring a note,
Or it's tipping down with rain or
We have not got a coat.

We have to go out at playtime
Whether we like it or not,
And freeze to death if it's freezing,
And boil to death if it's hot.

The teachers can sit in the staffroom,
And have a cosy chat.
We have to go out at playtime,

Where's the fairness in that?

[Year 5 child quoted in *Issues,* Summer 1986]

Children already know about power, change, justice and fairness. Being small and told by others what you can or cannot do for most of every day sharpens this understanding considerably.

They can also understand injustice and the unfair exercise of power at global levels, and begin to be involved in steps to change this. They can learn to recognise the realities of this observation, for example:

> The international trading system was devised by the rich to suit their needs; it ignores those of the poor.
> [Pope Paul VI]

The average sixteen year old of the 1990s will spend around one million pounds over a lifetime [quoted in Christian Aid (1992) *Trade for Change*]. As present and future consumers, children can start finding out about how poor countries are caught in the trap of producing raw materials such as bananas, coffee, rubber and sugar, which are then profitably shipped, processed and marketed by the industrialised nations. These same wealthy countries also discourage alternative development in the South by imposing high tariffs on imported manufactures and by high interest rates on the loans they have made.

Children can learn about this and start to look for 'people-friendly' as well as environmentally friendly goods. They can find out from organisations like Oxfam and Christian Aid how and where to shop in order to become fair global consumers.

Equality

The poem 'Complaints' opposite vividly highlights global issues of power, justice and inequality! At a more serious level, very many children in our schools experience inequality routinely and regularly. Research shows overwhelmingly that a child's cultural background, colour, gender and other physical characteristics have a profound effect on how s/he may be treated by others and, just as importantly, on that child's self-image and esteem. Teachers do not deliberately mistreat the children in their classes, but they too can be influenced by socially prevalent stereotypes and prejudices. Girls and boys are often given unequal access to important experiences — of leadership and autonomy for the girls, and of caring and responsibility for the boys. Children from different cultural backgrounds — Asian or Irish, Jewish or Greek — can feel that their heritage is second rate compared to the dominant culture of the school. Black children can experience overt racism and the more insidious inequality that springs from myths of 'cultural deprivation', leading some teachers to underestimate the children's potential.

Equality is not sameness but fairness.

Children's lives are microcosmic versions of the forces that define the wider world. They are well equipped to understand deeper issues of social and economic injustice and inequality. Furthermore, they have a natural sympathy and curiosity about the world.

Interdependence

> We travel together, passengers on a fragile spaceship, dependent on its vulnerable reserves of air and soil — all committed for our safety to its security and peace; preserved from annihilation only by the care, the work and, I will say, the love we give our fragile craft.
> [Adlai Stevenson, American Ambassador to the UN 1960-65]

Of all the metaphors used to describe our interdependence, 'spaceship earth' is perhaps the most popular. It is a key cultural archetype, full of rich imagery to which children readily relate. They can also grasp the dense web of human interconnection at an everyday level. Their clothing, from top to toe; their foods, from breakfast through to teatime; their games and comics; new films and favourite TV programmes are all likely to have been produced or made from components from a wide range of countries.

Children can also understand that this web of interdependence has a down side and an upside. The costs of crop failure in one country, for example, will be debt and hardship for the producers and greater expense for the consumers in other places. A positive aspect of the interconnected world is that the spread of communication technology brings people together, helping us to see and understand each other better.

Global education provides methods and resources to enable teachers to teach better and children to understand better the economic, cultural and environmental links that bind the world together. To return to the original metaphor: given our present knowledge of how delicate this ecological and economic web is, 'there are no passengers on Spaceship Earth. Everybody's crew.' [Marshal McLuhan, originator of the phrase 'Global Village'].

The World in our Daily Life

The World in our Jeans

In Sweden we consume a vast amount of textiles. We buy clothes to a value of over 30 000 000 000 Crowns per annum, including 12 million pairs of jeans to a value of 1 000 000 000 Crowns.

Jeans are made of cotton which we have to import, and in every pair of jeans there is roughly 2 Kg of raw cotton, which is the produce of roughly 10 square metres of productive cotton plant.

Sweden's Cotton Plantation

Anders has three pairs of jeans, so his 'cotton plantation' comprises roughly 30 square metres of productive land. In his infant group there are 15 children who between them own 68 pairs of jeans. As a consequence, their collective 'jean plantation' stretches over an area of not less than 680 square metres. How much space is that? The back-garden, a play-park, or a football pitch?

Sweden's 'jean plantation' is 12 million times 10 square metres. In other words, 120 square kilometres: and that is only for our jeans! Add to this the cotton which is used in our other clothes and we are up in an area 2, 3, or even 4 times the size of Malmo. Add to this again the acreage which is used up by our 'coffee plantations', roughly four times the Malmo conurbation in size; our tea plantations, our cocoa plantations, our peanut farms, and our tobacco. What kind of an area will we arrive at finally? Furthermore, how deep are our oil-wells and our copper and bauxite mines, how large are our cattle-ranches, our tulip fields and our banana plantations?

Who Benefits?

With 12 million pairs of jeans a year and over 200 different trade names, jeans production is a profitable business, but not for the cotton-picker. Ali is a cotton-picker in Turkey. For every kilogram of cotton he picks he gets paid 23 ore (that's 46 ore for a pair of jeans that may cost 2, 3, 4, 5, or even over 6 hundred Crowns). Where does the rest of the money go?

The largest proportion of this vast source of wealth actually goes to the 15 multinational companies who control 90% of the cotton trade. These companies are owned by international banks and American and Japanese financiers. None of the 10 million or more people who pick cotton every day in subsistence labour have any say whatever in pricing and distribution.

[Oscarsson (1992)]   *(In 1993 there were approximately 11.5 crowns to the pound).*

Making connections between the local and the global: strategies for primary pupils

1. First-hand experience
- Where do the things they eat, drink, wear, watch, listen to, play with come from?
- What is the origin of the raw materials of which these items are made?
- Who makes them and what are their lives like?

2. Personal histories
- What connections do they, their families, friends and neighbours have with communities elsewhere now?
- What connections were there in the past?

When questions like these are asked and researched, they will naturally and appropriately reveal issues to do with the meeting of cultures, about cultural and personal identity, about racism and colonialism.

3. Local connections
- What contacts does your community have with communities elsewhere — other regions, countries and continents?
- How do the different groups in the community keep in touch with the places they or their ancestors came from?
- Where do local manufacturing concerns get their raw materials? Where are their markets? What international contacts do they have?

4. Parallel lives
- What are the common life experiences of children here and people elsewhere? What experiences and conditions are similar to others', especially people in countries of the South?

Children's personal feelings of powerlessness can mirror the power relations between North and South, and equally, positive feelings, such as creative satisfaction and friendship, are universal.

Education for Citizenship

The aims of education for citizenship are to:
- establish the importance of positive, participative citizenship and provide the motivation to join in;
- help pupils to acquire and understand essential information on which to base the development of their skills, values and attitudes towards citizenship.
  [NCC (1990) *Education for Citizenship: Curriculum Guidance Eight*]

Learning about the world means learning about politics. That is, children cannot be expected to make sense of this world adults have created (either past or present) without some awareness that people act to fulfil wants, needs and ambitions in a world of finite resources. Thus far in human history, meeting one's needs and pursuing one's dreams has often resulted in conflicts and coalitions, with some groups and individuals taking more than others and holding on to it with little regard for fairness or even basic decency.

Children can clearly grasp these facts and begin to find out about the various structures and systems that make up contemporary society. They can be taught the skills of critical analysis and open debate to defend their own values and those of others.

'Political education' is not about discussing party preferences and it is certainly not about indoctrination. It is, in part, about learning to recognise the existence of bias in public life as different outlooks compete for acceptance. 'This means teaching about the nature of ideas, beliefs and opinions; how they are formed and how they can influence judgements' [John Huckle, 'Lessons from political education' in Hicks and Steiner (eds.) (1989)].

School *is* the appropriate place for this to happen; for children to learn about and openly discuss inequalities they might see around them, such as racism and sexism as well as wider national and international issues.

Later in this book (pp.74-75) there are some suggestions about the role teachers can play during discussions where controversial ideas might arise, and also activities for media education. The chapter by John Huckle referred to above is informative and helpful about handling controversial issues in the classroom. See also Carrington and Troyna (1988), Steiner (1989) and Stradling et al. (1984).

World studies, as its name implies, allies itself with a broad definition of citizenship. The key concepts of 'duties, responsibilities and rights'; of 'justice, democracy, respect for rule of law'; of 'community, roles and relationships in a pluralist, democratic society' [NCC, *Curriculum Guidance Eight*] are crucial for children to learn.

They need to be applied firstly to the 'communities' within which children operate daily — family, neighbourhood and school. Through an education that models the values of justice, fairness and mutual responsibility, children can learn to extend their commitment to these principles from the local to the national and also to the international. 'Citizenship' goes beyond consideration of one's country alone. To return to the spaceship metaphor: it is about loyalty to all the culturally, racially and linguistically diverse members of the crew. The case for this renewed 'paradigm of citizenship' is argued forcefully in James Lynch's *Education for Citizenship in a Multicultural Society*.

Environment

As our society becomes more and more urbanised, reflecting a world-wide trend, many children are being denied access to and understanding of the natural world. This is occurring at the very time when our relationship with the planet that sustains us has become so fragile and so important. Not only should children learn *about* the natural world, *in* natural settings outside the classroom, but they also need education *for* the sake of the environment. The importance of environmental protection is no longer promoted by merely a few 'cranks': it is universally accepted.

This teaching and learning must go beyond a superficial 'greening' of personal behaviour, vital though this is. Recycling and awareness of litter are, of course, valid beginnings for schools to make. Teachers can extend this by highlighting the choices we can make about consumption. They can inform students about the importance of life-styles based on a sustainable relationship with finite natural resources, and a just relationship with people in countries of the South.

Of all the goals of global education, this is perhaps the most challenging. It asks us deep questions about how we live our own lives and about how our own society and the world economy are organised. How do we individually

ANSWER:

The term precycled was coined by the City of Berkeley, California. The idea is to encourage consumers to buy food and products in biodegradable or recyclable packaging. Simply by making the correct buying choices, we can prevent excessive and unsound materials from getting into our waste stream. By doing so, consumers are "Precycling" while they shop.

Shopping Tips Include:

- Buy products which are recyclable in your city's recycling program.
- Ask for and buy products made from recyclable materials (Look for the "recycled" logo on product packaging).
- Don't buy polystyrene; buy paper equivalents.
- Buy products with extended shelf life in bulk. Examples include detergent, foils and wraps.
- Avoid products which use excessive packaging.
- Avoid "squeezable" plastic containers. These are made up of several layers of different types of plastic and are not recyclable or biodegradable.
- Write the manufacturer of products you frequently purchase and express your concern or support for their packaging practices.
- Buy fruits and vegetables loose, not pre-weighed and packaged in polystyrene containers with plastic wrap.
- Buy more durable products or products with a lifetime guarantee. Avoid disposable products such as lighters and razors. A disposable razor made from plastic and steel occupies space in the landfill for at least 450 years.
- Request an "Environmental Shoppers List" by writing the Recycling Office at 7501 North Jog Road, West Palm Beach, FL 33412.

Precycling is a wonderful term for something we can all practice.

QUESTION:

What Is Meant By "Precycling?"

answer these arguments, put to me by an 11 year old I had reprimanded for failing to pick up some litter?

Why should I, if nobody else did?
If I stopped to pick up all the mess I saw, I'd never stop.

To start with, such dialogues must take place in classrooms where there is a commitment to engage with values and an openness and respect between people. A world studies

The World Can't Afford Sweden

There are 1 000 000 000 Chinese. They have almost certainly many problems but make surprisingly little fuss about them. There are 8 000 000 Swedes. We make an awful fuss about our problems. Think if the reverse was the case, or if there were 1 000 000 000 Swedes, would the world cope with them as well as it copes with 1 000 000 000 Chinese?

We would consume more than 17 000 000 tons of Falun sausage each year, roughly equivalent to a herd of cattle the size of Northern Norway.

Furthermore, should every Swede suddenly decide to take an extra slice of toast for breakfast, we would have to exploit the hydro-electricity produced by six large rivers and build one new nuclear power station.

Would the world support 1 000 000 000 Swedes as it today supports 1 000 000 000 Chinese? I don't know, but we could think about it a while.

[Lasse Eriksson, Performer]

approach helps teachers create that atmosphere and also equips students with the necessary intellectual, social and action skills. This incident also highlights the fact that education about the environment needs to be not just about the world of physical objects and natural processes, but also about the world of values, choices and decisions.

Global education seeks to provide learning experiences through which people may take a place in society as informed, committed and active citizens who are capable of playing a part in making their society a better place in which to live by caring about the needs of all species, and speaking out and acting against social and ecological injustice.
[Fien (1992)]

Do we want to change our way of life?

It is becoming increasingly obvious that our planet cannot support the Western way of life. But what level of preparedness is there for changing our lifestyle? The Department of Future Studies conducted a survey in 1990-91 involving more than a thousand Swedish eighteen year olds who were asked to indicate their ideal kind of future society. More than half of these youngsters indicated that their first alternative prioritised a healthy environment. However, there were some inconsistencies in their indications. Their preparedness to reduce their level of consumption was very low. At the same time as they placed heavy emphasis on the environment in an ideal society, few of them seemed willing to make the kinds of personal sacrifice which would make real such a possibility. For instance, when they were asked to indicate how they felt resources might best be allocated in the future in order to accomplish their ideal, 'reducing one's personal level of consumption' came next to last. The survey also indicated that young women were more environmentally conscious than young men, and more ready to make personal sacrifices and reduce their level of consumption to the good of the environment.
[Oscarsson (1992)]

'The kids! The kids! Though terrible troubles hang over them, such as the absolute end of the known world quickly by detonation or slowly through the easygoing destruction of natural resources, they are still, even now, optimistic, humorous and brave. In fact, they intend enormous changes at the last minute.'
[Grace Paley (1979) *Enormous Changes at the Last Minute*]

Education for Life in the Future

In a world where change is increasingly rapid, we do well to ask questions about the future. What can we do together now in order to help create a more just and sustainable future?... All actions and choices, including choices *not* to act, have future consequences.
[David Hicks (1993)]

Preparing students for their lives in the future is a statutory responsibility placed upon schools by the Education Reform Act.

The curriculum must (also) serve to develop the pupil as an individual, as a member of society and as a future adult member of the community, with a range of personal and social opportunities and responsibilities.
[Quoted in DES (1989) *National Curriculum: From Policy to Practice.*]

Does this mean that they are to be schooled to expect more of the same, or will education offer space for visions of something different and better for individuals, communities and the planet as a whole?

Teachers can foster in children the belief and confidence that they do have the power to take part in change. The Guyanese-Canadian educator and diplomat, Robert Moore, argues that teachers can and should do more. They can act as 'Practical Visionaries', both instructing and inspiring students. A 'Practical Visionary':

- helps students get a clear understanding, through the learning experiences of the curriculum, of where we are *now* — what is going on in the world and how things have come to be as they are;

- helps release creative imagination as the students discuss and envision the *kinds* of future worlds they would prefer to live in;

- helps develop the skills, critical concepts and courage that are needed to make these visions reality.
  A visionary is not someone who sees things that no one else has ever seen before, or thinks thoughts no one has ever thought before, but rather someone who sees and thinks in new and different ways about what is already known.
  [Robert Moore (1992), conference lecture]

I am rich and pure and full of fresh thoughts,
Ready to take on the world.
I'm full of action,
Smart as anything,
And full of quality.
I am an egg ready to hatch.
I bring with me life.

[Child at Chalkhill Primary School, London]

The poem beautifully evokes... the concept... of confidence. The child is open to all the newness which the future has in store, and is marvellously confident of being able to shape personally the future's events and eventualities. As adults we are responsible for nurturing, protecting and resourcing such confidence, and for ensuring that it is warranted not only by children's own capabilities but also by the generosity and firmness of the world which we provide for them to grow up in, and which they will one day take over and run themselves.

[Robin Richardson quoted in Tyrrell Burgess (ed.) (1992) *Accountability in Schools*]

Priorities in Education for a Better World

These nine statements describe what I think are the essential ingredients for educating children to be active world citizens. I've ranked them in this diamond pattern on the basis of my priorities. What would your ranking be? Do you agree with these nine statements or would you prefer other ones?

Working through ideas is much more interesting when done with others. You'd be surprised at how strongly other people feel and how persuasively they argue! Both this Ranking exercise and the Sorting which follows are central world studies processes and are described in detail later in this book.

Education should...

Justice and Human Rights

Inform students about everyone's right to equal treatment and equality of opportunity and about the many ways this right is denied throughout the world, including in their own society.

Skills, Attitudes and Values

Help develop the social and intellectual skills, attitudes and values that will enable students to realise their own potential and equip them to work together co-operatively with others for a better world.

Self and Others

Help students to feel positive self-esteem and to respect and enjoy their own culture, and also other people and their cultures; to feel empathy with people whose life experiences are different from their own.

Perspectives and Judgements

Encourage students to recognise that people have different ideas, goals and beliefs about what is important and right. This should help them form their own ethical judgements, give them an open mind and the ability to listen to others.

Concern for the Environment

Teach children basic geography and ecology of the earth, and to respect the natural environment and all living things. They should be aware of their own responsibilities to protect, preserve and improve the quality of the environment.

Openness to Change

Help students learn to be positively open to change in themselves and others. Their schooling ought to show them how to conceive of different and better possible futures for themselves and others.

Learning

Make sure that students experience learning as fun, meaningful and stretching of all their abilities and talents, so that they are involved in it and will stay interested in learning all their lives.

Finding Out

Teach students about the various forces which affect everyone's life including the unequal distribution of power that exists in all societies. Inform them in as factual a way as possible about the past and present, and look to the future.

Interdependence

Bring about an understanding of the ways in which the lives of people throughout the world are linked and a sense of responsibility for other people and for the environment.

2. Moral Education

The eleven year-old quoted earlier probably failed to pick up the crisp packet out of essential human laziness. Nonetheless, he and all the others in the class had made a choice of non-action. How do we and should we help children develop the skills of decision making and the underlying moral framework for ethical choice?

> Education never has been and never can be value free... As a parent of three young children, I expect their school to have and communicate a clear vision of the moral values which it and society hold to be important. These include trust, fairness, politeness, honesty and consideration for others. I also look to the school to support our family in bringing our children to spiritual maturity. Spiritual growth in this context does not apply only to the development of religious belief but involves encouraging our children to appreciate what is right and wrong, to search for meaning in life and values by which to live. There are no attainment targets for these achievements, but to relegate their importance would be to deny the humanity of our children.
> [David Pascall (then Chair of National Curriculum Council) in the *Times Educational Supplement*, 29 May 1992]

David Pascall goes on to suggest that this can occur through the general ethos of the school, through religious education and collective worship, and through the teaching of the National Curriculum. Thus schools should provide opportunities for children to think about and discuss ideas that arise spontaneously or that are planned into their learning experiences.

Stages of Moral Growth

The belief that education plays a role in transmitting essential values has, in our century, been given further weight by theories of moral development, akin to those describing intellectual growth (see Piaget (1932) and Kohlberg (1985) inter alia). Their researches have led these writers to the conclusion that children pass through a hierarchical sequence of stages. While different authors identify different numbers of stages, the key characteristics of development are similar. Children are seen to move along a continuum such as the following:

- operating from an egocentric basis, relating judgement to their own wants;

- accepting the external authority of adults; fearing punishment and seeking praise;

- acknowledging that others hold different views and accepting their right to do so; seeking compromise and making 'fair deals';

- recognising the value of rules to maintain social order and the necessity of upholding them;

- generating for themselves an abstract, impersonal and universal set of rules based on 'justice, reciprocity and equality of rights, and respect for individual dignity'
[Kohlberg (1985)].

Whilst claiming that some sort of sequence is invariable, these theorists do not state that arrival at the 'top' level is automatic. Education can and should play a conscious role to enable the learner to attain this moral maturity.

Piaget, for example, strongly recommended a pedagogy that encourages rational discussion in groups, because this fosters both the independence of mind and the cooperative spirit that underlie a fully-fledged ethical sense. Children become 'moral beings' not merely by accepting and acting on the existence of rules, but also when they can comprehend the basic reasons and values that underpin such systems. He argued that children's 'spontaneous egocentrism' will be encouraged by working individually, and that this retards both cognitive and moral development if it is the only method of instruction:

> ... cooperation alone leads to autonomy.
> [Piaget (1977 edition)]

Through cooperation and discussion with others the child experiences basic reciprocity of treatment, as well as learning to accept the validity of different perspectives. Moving beyond their own narrow egocentricity, first to rely on adult authority and then to be informed by reciprocal dialogue with equals, young people can finally formulate an abstract conception of goodness and justice.

Attitudes and Values

Much of this book is concerned with processes that can help students clarify their fundamental values and articulate them clearly, as well as their attitudes to specific issues. I understand values and attitudes to mean the beliefs one has about what is best for oneself and others. Values are more fundamental and enduring ideals of absolute qualities, and can be very concrete (eg. to value 'freedom from hunger' is to want all people everywhere always to have food).

Attitudes:

> ...are derived from values... Thus while values give rise to the attitudes we might have towards particular situations, attitudes mediate between values and behaviour. In this way, attitudes are expressions of opinion about what should happen in a particular situation, and guide decisions and actions about specific situations that arise in everyday life.
> [Fien (1992)]

Education with a moral purpose would enable learners to understand what their own values are, to compare these with spiritual and ethical teachings and with other people's values, so that they can develop the confidence and willingness to make moral choices. It will also help them evolve strategies to cope when they realise that there may be a conflict between their beliefs. Holding a value or having an attitude about something does not lead to any specific action or, necessarily, to any action at all. Inaction is itself a moral choice. Being aware of how and why we choose to behave is part of the equipment for a fully human life.

The principal of an American High School sends this letter to his staff on the first day of school:

Dear Teacher,
I am a survivor of a concentration camp.
My eyes saw what no man should witness:
Gas chambers built by learned engineers,
Children poisoned by educated physicians,
Infants killed by trained nurses,
Women and children shot and burned by high school and college graduates.
So I am suspicious of education.
My request is this:
Help your students become human.
Your efforts must never produce learned monsters, skilled psychopaths, educated Eichmanns.
Reading, writing and arithmetic are important only if they serve to make our children more human.

The Teacher's Role

Caring

The teacher's voice is a moral voice, always concerned with the good of pupils.
[Nodding (1984)]

Writers like Nel Nodding and Carol Gilligan (1982) argue that the development of a fully mature moral and ethical understanding does not stop at the attainment of an abstract and universal set of principles. They believe that the ethic of love, caring, compassion and responsibility to others, *in addition* to an intellectual conviction that basic rights must be respected, will deepen and enrich that commitment. This is a profoundly holistic position, acknowledging and building on the dual characteristics of human nature — thought and feeling.

Thus to be a moral educator a teacher will:

- **live** the ethic of caring by letting each student know s/he cares for their basic well-being and wants them to attain their best; genuinely accepting them as they are and also allowing for the possibility of growth;

- **model** the values of caring and fairness in all his/her relationships;

- **teach** all subjects in ways that illuminate their fundamental social aspects, i.e. how people's lives are and have been affected by the consequences of human thought and action and what our responsibilities are to each other and to the natural world;

- **engage in dialogue** about ideas and values.
[Drawn from Nodding (1984)]

Balance and Controversy

The role of the (environmental) educator is not to tell students how their values should be applied on particular issues or how they should act as a result. That is, the attitudes students form towards particular issues are their own business.
[Fien (1992)]

Teachers cannot and should not avoid issues of a moral and controversial nature; they will engage in them in a professionally ethical way. Through modelling open-minded, constructively challenging bias, affirming individuals and promoting fairness and non-violence, they are being 'moral educators'. Equally, they must seek actively to raise concerns about social injustice and environmental sustainability. Later in this book (pp.74-75) there are suggestions for specific procedures for work about attitudes and values.

2

The World Studies Classroom and School

The Key Ingredients

Your relationship with children

- high expectations of each and all
- explicitly valuing and affirming each child's contribution
- enhancing self-esteem and encouraging affirmation amongst the child
- constructively challenging bigoted behaviour and attitudes

The school and classroom environment

- an affirming atmosphere based on mutual respect and trust
- displays reflecting our culturally, ethnically and socially diverse society and world
- displays sensitive to the languages and cultures in the school
- visitors, maps, plants bringing the world into the school
- resources which are up to date and avoid stereotypes

Classroom organisation and methods

- physical organisation encouraging independence and responsibility; communication and co-operation
- what counts as acceptable and unacceptable behaviour has been jointly negotiated
- a range of teaching styles
- a regular use of discussion-based, co-operative activities
- supportive assessment
- pupil self-assessment

The skills you encourage

- making good relationships with others
- cooperation and sharing
- critical thinking
- taking responsibility for own learning
- action skills for citizenship
- reflection

The attitudes you encourage

- interest in learning and courage to take intellectual risks
- concern and empathy for people and the environment
- commitment to fairness and justice
- open-mindedness and questioning

What you teach

- current and topical issues
- about the local and global and how they connect
- about justice, fairness and interdependence
- making links between the children's experiences and the content of the curriculum

The Whole School

While the 'world studies' classroom above can be achieved by anyone, anywhere, who has a commitment to these principles, a whole-school approach has a more significant impact on children's overall development. Where this whole-school approach prevails:

- **Relationships** would be based on mutual respect and genuine care.

- There would be clear public **policies** to support equal opportunities. These would address issues such as bullying, racist or sexist verbal abuse, and the effects of gender, class or ethnic stereotyping. Such policies would be designed, monitored and implemented by all the staff (teaching and non-teaching), the governors and, in ways appropriate to their age, the students.

As a staff, we are re-evaluating the very ethos of the school, and the activity (children ranking statements about classroom organisation and school rules), *could prove to be beneficial in gaining some kind of perception of the school through the eyes of a child.*
[Teacher, Year 3, Stockton-on-Tees]

- **Activities** such as assemblies which involved everyone would be occasions to celebrate effort and achievement and to share feelings and values. Local and global concerns would be discussed in ways that allow everyone to contribute.

Avove and below: Claremont Junior School, Moss Side, Manchester

- **Cooperation** is modelled throughout the school as children see teachers sharing planning, ideas, resources and support; the head consulting widely and promoting trust; the contribution of non-teaching staff being explicitly recognised.

- **Parents** are welcomed and valued.

Claremont Junior School, Moss Side, Manchester

The Whole Curriculum

One purpose of this book is to offer examples of the many opportunities for a global approach that exist in the taught curriculum. These have to do with *how* and *what* you teach and the children learn. Processes, learning styles and curriculum content are described in detail in Parts II and III.

• **Core concepts**:

The taught curriculum rests on a foundation of core concepts which bring coherence to the process of understanding the distinctive features of each subject. A world studies approach helps give meaning to basic ideas such as **time, place, cause** and **effect, similarities** and **differences, interdependence** and **change**. *Concepts such as these are the essentials that you hope students will understand and remember long after they have forgotten the specific facts you will teach them.* The ability to develop and apply generalisations is a key outcome of an active learning process.

• **Cross-curricular dimensions and themes**:

The core dimensions of equal opportunities and education for life in a multicultural society will be powerfully reinforced by global education techniques and resources. The five cross-curricular themes (**economic and industrial understanding; careers; health; environmental education;** and **education for citizenship**) provide rich possibilities for bringing together the local and the global; personal concerns and communal responsibilities. Some suggestions for planning with these in mind are made in the second section.

• **Action skills**:

The 'opportunities, responsibilities and experiences of adult life' for which education must, by law, prepare students (ERA, 1988; Section 1), extend beyond passing examinations and getting a job. They are to do with personal fulfilment, civic duty and social engagement. Students can become empowered to recognise the potential for change in society and their part in this. Children in primary schools can begin to acquire the skills and confidence to take part. They can:

• participate in decision-making in the classroom and more widely throughout the school. Class debates about school, local, national and international concerns, and student councils to participate in decision-making, should become a feature of schools genuinely concerned to foster citizenship.

• be involved in action for the environment, such as recycling waste paper, reducing energy consumption, monitoring animal welfare. They may then promote these ideas to friends and family.

• take part in community programmes to assist and befriend the elderly and infirm, and improve local services and amenities like parks and playgrounds.

• find out about the work of national charities that help people both in this country and overseas, and join in. What children have done and can do is described in books such as *A Million Ways to a Fairer World*. [Schoolchildren and Oxfam (1992)]

Global Education and the National Curriculum

How would you sort each of these 25 goals for education in terms of the diagram below? The overlap is where the 'entitlement curriculum' takes place. Place an A, B, or C beside each objective

Knowledge and Understanding

- To know about one's own society, culture and history.

- To know about other countries, cultures and histories.

- To know about the links between our lives and others throughout the world.

- To know about the various forces that shape our lives, including the major inequalities of wealth and power in the world.

- To know about the basic geography of the earth and how plants, animals and people co-exist.

- To recognise that the mass media is the main channel of information we have about the world and to be aware of bias and selectivity.

Skills

- To be able to express ideas and opinions and explain facts clearly through talking and writing.

- To be able to work collaboratively and cooperatively with others to solve problems and share ideas.

- To be able to handle controversy and to identify solutions that take others into account.

- To be able to use one's own judgement to decide on moral rights and wrongs.

- To be able to imagine the feelings and beliefs of others.

- To be able to negotiate and make decisions about matters which affect ourselves and others.

- To recognise bias.

- To approach issues with an open and questioning mind.

- To be able to change our ideas as we learn more.

- To listen to others' points of view.

Attitudes

- To have an optimistic concern for local and global issues.

- To be curious to find out more about people and issues.

- To have a sense of one's own worth and to believe that one can meet challenges with competence.

- To value, appreciate and enjoy a diversity of culture, including one's own.

- To be prepared to stand up for one's own rights, and for those of other people.

- To care about and for the environment.

- To be aware that we can influence the kind of future we will have, personally and globally.

- To be willing to take part and work together with others to promote democracy, and to work for a more just world.

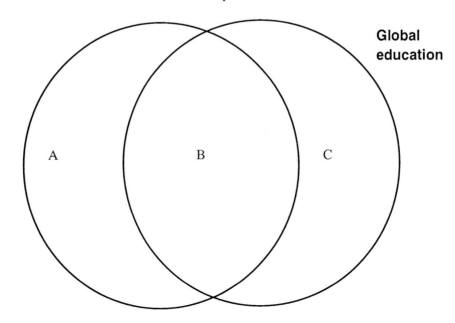

The basic curriculum

Global education

A   B   C

A letter from the Japanese Translator of the *World Studies 8-13 Teachers' Handbook*

Tokyo
13 February 1992

Dear Miriam,

I'm really excited and wanted to share this experience with you straight away. This evening we went out with a group of reporters from the *Japan Times* (an English language paper here in Tokyo); *Asahi Shinbun* (the *Independent* or *Guardian* equivalent in Japan); NHK (the national TV network) and also the chief editor of the national teachers' weekly. When we translated the *World Studies 8-13 Teachers' Handbook* in 1991, *Asahi Shinbun* had actually reviewed it by reproducing two of the activities! I'm sure you want to know what their judgement was. The article, published in November, included this:

'How can we teach children of age eight through thirteen about our modern world? As an effort to answer that question, a teaching manual was put together in Britain and translated into Japanese. This World Studies Manabikata/Oshiekata Handbook has in it plenty of seeds for such classroom lessons that would be fun.'

I think also you'll be really interested in what the editor of the teachers' paper said. He thought we're doing the right thing at the right time, and he said this in a really enthusiastic way.

I don't know... perhaps there should be a sensational campaign in Britain to say 'Don't Japanese Our Education — do we want our children crushed to death by school gates?' Our education is so rigid and inflexible, it doesn't suit living natures. That's why these many people here are interested in the world studies approach. They feel that what we have is not right and they are trying to find a way out. Very many Japanese feel our system is wrong and wonder why on earth you seem to want it in Britain!...

Anyway, I have just wanted to share with you the feeling I've got this evening that our approach will be gradually adopted in my country. I hope you're fine and that you are not depressed or tired by what is happening in your education system. You have enthusiastic colleagues here!

Lots of love,

Noko

3

World Studies in Schools Now

Evaluating the effectiveness of active learning methods

My interest developed out of a sense of and for justice. Not to impose my views, but to allow students the opportunity to realise that they are part of one world, and that what they do can, and may, affect people in their own area and elsewhere around the world. Students also deserve to have interesting lessons — to look at, consider and voice opinions about issues! To deny them this opportunity is to deny them the truth.
[Teacher, Year 9, Birmingham]

This book came to be written after an intensive investigation into how far the discussion-based, experiential and cooperative groupwork activities described in *World Studies 8-13: A Teacher's Handbook,* in *Making Global Connections: A World Studies Workbook* and other global education books do contribute to the process of children developing the skills and attitudes described above. Do these kinds of activity help them understand very basic concepts — like **interdependence, justice, change**? Will children demonstrate greater tolerance and understanding of difference — different places and ways of life — and greater intolerance of racism, sexism and all kinds of discrimination? After a decade of world studies and development education, and in the light of the new curriculum, it seemed vital to find out.

This enquiry was carried out in two ways. One was to ask the people who had been involved with and used global education approaches over the years for their judgements.

Almost two hundred people expressed their opinions, through direct interviews, anonymous questionnaires or personal letters. Their judgements and comments and those of teachers and children in schools now are the source of many of the statements made throughout this book about the effectiveness of global education.

What about world studies now? With all the changes teachers have had to absorb, how do they regard the methodology and the content of the global approach? A group of forty teachers throughout England, from Tyneside to Bournemouth, took part in a classroom research exercise during 1991-92, at the very time when they were also introducing the new History and Geography curricula. The three core activities they used — Diamond Ranking, Jigsaw Photographs and Magic Microphone — are described in Part II, Chapter Nine.

These teachers watched and listened to small groups of children, aged between 6 and 13, over two and a half terms. The majority were in the 7-11 age group. The children were involved in activities which gave them scope to talk, listen, work cooperatively, make decisions and consider some wider issues. The topics they discussed included the environment, views about other countries, gender roles, how their classrooms and playgrounds were organised, and their hopes for the future. The teachers planned lessons within the framework of the National Curriculum, recorded what the children did and said, and assessed whether each child was growing in awareness, cooperation and communication. The conclusions they reached were that yes, they can and they do, and yes, such work is really vital because of the attitudes children have towards themselves and others.

Numbers of children and schools involved

	evidence from both terms	autumn term '91	spring term '92	total number
schools	21	31	24*	34
classes	27	42	30**	45
children	216	336	240	360

* Three new schools took part   ** One school where five classes had taken part dropped out.

Observations arising from this research

A. Children's learning: some general conclusions

- Children really enjoy working in this active, open-ended way.

- The teachers who took part in interviews, questionnaires and in the classroom exercise generally agreed that these approaches do develop communication and cooperation skills. A large number also felt that the children's thinking skills were extended.

- Children's awareness and understanding of global issues can be enhanced through this approach if teachers provide opportunities and use resources that address global issues.

- Children's ideas and attitudes are powerfully influenced by experiences outside the school — by the significant adults in their lives, by the media, by the interchange of opinions within their peer group.

- Many children, especially amongst those with no family or historical links to the South, have ideas and attitudes which are in a general sense, 'negative'. They see life in the South as unattractive, poverty- and disease-ridden; people from other countries as having strange customs; a person's gender as determining what is 'appropriate' behaviour for them. *'Different from' is generally construed as 'worse than'.*

- Children can and do become more open-minded and prepared to question these assumptions in the context of discussion activities when they can examine evidence that challenges them.

- Discussion activities that encourage them to engage with evidence and decision-making can contribute to greater flexibility and tentativeness — the ability to question assumptions and accept uncertainty. Parts II and III of this book provide more detail about such activities.

B. Children's learning: specific research findings

- Children gain confidence and communication skills through addressing issues and sharing opinions in small groups.

- Structured active learning exercises help children to make gains in individual oracy skills (e.g. expressing thoughts and feelings, listening) and in cognitive processes (e.g. forming and testing hypotheses, presenting arguments, analysing ideas).

- These activities also lead to gains in working effectively and cooperatively with others.

- Development of a more positive self-concept through these methodologies appears to be more age-related.

- Children in the 6-14 age range enjoy participating in discussion activities which have a clear structure and direction, and for which they can see a purpose.

- Children can identify the various skills they are using in these activities, eg. listening, explaining, and so forth.

- Even quite young children are able to perceive and articulate the more implicit characteristics of these discussion activities, eg. the importance of attending to what others think.

- Up to 70% of children investigated believe that they are 'learning' through open-ended discussion activities.

- Children can develop the skills, knowledge and understanding described in the World Studies 8-13 objectives if they are given opportunities to consider appropriate and relevant information, and to engage in active learning processes.

- They can also be working towards the specific learning objectives within the National Curriculum at the same time.

Very similar findings to these are reported from other recent research into how children function socially and intellectually in groups, as well as how they feel about the experience. See Bennett and Dunne (1992) and Galton and Williamson (1992).

C. World studies and the whole school

- The majority of teachers in the classroom project as well as the others contacted believed that a *whole-school approach* would have a more significant impact on children's overall development (conceptually, socially and in skills and knowledge).

- A whole-school approach is characterised as one where the general atmosphere is caring, where the individual (child and adult) is both valued and respected, and where exploration of issues through discussion and exchange of ideas is encouraged and supported.

- The support of the headteacher and a sympathetic attitude in the school contribute importantly to a teacher's involvement in world studies work. It is not a determining factor: there are committed headteachers with uninterested staff as well as enthusiastic teachers with neutral or negative headteachers and colleagues.

D. General conclusions and reflections on the classroom investigation

There is no irrefutable evidence that working in collaborative groups or participatory exercises, or discussing global issues such as the environment, development and human rights in an open-ended way, make young people any more likely to take part in social action outside the school than any other style of education. Neither can this investigation, in common with others that have preceded it, prove that specific techniques or curricular input can be used to form attitudes (see, *inter alia*, Jungkunz (1987), Mares and Harris (1987) and Unesco (1965)).

Nonetheless, the evidence of this research points to positive gains in understanding and skills, and to a greater willingness to consider a range of perspectives. The classroom investigation, the interviews, the written testimonies and the questionnaires all suggest that when children work in small groups, discussing an issue and sharing opinions on it, they gain confidence and skill in communication. Both the classroom study and the many people who shared their experiences with me testified that you can see a positive change in the overall atmosphere of the classroom and school. This is surely a good thing for all involved in the daily experience of school life and a highly convincing argument for world studies.

Or is it this...?

Tries to counter inequality and injustice

An open mind, and ears that listen to and take account of others

Recognises gaps in knowledge of global issues

...

and is committed to finding out more

A caring heart

Accepts the value of active learning and uses it as much as possible

Still needs stamina!

Is it this?

Serene, warm, involved. Totally calm in all situations

Clear thinker, forward planner. Yet capable of brilliant spontaneous lessons

Highly creative at arts, crafts, structuring all hands-on experiences

Tireless champion of all good causes

Inexhaustible energy

Complete knowledge of global history, current issues, geography

Making Global Connections, Hicks and Steiner (eds), Oliver & Boyd, 1989.

World Studies: Experiences, Views and Visions

The diagram on page 22 is the professional and personal profile completed by teachers who took part in an investigation into the effectiveness of world studies-methodologies. The original was spread over two pages to give plenty of room for teachers' opinions and views. The feelings of these 'world studies' teachers about why and how they teach, and also about what they want to achieve, are very similar to those reported by Jennifer Nias after a ten year study, in *Primary Teachers Talking* (1989).

Teaching is not just a job; most of us do it because we have a strong concern for others and a vision about helping children grow to be happy and productive people.

Discussing their 'purposes of education', most of the people responding to the questionnaire which follows used phrases such as '*develop children's full potential*', '*develop the 'whole' child*', '*develop skills useful for all of life*', '*produce citizens who are confident, knowledgeable and able to take their place in the world*'.

What are *your* thoughts and feelings? Whether you are new to global education or have been using these ideas for some time, you too may find this an interesting exercise.

World Studies: Experiences, Views and Visions

1. Experience

I have been a teacher for................ years. I have worked in this school for.................. years.

This class is new to me/ I'm familiar with these children.

In general, this school is/is not supportive of a world studies approach.

I am coming fresh to/have some experience of/am very familiar with an activity and issue based way of working.

2. Views and Visions

To me, the purposes of education are:

I would describe my teaching style as:

I think children learn best when:

In my judgement, world studies/global education is about:

I find world studies/global education sympathetic because:

I'd know that world studies was successful in the school when I'd see or hear

    a.   in the classroom:

    b.   in the playground:

    c.   when my colleagues also:

    d.   when the headteacher:

    e.   when the children, wherever they were:

Things going on in the world which depress or worry me are:

Things going on in the world which excite me are:

I think I'm an optimistic/pessimistic person.

4

Learning from Experience: Approaches to Assessment

'Five more smiles an hour': Learning and development in global education

In this chapter I discuss how a world studies approach to assessment can help you find out about how the development of the whole child is taking place. We look at how we might recognise when a child is developing the skills, attitudes and knowledge of a junior 'global citizen'. We also review some principles of the assessment process and how the exercise of finding out what children 'know and can do' can be related to our definition of world-awareness. The criteria are drawn from what teachers experienced in world studies believe are both reasonable and achievable.

> *Within the next few years, as the National Curriculum develops, I feel that the esteem of many of our children will be threatened and/or suffer and the profiling system, into which I incorporate world studies strategies, can counteract this.*
> [Manchester teacher (1992)]

Assessing 'sensitivity' and understanding?

World studies has been an influence on the curriculum since the 1970s and the *World Studies 8-13 Project* in particular since 1980. (A useful overview of the movement for education for international understanding is Graham Pike's 'Global Education: Learning in a World of Change' in Dufour ed., (1990).) Teachers, headteachers, parents, inspectors, and HMI have stated repeatedly that 'it works', that children are attaining the skills and learning about the kinds of issues, in the kind of atmosphere and in the kinds of ways that give them a good start for becoming independent and open-minded, concerned people. The comments and observations of two hundred such people underlie this book.

From: C. McFarlane and S. Sinclair (1986) *A Sense of School* (Birmingham DEC)

With recent attention focused on appropriate and consistent ways of assessing and recording attainment in education, it is important to look at world studies approaches in similar ways. Global education addresses the concepts, attitudes, skills and knowledge (CASK) that prepare children for life more widely, in their school careers and beyond. The kinds of evidence that teachers need to see, to check that their efforts in planning and teaching are succeeding, can be less clear cut and appear less straightforward than in some other areas of learning. This is because learning in world studies is about integrating objective knowledge, cognitive and social skills, and personal values in a way that is personally meaningful to the learner.

You can find out whether children know what the words *cooperation* or *justice* mean; you can't give a mark out of ten for how cooperatively or justly they behave. You can test if they know facts about both their own and other countries and cultures; you can't grade their sense of interdependence or lack of prejudices. However, this does not mean that it is either inappropriate or impossible to attempt to see if these kinds of skills or attitudes are growing. Yet, as in Religious Education, there are elements of global education which are not appropriate to assess:

1. **matters which pupils may wish to keep to themselves**

   This means that pupils should never be pressurised into disclosing personal or private information, and no assessment or judgement should be made of their willingness or unwillingness to do so.

2. **whether pupils' own beliefs and values are 'right' or 'wrong'.**

   [The Regional R.E. Centre (Midlands), Westhill College (1991)]

What you are looking for and how you define development are the key questions. Are 'performance indicators' and attainment targets the most appropriate concepts in such contexts?

At root here is a fundamental dilemma. Those personal qualities that we hold dear — resilience and courage in the face of stress, a sense of craft in our work, a commitment to justice and caring in our personal relationships, a dedication to advancing the public good in our communal life — are exceedingly difficult to assess. And so unfortunately, we are apt to measure what we can, and *eventually come to value what is measured over what is left unmeasured.* The shift is subtle, and occurs gradually. It first invades our language and then slowly begins to dominate our thinking. It is all around us, and we too are part of it.

In neither academic nor popular discourse about schools does one find nowadays much reference to the important human qualities listed above. The language of academic achievement tests has become the primary rhetoric of schooling.
[Committee of the National Academy of Education, quoted in *Education Counts: an Indicator System to Monitor the Nation's Educational Health*, Special Study Panel on Education Indicators, Department of Education, Washington DC (1991)].

In this area of assessment, as in all others, common sense, honest and open sensitivity to children and a personal awareness of the world are the tools a teacher needs. Whether in the realms of knowledge, skills or attitudes, or in grasping the key concepts that bind the content of separate areas together, looking for and assessing development will be based on 'sensitive attention to the initial conditions'; knowing the class, child by child, and being attuned to those shifts, however small, that can show an aware observer that something has grown or changed within the child. It may be in her level of self-confidence that gives her greater fluency in expressing thoughts or taking more initiatives. It may be the things he says about something he's heard on the TV or in the way he handles himself in disagreements with others.

These developments are all observable and they are 'assessable'. By this I mean that a 'tuned in' teacher can describe whether there is *more or less* of a particular kind of behaviour, whether it happens *more or less often,* and *for longer periods of time,* what *kinds of* work and social *strategies* the child is choosing. This is not to suggest some form of crude measurement system of pluses and minuses in social skills and 'correct' attitudes, what might be called the 'good citizenship complex', in which personal quirks and rough edges are not allowed! Knowing the directions in which you and the school policy — as defined by staff, parents and governors — hope students will be moving, you can begin to form conclusions about individuals and plan opportunities.

In education there are very few times one can say that input produced that output, but over a period of four or five years I am sure that the ethos, the personality, the character of the school reflected by the children has changed, in the way we wanted it to change... We are very proud of the children, the product at the end of the day, because they are, on the whole, confident, articulate, pleasant, well adjusted children who in school work well together with other children, with adults and with strangers who come into the school. We have children who are aware of issues that arise from the work we intended to aim at in terms of cooperation, understanding of other

cultures, sensitivity towards other people's feelings, fairness and justice. It's particularly noticeable that our Year 6 children are able to articulate some quite abstract concepts and I think that's quite a significant achievement. I don't think they would be doing that unless they had been through four years of world studies, to whatever degree.
[Headteacher: urban inner city school (1992)]

Individual development can be recorded in the personal profiles, which has the additional advantage of involving the children in registering their comments too. As you enrich the programmes of study with the global dimension, you will be providing 'added value' to standard assessment. The attainment that is being recorded will be enhanced and expanded when the perspectives of global education are woven into the curriculum.

World studies and assessment: education *about, through* and *for* global awareness

A classroom run on the lines of cooperation, affirmation, and genuine equal opportunities will be a much easier place in which to observe real learning. Relationships which are equal and friendly enable children better to display competence and to extend their expertise. Two decades of research into the impact on learning of positive self-esteem and an affirming classroom bear this out (see Bibliography). A recent work, *Group work in the Primary Classroom* (Galton and Williamson (1992)) provides striking evidence of how children often regard the classroom as hostile territory in which they will be judged failures. This will be discussed in more detail below.

A world studies approach to assessment is about...

Values

> Education is inherently about values: it reflects a vision of the kind of world we want our children to inherit; a vision of the kinds of people we hope they will become; a vision of what it is to be an educated person.
> [Alexander (1992), p. 188]

Where are you starting from? Where do you want to get to? Do your basic values about the purposes of education and the practices you adopt to provide this, match? Do you regard assessment as a tool that will enable you to meet children's needs and help them realise their potential?

(All the boxed statements which follow come from the group of teachers evaluating global education methods during 1991-2.)

To me, the purposes of education are:

To develop children academically, socially, spiritually, aesthetically. To encourage each one to be critical and aware human beings.

To expand people's horizons, thoughts etc., to give confidence to each student, to make them feel positive about themselves so they can try to deal with life's problems.

Success for me is when children freely discuss issues together without my involvement. When they comfortably discuss and argue their own points of view.

Feelings

Where are your children and you yourself starting from? Extensive research has demonstrated the importance of self-esteem for engagement with learning, for getting on with others, for wanting to succeed. Is your classroom one where you value yourself as well as the children? Do they value themselves, you and others? Is assessment about recording success, no matter how small?

I think children learn best when:

They are... Happy. Relaxed. Confident. Motivated. Independent. Feeling involved with the work. Have some ownership of the activity. Cooperating.

They are offered their particular learning style — and have the opportunity to develop others. Children will only learn when self-esteem is raised and they understand their self-worth.

Quality

This is about the quality of the classroom environment and school, the quality of the learning experience for the children and the quality of the teaching experience for you. Do you all talk to each other in a friendly way? Do you listen to each other? Are the children keen to carry on with

---

I think children learn best when:

They are in a secure learning environment where both motivation and expectation are high.

They are respected and empowered.

They are confident that their views matter and are taken seriously, and that they are operating within a well-structured system.

I'd know a world studies approach was successful when my colleagues:

Feel confident to discuss the real world with the children.

Show a wider interest in other cultures.

Cooperate/collaborate/affirm each other.

... when the headteacher:

Shows a concern for equality of opportunity and about global issues.

Gets complimented on the lovely school atmosphere.

Makes this approach an inherent part of school policy.

Smiled more!

their work? Do they know what they have to do and why? Is there a balance of individual, group and class work? Above all, do they know that you have high expectations of each of them and confidence that they'll achieve them?

Criteria

A world studies approach to assessing children's development is based on these simple criteria:

- Will the assessment process, in whatever area of the curriculum, be enjoyable for them and low in stress for you?

- Does it increase self-esteem and motivation? Is it designed to emphasise each child's success (however limited) rather than to highlight failure?

- Does it involve the students in feedback and evaluation of the learning activities?

- Does it value the idiosyncratic and episodic nature of 'evidence' and is it open to unanticipated outcomes?

- Do the range of assessment techniques suit the different learning and communication styles and abilities that children all possess? That is, is there oral as well as written feedback, do drawings and imaginative stories also count as evidence? Are open-ended questions that invite opinion and imagination used, in addition to questions that

A group of teachers in South Shields were asked to annotate this cartoon of the 'World Studies Teacher' taken from *Making Global Connections.*

Is it this?

Serene, warm, involved. Totally calm in all situations

Clear thinker, forward planner. Yet capable of brilliant spontaneous lessons

Highly creative at arts, crafts, structuring all hands-on experiences

Tireless champion of all good causes

Inexhaustible energy

Complete knowledge of global history, current issues, geography   admit limitation but encourage student to help + be enthusiastic in search for information

Or is it this...?

Tries to counter inequality and injustice

An open mind, and ears that listen to and take account of others

Recognises gaps in knowledge of global issues
... and is committed to finding out more

A caring heart

Accepts the value of active learning and uses it as much as possible

Still needs stamina!

This image seems the one that most appeals to me. Someone who is idealistic and passionate in their optimism about the world. In this image there is a more positive discrimination for good — an evangeli[cal] attitude fused with practical advantage for each huma[n] + animal in achieving a positive result.

A group of teachers in South Shields were asked to annotate this cartoon of the 'World Studies Teacher' taken from *Making Global Connections*.

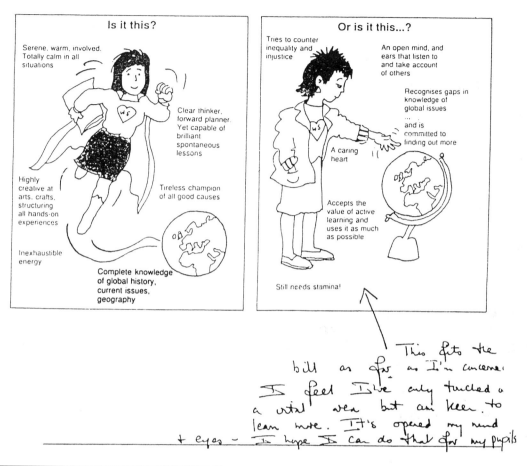

require factual accuracy? Are resources such as photographs, media extracts, drama used to stimulate responses whatever the area of the curriculum, and not only in English?

- Are the techniques for observing and recording an integral part of the learning process?

- Do you know what you are looking for? If you're clear about what it is, you're more likely to see if it's happening!

Opportunities

Assessment is about looking deliberately for windows that allow a glimpse into what is happening in children's minds as they process information and experience. It is always speculative and open to inaccuracy! World studies assessment looks at how children gain independence and self-esteem from the skills and knowledge they acquire through both the taught curriculum and through the intentional use of positive teaching and learning strategies by teachers and schools. This is the next step after the 'can do and knows about' which result from the snapshot of formal Attainment Target led assessment (AT henceforward). It asks how children comprehend and integrate

basic ideas about the world as they attempt to make sense of and understand life around them. A world studies point of reference is about making connections.

- It is about ways of finding out about, but not judging, attitudes and underlying values.

- It is *formative* as it can describe where the child is up to now, so as to see where s/he might be helped to go on to next.

- It is *diagnostic* so that the teacher can work out what to do to promote further growth.

- It is fundamentally *evaluative,* enabling the teacher to judge how effective current teaching strategies and classroom organisation are in attaining the goals set.

- It is *normative,* based on agreed expectations amongst teacher, school and parents about children's potential behaviour. This would show whether the child is acquiring the planned-for capacities, *and choosing to use them.* (Sharing her list of 'performance indicators' after years of world studies work in the classroom, a London teacher recounted how, on more than one occasion, parents whose children were 'cripplingly self-conscious', explicitly remarked on the obvious growth in self-confidence brought about by her use of world studies methodologies.)

- It is *ipsative* in that each child is compared only to her/himself, to how s/he used to be at an earlier stage and what s/he is saying and doing now. The overall frame of reference is what others in the class are doing and saying. Thus activities can be planned that will help each child move onwards, within the context of class or small-group activities.

Some principles

Global education deals not only with unbiased information about the world but also with opinions, attitudes and values, which cannot be easily pinned down and measured. In that sense, it calls for greater sensitivity than some other kinds of assessment. Objectivity — fairness, consistency and absence of personal bias — is always essential when considering how children are responding to the effectiveness of a teaching programme. Objectivity, in the sense of being 'scientific' and controlling the variables so that identical conditions exist for each and every individual being assessed, is neither possible nor desirable. Learning (remembering and integrating information and skills) happens at too many levels and in too many individual ways. Each person has evolved their own strategies for learning and relating to others; each person reacts differently at any given moment, having 'good' days or 'bad' days, undertaking tasks with greater or lesser enthusiasm and ease, depending upon all sorts of reasons, most of which are really beyond our knowing.

Yet relating to children in a personal or *subjective* way is inappropriate if generalisations prejudice the accuracy of our judgements; when we think that a child's class, gender, colour, cultural or family background *determine* how that child will think or act or behave at any given moment. (We can all recall staffroom conversations about '*That family! They're all alike!*') These factors may well be an influence but are in no sense predictors of future actions. Making decisions and drawing conclusions about each unique child is the essence of being a teacher and the core of professional expertise. It is subjectivity tempered by experience and open-mindedness. A good teacher expects to be surprised by every child s/he teaches.

Reporting her work on the Cambridge Institute of Education Project, 'Observation and its possible effects on the Assessment Process', Doreen Ponting concluded that she had learned:

1. To value my own experiences and judgement about the children based on evidence which I collected about them through close observation.

2. The value of knowing what a child can do at any given moment in time measured against her own abilities and not those of others.

3. The value of organising myself to document incidental occurrences of importance in the classroom, as well as actually organising specific assessment tasks, which were embedded in on-going learning.

4. The absolute necessity of being able to think positively about the whole business of assessment and making it a meaningful part of curriculum planning.

5. The involvement of parent and child in the gathering of information throughout the school life of the child.

6. The acceptance that observation of our children will also involve observation of our own teaching skills and classroom management. We must use this positively to improve the learning in which we are all involved.
[D. Ponting (1990)]

Some starting points

Looking for potential outcomes of working in a world studies way, that any child in any school could exhibit, can be approached from various perspectives.

- *What is the starting point? The child's, the teacher's, the school's?*

What seem to be the values of the community in which the school operates? What, in general, appear to be the 'local' attitudes to race, gender roles, education in general, models of schooling (e.g. more or less formal modes of organisation; parental involvement)?

- *What do the children need?*

In their daily lives? In their relationships within the school? As future citizens, workers, and happy fulfilled people? What do you hope they will remember after they have forgotten some of the specific facts you teach them?

- *Where do you stand, what counts for you as a person and as a teacher?*

What are your preferred teaching styles? (In *Primary Teachers Talking: A study of teaching as work*, Jennifer Nias offers an enlightening account about what teachers feel and think about 'being a teacher'.)

Practice is not just observable, codeable and measurable behaviours but an array of ideas, values and intentions, and, in action, diagnosis,

I would describe my teaching style as....

- *Informal with a disciplined structure.*

- *Mixed. At times I use whole class teaching (global education is so open-ended it is ideal for use with mixed ability classes). More frequently I have integrated (i.e. mixed subject) sessions or single subject sessions with differentiated activities.*

- *Formal and informal, depending upon the activity, certainly child-centred approach using a cross-curricular method.*

- *Cross-curricular and one which encourages open interactive learning through collaborative learning techniques and strategies. My teaching style has been influenced by 14 years of multicultural teaching.*

- *A mixture of methodology to try to cater for the range of learning styles which the children will have. Hopefully it is one which arouses their interest and stimulates them in and outside the classroom.*

- *Child-centred, caring, liberal but with discipline.*

- *A hotchpotch: supportive/ motivating/ non-authoritarian.*

- *Mixed. Some class lessons, a little group work. Warm, friendly, caring.*

- *A mixture — the ingredients determined by each new recipe selected by the government!*

[World Studies Active Learning Classroom Investigation (1991-1992)]

decisions and judgements. Practice is thought and thought is practice.
[Robin Alexander in A Blyth (ed.) (1988)]

(You might find it helpful to try out for yourself the personal profile exercise answered by these teachers. (See p.22).)

- *Where do you want to get to?*

Does the school's policy support you?

What should an enriched, enlightened and empowered citizen know, be able to do, and what democratic beliefs demonstrate while still at school? [*Model Learner Outcomes for International Education*, Minnesota Department of Education (1991)]

How do you, the school, and the community answer this question?

- *How do you plan to get there?*

It may be through the classroom environment, long-term planning for learning, individual lesson plans, (activities and resources used, teaching style(s), organisation, debriefing techniques). Building in the world studies dimension throughout the curriculum and planning specific classroom activities are both discussed in greater detail in Part III.

- *How do you know when you have got there?*

There are specific moments when you can tell it's working. More generally the effectiveness of world studies is demonstrated by a class's ability to work together co-operatively, to reason, to listen to peers without interrupting, to discuss contentious issues confidently without resorting to personal abuse. (Perhaps the proof is in what children are not *doing rather than in what they are doing: not shouting each other down, not insulting, not fighting, not competing, not moaning etc.) To sum up, I know world studies is effective when I can trigger a situation in a classroom and then drop back as children move into groups and an industrious hum pervades the air, punctuated by the odd shriek of enthusiasm or joyful laughter.*
[Former teacher and co-ordinator of northern LEA World Studies ESG programme, currently Educational Consultant, Wales (1991)]

'Performance Indicators' for global education?

The language of evaluation and assessment has become routine educational parlance. We all talk easily now of *understanding, competence, levels, performance. Taxonomies of behavioural objectives* are produced to help overstretched teachers more easily to record children's growth as they pass through their hands.

I know from my own experience that I have forgotten much of what was taught me during a fairly 'successful' school career. I remember well, by name, those teachers who were exciting and kind and those who were mean and unfriendly. I can name the capital cities of countries that no longer exist. I trust shopkeepers to give the correct change and no longer bisect triangles nor dissect frogs. I can no longer list with any confidence the 'causes' of all the wars and conflicts I learned about because, as I learned more, my awareness of the complexity and sheer messiness of human life has made such reasons unbearably simplistic. Nor could I accurately answer many questions on a KS2 test in most subjects, because I have either forgotten the information or because I never knew it, as knowledge has proliferated so much since my school days and as it will continue to do. Most 8 year olds know more about maths, technology, and computers than I do. What level would I be?

> It is conceivable that an 8 year old, an 11 year old, a 14 year old and a 16 year old could all be assessed as having achieved level 4 but not level 5... These pupils are manifestly not the same in ability, in potential or in any other respect except that they have achieved the same ideas or skills. There seems to be worrying potential in labelling pupils with their levels.
> [Wynne Harlen in *R.E., Attainment and the National Curriculum* (1991)]

Global education supports the view that most learning takes place in a non-linear way, that people learn not only at different paces but in different styles. We're all aware of these differences in the children we teach and in ourselves, using words like *imaginative* and *creative, logical* and *analytical, commonsensical* and *intuitive, practical* and *theoretical*. Thinking styles and how they affect our relationship with schooling have been discussed above. Thus we need to vary teaching styles and the way learning experiences are organised.

This does not mean that it is inappropriate to look for 'development' in the skills, knowledge, grasp of concepts and refinement of attitudes associated with world studies. Children do 'get better' at doing things, can be seen to be choosing more constructive strategies and to be asking more aware and reflective questions. They can also go beyond this.

In its characteristic usage, within traditional kinds of learning assessment, understanding refers to something entirely intellectual and cognitive: knowledge in the head rather than in the heart or bones... (Furthermore) Young people, like all of us, have no chance of escaping the stereotypical understandings implicit in their local life-worlds, unless they can acquire new concepts that make genuine, intuitive personal sense... At one level the task is that of widening social vocabularies. But, of course, the learning must go beyond merely enabling young people to talk glibly in a new terminology: the concepts need to be grounded in lived experience, local situations, personal choices and possibilities.
[P. Salmon in S. Warner Weil and I. McGill (eds.) (1989)]

If we went looking for signs of growth in the skills and understanding for world-awareness, what could we see? Using the **CASK** objectives of concepts, attitudes, skills and knowledge described earlier as a starting point, it is possible to set out a baseline of things that could be seen, heard or read. The examples which follow are representative samples from each of these four components of development. They are quoted from the ideas of a wide range of teachers, advisers and inspectors and workers in the field of global and development education who met specifically to consider what indicators of global education might look like. The examples are in no sense intended to be comprehensive, but suggest what the real children we work with could be beginning to do.

Development in world studies: a broad framework

I. Short term

Time span

a. *Classroom and playground behaviour:* accepts responsibility for own actions in the classroom and playground; can cooperate and take part in group activities, can settle disagreements without fights; speak clearly and confidently, listens to others.

b. *Engagement in learning:* (can work without the teacher, alone and with others; takes initiative, asks good questions and shows enjoyment.

c. *Changing levels of awareness and knowledge:* aware of self, curious about others, about events in the locality, events in the world; takes an interest in finding out both inside and outside the classroom.

These developments can be seen with one teacher, during a term, and over a year and, increasingly throughout the years of primary school.

d. *Beginning to express responsibility:* for other people and for the environment, both within and outside the school and the home. Looks for ways to do something about issues that concern him/her.

e. *Open:* to change and to tentativeness; beginning to tolerate complexity and uncertainty.

II. Medium term

More, and more frequent evidence will be seen of the developments listed above. Also he or she will begin to articulate interests in local/world affairs and take part in group activities throughout the curriculum with pleasure and confidence.

These developments will be seen during the time spent overall in formal education. There will be varied opportunities for developing 'world-mindedness'

III. Long term

Reflected in the choices made in adult life: about personal relationships, consumption, tolerance to people different from oneself, commitment to opposing injustice (economic, social, racial) at local and global levels. Hopefully, they will be confident and happy people, strong in character, appreciating their own qualities and sensitive to others, possessing a sense of justice and an optimistic concern and wish to be involved in local and global matters.

"Look, don't judge me by the clothes I wear, the car I drive. the books I read, the food I eat, the music I like, the friends I see, the money I earn, the place I live, the job I have, the things I say, or the way I act. OK?"

Progression in world studies objectives:
what a child might say, do or otherwise demonstrate

CONCEPT: Fairness

Fairness involves respecting the rights of other people and seeking solutions to conflicts which take into account the interests of all parties.

Level 1

— can take a turn in a group, willingly rather than reluctantly

— can list some of their rights

— can recognise inequalities in stories

— can 'cool off' in playground quarrels

Level 2

— can encourage others to take a fair turn

— can discuss school rules and make suggestions

— can recognise stereotypes in stories

— 'cool off' sooner

Level 3

— can organise a group so that all take a turn

— can recognise that responsibilities match rights

— can give examples of inequality and injustice in the world (local and global), e.g. sexism, apartheid, inequalities of income

— can identify acceptable compromises to conflicts with others in their lives

Level 4

— can accept that some may need a longer 'turn'

— can explain why rights and responsibilities go together

— can offer reasoned views on how to create change

— can challenge stereotypes constructively

— can begin to accept that not all conflicts have easy solutions

---

KNOWLEDGE: Future awareness

Thinking about the future at a personal, local, national, and global level. Becoming aware of ways in which their actions can influence the future.

Level 1

— 'We're getting a dog at Christmas'.

— 'I need to save up for Mum's birthday'.

— 'I'm going to be a pilot'.

— developing a sense of time.

Level 2

— 'I will have to take it for walks'.

— 'We will be moving house when I'm 10'.

— 'I hope the rainforests don't all get chopped down'.

— developing ability to predict.

Level 3

— 'I would like to go to the new high school'.

— 'Too much litter is bad for the environment, I'll be more careful'.

— 'I won't smoke when I grow up'.

Level 4

— 'It would be great if our city staged the Olympics'.

— 'We need to do something about the rainforest, I'll tell my parents not to buy so much paper'.

— 'I hope it's easier to have a job when I grow up'.

SKILL: Cooperation

Being able to work with others and accept a variety of roles that involve listening, explaining, sharing, negotiating and compromising.

Level 1

— can work with a partner taking turns to listen, speak, and share ideas and resources

— can use the term 'cooperate' appropriately

— can disagree with others and explain why

Level 2

— can work this way in a friendship group

— can relate cooperation to life outside the school

— can accept others' differing and critical viewpoints

Level 3

— can work in a mixed group, not all self-chosen

— can negotiate between differing outlooks

— can identify issues (local to global) where cooperation is not occuring

Level 4

— can work with any group, of mixed gender etc.

— can suggest alternative solutions to personal, local and global issues using cooperative tactics

ATTITUDE: Empathy

Being willing to imagine the feelings and perspectives of other people, in the present and the past, around us and in more distant places. Without empathy for the thoughts and feelings of others, children will have difficulty understanding the processes and purposes of democracy, cooperation and consensus.

Level 1

— can accept that there can be more than one side in a disagreement

— can share feelings and explain behaviour

— can describe the feelings of characters in stories

Level 2

— can recognise that another child or adult has reasons for wanting something different than you

— can express awareness of the different life experiences of others in the class

Level 3

— can explain that people do things differently because of their background and situation

— can challenge the use of insults in school based on gender, disability, nationality, poverty

Level 4

— can challenge stereotypical statements made about people different from themselves

— can make and articulate judgements about the fairness and justice of current and historic conditions of the world

The final picture?

These are a small sample of some possible behaviours we might hope to see as the child progresses through school and has opportunities to find out about the world, to work collaboratively, discuss ideas and share feelings with others. Pages could be filled with checklists of even more. While compiling such lists might help describe an overall picture, it would still leave an important question unresolved. For in the end, how and what a person takes away from an educational experience is unpredictable. Even when we believe we can see 'change' in the kinds of attitudinal and conceptual areas that global education covers, we will not be able to say with total certainty what the chief influences were.

Is the change we see due to natural maturation and development? Views they've learned but do not believe, saying and doing what they think teacher wants to hear? A momentary response to the strong personality of the teacher or classmate? The impact of a range of out-of-school experiences eg. family, friends, faith community, media? A teacher is only one small part of what goes into children; skilful jugglers, they co-exist in so many worlds at once. But it is still well worthwhile to look at what is happening in these areas and imperative to continue to work towards this goal.

I must admit that at times I was frustrated — especially if individual children did not respond in ways that I had anticipated, but I think that it is important for teachers to realise that they may not see immediately the fruits of their work, but that they may be only a small part in a much longer process of individuals reaching their full potential.
[Teacher, Stockport (1991)]

PART TWO

Putting it into Practice

5

Organising Learning in the World Studies Classroom

This section of the book describes how you can weave the objectives of global education into your planning. It looks at three aspects of organising learning: **active learning exercises**, **group work** and **topic work**. These help children to develop and to learn social and operational **skills**, **knowledge** about the world through the curriculum, knowledge about themselves and other people in the school and positive **attitudes** towards learning, themselves and others.

Active learning is described from two perspectives. One part of this section describes a core of active learning procedures which are compatible with any and all aspects of the curriculum. The other part provides exemplar activities that you can use with specific subjects. They help enliven the subjects of the National Curriculum and make them more stimulating. More broadly, the explicit focus on *self-esteem, communication, cooperation* and *critical thinking skills* throughout the curriculum make these ideas integral to all learning and not just fun activities for special occasions.

The planning, general methodologies and specific activities described in this book are all based on promoting a global approach in the classroom. Every child really does have an entitlement to learn about this world and how interesting it is!

Starting with the Learning Process

World studies is a dimension across the curriculum, infusing each subject with a global and equal opportunities perspective. It provides even greater coherence to cross-curricular planning.

☐ **Education is about 'wholes', not bits; interconnectedness, not fragmentation.**

The real purpose of education is to help children survive and prosper in a complex world. It is about helping them make sense of all the different bits — counting, measuring, analysing and describing the physical world; finding out about, remembering and appreciating history, stories, art, music; getting along with other people. Subjects and facts are the bricks, with general concepts and stretching learning activities the mortar that hold them together.

☐ **Education is about understanding, connecting, storing and retrieving**

A head filled with unconnected facts is like a well-stocked but chaotic stockroom. You need to know what's there and how to get at it!

☐ **Education is not a tidy, linear sequence. It is unpredictable, happening in leaps and bounds.**

☐ **Education is about how different personality types engage with learning and with the social disciplines of the school.**

Teachers value each child's uniqueness. They also see a gallery of characters — the methodical and reflective; the impulsive doers; the individualists, whether introverts remaining alone or extroverts seeking constant feedback from others; the collaborators, wanting to give and receive support.

☐ **Education is about working with people's actual thinking processes.**

People are not like computers, laying down 'bytes' of information in an identical manner. We have different thinking styles, just as we have different body shapes and personalities. These influence the ways we approach the whole learning experience and how we process it.

(i) Some people start by seeing 'whole' and then engage with the separate elements, relating them to an overall hypothesis or general picture.

(ii) Others build up their picture bit by bit, examining each 'piece' separately to see what it all adds up to.

(iii) People more comfortable with reasoning and analysis like to deal with the concrete and specific and to weave their understanding out of abstract generalisations.

(iv) Others respond through instinct and intuition, feeling their way towards understanding.

Different areas of the curriculum call for different thinking styles and skills and planning a mixture of activities allows each 'type' opportunities for success. (Pike and Selby,

A Global Approach
is based on justice, equality and interdependence.

People

- how they live (development, justice, the future, systems and structures)
- how they are different (culture, environment, choices)
- how they are the same (human rights, values, interdependence)

Environment

- the interdependence of all life
- aesthetic and spiritual connections
- sustainable development
- responsibility
- optimistic concern/concerned optimism for the care of the planet

A global approach in the classroom is about :

Learning

- self-esteem
- co-operation and collaboration
- empathy
- critical thinking
- clear and courteous communication
- valuing feelings as well as reasoning
- generating action based on unbiased information and clear values
- positive commitment to oppose prejudice and discrimination

Making Connections

- recognising common and basic human needs wherever and however people live
- understanding how we are connected to our cultures and places
- understanding how other people feel the same about their places and cultures
- recognising that localities are interconnected and interdependent

A global approach to the methods and content of learning lies at the heart of developing 'world-aware' people. Five skills a world-aware person might have are:

:
> '1. *to see modestly*
>
> 2. *to listen carefully*
>
> 3. *to think globally*
>
> 4. *to feel fully*
>
> 5. *to act responsibly*'

To 'see modestly' means to recognise that no-one ever sees the whole picture, or has the only truth. Where one stands determines what one sees, and we are all limited by the perspectives of our culture, class, age and gender. [Hampson, T. and Whalen, L. *Tales of the Heart: Affective Approaches to Global Education*]

David Hicks (*Making Global Connections*) and David Selby and Graham Pike (*Global Teacher, Global Learner*) offer excellent, more detailed definitions of the global perspective.

(1988) and Pollard and Tann (1987), both describe varieties of thinking style and strategies for taking them into account.)

☐ **Education is about knowing what you think when you hear yourself say it.**

We know this from our own reflections on experience, as well as from the research and analysis of theorists like Bruner, Piaget and Vygotsky. It is also confirmed by the recent work of the Oracy Project (see Bibliography). Learning is an intellectual *and* a social activity. Children need to 'think aloud' through talk and through writing, without the fear of being criticised for getting it wrong.

Weaving the world studies objectives into your planning

There are many formats for planning the match between content and learning activities; perhaps your school already has its own. Some suggestions are offered on pp.60. *World Studies 8-13* is based on the CASK model, that is the belief that there are a core group of concepts, attitudes, skills, and general areas of knowledge common throughout the curriculum, whatever the subjects being learnt. *World Studies 8-13: A Teacher's Handbook* [Fisher and Hicks (1985)] first used this model to draw together the core ingredients of world studies learning, for what are now Key Stages 2 and 3.

Each field of the curriculum does indeed have its own unique and particular nature for which teaching must be planned, yet 'education' is essentially the process by which we come to perceive the distinctiveness of each but within a sense of wholeness and interconnectedness. The following pages suggest some learning outcomes that are particularly relevant for developing a global perspective that you could plan for, whatever the area of the curriculum. *Global Teacher, Global Learner* [Pike and Selby (1988)] provides an in-depth discussion of the holistic nature of global education and suggests a detailed framework of objectives.

Concepts

These are the binding elements of learning, the organising principles to be found in all subject areas and disciplines. They are not just abstract notions, but reflect basic processes we take part in daily. A concept like *change*, for example, explains what is occurring in a scientific experiment, in a mathematical exercise, what happens over time to all of us and to the places we inhabit. In some senses, all learning is about moving from the specific to the general, making sense of the world by seeing how things connect.

Causes and consequences, change, conflict, co-operation, power, interdependence, similarities and differences and values and beliefs.

All of these concepts underpin the learning anticipated in the Programmes of Study and in the cross curricular themes. They are very definitely within the grasp of KS2 children, and in many cases of children under the age of seven.

In the course of the school day, in their relationships with peers and adults, young children do in fact have simple, concrete experiences which contain elements in common with larger world issues. (They) regularly:

- Call each other names, sometimes gender- or race-related (prejudice)
- Exclude others from play for arbitrary reasons (discrimination)
- Argue over materials (resource distribution)
- Protest that rules are 'not fair' (human rights)
- Fight (peace and conflict)
- Use up consumable materials, sometimes unwisely (environmental awareness)
- Decide what activities they will take part in: write letters, pick up litter or plant flowers in the school grounds (awareness of human choice and action). [Susan Fountain (1990)]

Attitudes

Children's attitudes towards themselves and others contribute to their capacity to learn. Their attitudes about fundamental issues: the environment, gender roles, the colour and class differences between people, also have an impact upon the classroom. These ideas are brought from home, the 'streets', and the media. They can be affected by those seen to be valued in the classroom and school, but whatever their origin, they affect learning and behaviour. So you can decide, legitimately, to look for evidence of those attitudes which the school and parents have agreed help the learning and development of happy children. That way you can plan experiences that will enable children to develop morally, socially and intellectually.

The evidence to guide your planning will consist in what the children say or do in specific situations and how they do or say it. 'Whenever pupils express their own ideas or react to situations, they offer insights into the way their attitudes are forming and developing.' [Westhill R.E. Syllabus, *op. cit.* See also Chapter One for some reflections on attitudes, values and moral development.]

Part of the teacher's role is to help the children themselves to become aware of their attitudes and how they affect their actions, choices and behaviour. This is an area of subjective judgement, where you will use your experience and sensitivity and where the children can also participate through self- evaluation. There are many attitudes thought to be appropriate to schools and learning, covering issues such as approaches to work and the other children and adults in the school community. The following are particularly relevant to a 'globally minded' person.

- **Self-esteem**: accepting oneself and seeing oneself in a positive light, being prepared to acknowledge one's abilities and to learn from one's mistakes. Key components are the feelings of *'security, identity, belonging, purpose* and *competence'* [Robert Reasoner, *Building Self-esteem* in Borba (1989)].

- **Affirmation**: '... positively communicating to others those aspects about them which please and satisfy us' [Whitaker (1984)].

- **Dignity**: having a sense of one's own worth and of one's own particular social, cultural and family background and also of the equal worth of others.

- **Positive curiosity**: being interested to learn *about* and also *from* people and life-styles different from one's own and about the world around one generally.

- **'Earth awareness'**: 'show by our own lives that we're prepared to care for the earth e.g. not dropping litter, switching off lights, using resources unwastefully', [teacher and freelance-writer on Development Education, Lancashire].

- **Empathy**: being willing to imagine the feelings and viewpoints of other people, those around one and in cultures and situations different from one's own.

- A sense of **Justice, fairness** and **human rights:** understanding that all people are worthy of equal treatment and being willing to stand up for one's rights and for theirs. Choosing democratic processes such as discussion and negotiation to achieve more equality. Expressing awareness and concern about unjust situations both locally and globally.

- **Open-mindedness**: being prepared to approach people and ideas without preconceived notions and to change one's ideas as one learns more.

Fortunately, there is no proof that there actually are techniques you can use systematically to form attitudes, nor would we want there to be! Nonetheless, attitudes such as those described above will be encouraged in a world studies classroom.

Skills

The essential skills for globally aware citizens can be fostered throughout the formal curriculum. They are the skills to do with **oracy** and **co-operation**: talking to and learning from others, taking your turn, clarifying your thinking and justifying your ideas to others, negotiating, expressing opinions and personal views, recognising the difference between fact, opinion, fantasy. (See Bibliography and National Oracy Project (1991) inter alia).

Also central are **conceptual** or **thinking skills**: investigating and interpreting evidence/data, predicting, hypothesising, making generalisations, evaluating. Thinking and communicating ideas clearly are necessary capabilities. So are those **social skills** to do with communicating feelings and beliefs: appropriately expressing thoughts and feelings verbally and in other ways, listening to others, tolerating difference, accepting criticism, criticising others constructively, resolving differences/conflicts non-violently, taking an active cooperative role when working with others, considering what it's like to be in another's position.

> *The children have become more skilled at co-operation through the work we've done together. They choose to co-operate with each other not because it's 'nice' and will please the teacher, but because they recognise that it's the best way to deal with complex tasks.*
> [Teacher, Newcastle (1992)]

Knowledge

Starting from a world studies perspective some key ideas defined below can both describe and explain the world at local and global levels, past, present and future. In fact, these concerns enrich the bare bones of the programmes of study, fleshing them out with relevant, interesting content.

Thus children can discuss **what's going on in the wider world** and how people are trying to **resolve conflicts**; the **culture** and **values** of their own societies and of others, past and present; **human rights** and injustice, both in their own society and elsewhere in the world, brought about by inequality of wealth and opportunity and also by prejudiced ideas about people's gender, colour, age or impairment. Very importantly, they can find out about what people in the past and present have chosen to do to **change** this; about the **environment**, what people are doing to take care of the natural world, as well as the damage occurring; to think and speculate about how their choices and actions can influence what the **future** might be like.

> Monocultural education is unlikely to develop the faculty of imagination which represents the ability to conceive alternatives... Imagination does not develop in a vacuum. It is only with exposure to different societies and cultures that the imagination is stimulated and the consciousness of alternatives becomes an inseparable part of the way of thinking!
> ['The Gifts of Diversity', B. Parekh quoted in Pike and Selby *op. cit.* p.30.]

Objectives for world studies

Concepts

- **Causes and consequences** — to know that our own and others' decisions can have both helpful and harmful effects for ourselves, others and the environment.
- **Change** — to recognise that change is a constant part of life and that we can all work to try and make it change for the better.
- **Conflict** — to be aware that whilst differing wants, needs, beliefs and values can lead to conflict between people and groups, it is possible to work them through.
- **Co-operation** — to understand that we live and work with others all our lives, and that it is rewarding to get on well.
- **Fairness and Justice** — to understand that all human beings, whatever their differences, have the right to be valued and treated equally. We all have the right to food, shelter and just laws.

- **Interdependence** — to be aware of how we are all connected and interdependent with other people and with life on earth. The actions of each one affects the others.
- **Power** — to understand that individuals as well as groups can have influence over their own lives and what goes on in the world. Power is distributed unequally and this affects people's life chances, rights and welfare.
- **Similarities and Differences** — to be aware that while each of us is unique and has a different appearance, ideas and traditions, people share the same basic needs, including the need for love and acceptance.
- **Values and Beliefs** — to recognise and accept that people have differing dreams and goals about getting the best out of life.

Knowledge and understanding

- To know about one's own society, culture and history.
- To know about other countries, cultures and histories.
- To know about the links between our lives and others throughout the world.
- To know about the basic geography of the earth and how plants, animals and people exist.

- To know about the various forces that shape all our lives, including the major inequalities of power and wealth in the world.
- To recognise that the mass media are the main channels of information we have about the world and to be aware of bias and selectivity.

Attitudes

- To have an optimistic concern for local and global issues.
- To be curious to find out more about people and issues.
- To have a sense of one's own worth and to believe that one can meet challenges with competence.
- To value, appreciate and enjoy a diversity of cultures, including one's own.

- To be prepared to stand up for one's own rights and those of other people.
- To care about and for the environment.
- To be aware that we can influence the kind of future we will have, personally and globally.
- To be willing to take part and work together with others to promote democracy and to work for a more just world.

Skills

- To be able to find out and record information; and to distinguish between fact and opinion.
- To listen to others' points of view
- To be able to express ideas and opinions and explain facts clearly through talking and writing.
- To be able to work collaboratively and cooperatively with others to solve problems and share ideas.
- To be able to handle controversy and disagreement and to identify solutions that take others into account.

- To be able to use one's own judgement to decide on moral rights and wrongs
- To be able to imagine the feelings and beliefs of others.
- To be able to negotiate and make decisions about matters which affect ourselves and others.
- To recognise bias.
- To approach issues with an open and questioning mind.
- To be able to change our ideas as we learn more.

Looking for Evidence: what teachers have found

What does this all look like when you are planning lessons and the assessment opportunities they can afford? You can integrate one or more of the concepts, attitudes, and areas of 'global knowledge' into whatever planning format you use, whether for a period of work or a lesson. Collecting evidence for development in these areas can dovetail with the work you're doing in other parts of the curriculum.

- **Geography**

  For example, listening to the kinds of statements the children make as they investigate life in their own locality and in localities elsewhere in the U.K. and overseas, can show not only gaps in information but the preconceptions, negative and positive, children have of how other people live .

  A Y5 class studied, one by one, the cut up parts of a photograph showing three people in India standing in front of their shanty home behind which stands a modern city of high rise buildings. (Photo 24 from the excellent 'Doorways' pack of homes throughout the world. See Bibliography). This JIGSAW activity is fully described below.

  One group picks up on the fact that the people are smiling —the implication is that if they are living in these conditions they should not be happy. It is suggested by this group that the people may not live in this dwelling — they may be friends or relatives who are posing for the photo. (Is this indicating a development of questioning; who took the photo and for what purpose?) Some groups wondered whether the dwelling was a tent and if the people were camping. Was this a type of holiday village? (Are they trying to make sense of the picture by drawing on their own experiences?) All the groups expressed surprise on seeing the final piece of picture and a certain reluctance to accept that it was the same country as the original pieces. 'It's two different countries.' 'It's two pictures stuck together.' (Is this the beginning of understanding that evidence can be doctored... that a photo may not always tell the whole truth?) On further questioning, some pupils did agree that India would have rich and poor people; houses and more 'primitive' dwellings, but they obviously found it difficult to accept both images on the same photo.
  [Teacher, South Shields, Tyne and Wear]

- **Design Technology**

  When they compare the artefacts of different societies and the solutions to design problems in different environments.

- **Maths**

  When they engage in everyday maths activities:

  As someone who has used these approaches over several years I am aware of the strong influence it has had on my approach to teaching in other areas, e.g. maths, science, technology. I've changed my view of what is acceptable or unacceptable in these subjects, for example what I saw as 'copying' in maths, I'm now more likely to see as peer tutoring. I use children as teachers now in paired work, making sure that the pairs are well matched, of course!
  [Deputy Headteacher, Manchester]

- **Religious Education**

  From their reactions to your preparations for a multi-faith assembly.

- **History**

  When they discuss the lives of children in Victorian times or in Ancient Egypt; when they consider the issues involved in Invaders and Settlers, whether the native Britons and those who came here, or the interactions of other explorers with those they encountered.

  After looking at a drawing of labourers constructing a pyramid, also presented in a piece-by-piece jigsaw (an activity that was evaluated by Elena (Y5) as 'Brill, fab, excellent!'), the children gave their first reactions, going round a circle and each talking in turn.

  'I felt the way they did and wanted to know more about it.'

  'I learned they can keep bodies for hundreds of years —it's amazing!'

  'I was surprised by the picture and how poor they were.'

  'I didn't like it when I saw the slaves working.'

  'Next time I'd like to learn more about when they mummified people.'

  'It was interesting the way you had your first ideas and changed your ideas when you saw a different piece of picture.'

  [Kimberley, Daniel, Eleanor, Hayley, Victoria, and Oliver, Year 5, Bournemouth (October 1991)]

Children from Hartburn Primary School, Stockton-on-Tees, Cleveland

The companion activity was writing about slavery inspired by the images of the labourers. 'The thought of writing is usually boring, but I really wanted to do this!'
[Kimberley]

- **Personal and Social Education**
  From their behaviour when a visitor from another country or culture or with some impairment comes to the school; or in the playground during the seemingly perennial conflict about who plays what where .

- **Science and Geography**
  In the way they share their understanding of environmental processes.

A Manchester teacher describes how a diamond ranking activity (see pp 80) helped her Y5 class extend their understanding. The images she used are included on page 82.

I feel that this activity was extremely successful. The main reason for this I feel stems from the fact that the children entered into the activity with a fairly comprehensive knowledge of the environmental issues depicted in the pictures. This surely gave them the confidence to discuss these and make valued opinions and decisions. A great deal of discussion took place. It was interesting that one group decided to look at the aesthetic damage to the environment whilst the other groups based their decisions on the long-term consequences.

There are numerous 'diagnostic opportunities' to see how the values and skills associated with a global perspective are developing.

Date:	**Lesson Evaluation**

Activity: **Main resource(s):**

My main objectives for this lesson: National Curriculum & world studies understanding

a. skills: **d. Subject areas to be covered:**

b. attitudes:

                                           e. A.T.(s) focus:

c. concepts:

What did the children actually **do** during the activity?

What exactly did I do?

How do I know this learning was taking place? How did the children let me know this through what they said, wrote or communicated in any other way?

Which, if any, of the objectives above require more attention?

Lesson Evaluation

Date: 18·2·92   Activity: RANKING   Main Resource: DOORWAYS PHOTOGRAPH PACK

What did the children actually **do** during the activity?

The children ranked the photographs. Initially they used discussion but when they reached an impasse they used various strategies such as voting or turning photographs face down, shuffling and choosing. There was a lot of interaction, discussion and the giving and receiving of ideas & information.

What did I do? I watched and listened. I sat in at each table for a short time and for most of the time sat between them. They required little from me, only asking if it was acceptable to use a 'choosing' strategy when they couldn't arrive at a decision.

What World Studies Objectives were they learning? [in some cases further development of these skills]

a. **skills**
Enquiry
Communication Skills
Critical Thinking

b. **concepts**
Communication   Similarities & differences
Co-operation   Values & beliefs
Fairness

c. **knowledge**
Ourselves & others
Rich & poor

d. **attitudes**
Curiosity   Appreciation of other
Empathy.   cultures.
Human dignity

How do I know this learning was taking place? What sorts of things did the children say, write or communicate in any way? The children communicated freely with lots of exchange of ideas and knowledge. They affirmed each others ideas and choices and at times put forwards reasoned disagreements. They made strenuous efforts to make sure the ranking was done with everyone's agreement. They questioned the fairness of poverty especially in relation to photograph 17. Derogatory comments about living in a caravan were questioned by some.

Did the activity help me become aware of which objectives required more attention? Which one(s)? The children need further work on rich & poor on a more local basis (we have recently done some related to Victorian times). Also they need further understanding of interdependence of people and how the actions of some influence the life of others. There is a definite racist attitude towards travellers and I intend to do some positive work in this area.

Did it help me meet National Curriculum objectives? Which ones?
English A.T.1 levels 4-6, depending on their personal level of articulation.
Geography AT2 & AT3 were certainly touched on [if I had been able to make more input there would have been a more concentrated degree of work here.]

6

Active Learning: Planning for Feelings, Thought and Action

Rationale

All learning is of course 'active' as the learner engages with absorbing, remembering and attempting to understand new knowledge and experiences. The term 'active learning' refers to structured experiences that require individuals to interact with others and to reflect on the experience afterwards. The key words are **Experiential**, **Participation**, **Ownership**.

> Active learning techniques such as group discussions and problem solving, role plays and simulations, and co-operative games are often used in global education because they are ways of organising learning that combine both thinking and feeling, group discussion and individual reflection. They are ideal vehicles for enquiry learning, ...creating situations in which pupils can formulate questions and find answers for themselves. World studies focuses on learning to learn, solving problems, clarifying values and making decisions.
> [Fisher and Hicks (1985)]

The main components of experiential learning are engagement with some idea or topic through discussion and action (including individual research); reflection with others on what has been discovered or experienced; and personal evaluation of these processes, both about what has been learnt and the meaning this has for the student.

> The essential key feature of experiential learning is the opportunity afforded to the learner to reflect on the nature and meaning of particular learning activities and to consider their relevance and meaning in the learner's life.
> [Whitaker (1984)]

The evaluations of Key Stage 2 children quoted throughout this book are evidence of their analysis and reflection on learning.

☐ **Activity based learning can help children become more deeply engaged with both information and the concepts that underpin the work.**

Ownership is about interest and commitment, about being involved in discovery and about taking responsibility for oneself. Children can make their own interpretations, reflect, try their thinking aloud, reformulate their understanding after feedback from others and move on.

☐ **Active learning provides an acknowledged space in which it is legitimate to explore feelings.**

Feeling is an important ingredient of understanding. Structured activities typically involve opportunities for children to acknowledge and articulate feelings and to experience empathy. This can be in relation to other members of the group — 'Can I understand how you feel about this?' — and to others outside it, imaginary characters or people in other cultures, places or times — 'What would it feel like to be you, to have your experiences?'

☐ **Active learning respects different ways of learning and knowing.**

Children will be able to explore complex issues and concepts in ways they can understand and relate to their own current levels of experience and understanding. These kinds of experiences help children to value their own contributions and also to remain open to absorbing the insights, perspectives and knowledge of others around them. Importantly, this includes their peers as well as authority figures such as teachers, media, textbooks.

☐ **A classroom is which active learning is a frequent feature will be based on affirmation and mutual respect, trust and tolerance. Indeed, regular use of these activities can only make the classroom a better and happier place!**

The activities throughout this book are based on this model.

Some themes in the global classroom

Understanding news

Getting on with others

Understanding other peoples

World tomorrow

7

Groupwork: Planning for Communication, Co-operation and Critical Thinking

'I thought it was hard at first, but when we started working I found it easy.'

'I liked to work with friends.'

'I think it's a good idea to ask what other people think.'

'It is better than working on my own. I don't know what to do on my own.'

[Year 3 children from various schools.]

These children from schools around England (and the other children quoted throughout the book) were taking part in the classroom research into the effectiveness of cooperative active learning described earlier. Their teachers concluded that working in small groups and using these activities contributes significantly to children developing communication, cooperation and critical thinking skills. [Steiner (1993)]

Why Groupwork?

Groupwork is central to the successful operation of the National Curriculum. This has led to renewed interest and research into how it best works.

> Grouping pupils within the class enables resources to be shared; fosters the social development which primary schools rightly believe to be an essential part of their task; and above all, provides for pupils to interact with each other and their teacher.
> [Alexander, Rose and Woodhead (1992)]

Monitoring children's behaviour and development within groups settings was deliberately planned into the statements of attainment throughout the entire curriculum as an assessable activity (see, for example, *A Guide to Teacher Assessment*, Pack C; SEAC (1990)). Recent classroom research has resulted in a number of stimulating and useful books about groupwork, process and practice (eg. Bennett and Dunne (1992); Galton and Williamson (1992); and

other titles in the Bibliography). In *Teaching Talking and Learning (Key Stage One and Key Stage Two)* the National Oracy Project team have also provided a powerful argument and useful guidance for organising learning in groups.

Groupwork, and the physical organisation of the classroom into blocks of desks to facilitate it, are a staple feature of our primary schools. The National Curriculum rests solidly on this foundation. What are its key features and why is *cooperative* groupwork one of the organisational devices most congruent with world studies?

I.   How learning takes place

As mentioned earlier, theories of learning support the belief that talking out loud and listening to what others say is one of the chief ways that we learn, at whatever age.

☐ **Children need to hear what others more informed and experienced than themselves (teachers and other adults) think and to interact with them both through listening and in conversations.**

This helps move the child beyond what s/he already understands and can do, towards new skills and knowledge. (D. Wood (1988) provides an excellent overview of the main thinkers and theories.)

☐ **Children need to go beyond the apprentice relationship and to talk, purposefully, with each other; to be challenged cognitively and socially by their peers; to explore their own conclusions, tentative hypotheses, emerging opinions and values. They also need a purpose for this thinking and space to do it in.**

In small groups, children are often prepared to be tentative, to take chances in exposing what they are unsure of, and to use language exploratively. Understanding is more likely to be achieved when children are allowed to make their own language to express it, and to check against the understanding of others.
[National Oracy Project (1991)]

Learning is both individual and social. The increasingly sophisticated understanding we have about how personality type and thinking styles affect how children process information and acquire new skills, also points to the dynamic impact of groupwork. See Pollard and Tann (1987) for example, for practical insights into cognitive processes and personality characteristics and the relationship between them, and for useful strategies for planning learning with these elements in mind.

'It got us to say what we felt.'

'You get a chance to say exactly what you think.'

'Good for learning to work with each other and compromising.'

'I prefer working in twos.'

'You can express your feelings a lot more.'

'You get to know other people, not just your best friends.'

[Year 6 children from various schools]

☐ **Purposeful talk helps children mature both conceptually and socially and small groups working towards a common goal are a very effective way of enabling this.**

A child participates as an individual within the collectivity of the whole class and this experience is vital for the formation of personal autonomy and identity. Within a group, the child remains an individual but must also work more consciously at collaboration and clarity of meaning. It may not make that much difference to an individual, on an affective level, if the others in the class as a whole understand what s/he is communicating (although on a self-esteem level all successful exchanges are important). But in a group, it makes a great difference, as one is both more exposed personally and more committed to helping the group achieve its goals.

☐ **Children can gain deeper understanding of abstract concepts through structured group tasks which require them to talk through their ideas, listen to others and collectively arrive at some form of conclusion.**

Present research on children involved in collaborative problem solving (eg. on the computer) shows that they can make significant gains in understanding and higher order thinking, *particularly if they have had training in discussion and co-operation skills.*
[Open University research reported in the T.E.S. (14/8/92)]

II. Social Relationships and Learning Skills

It has always been the case that schools have seen their purpose and role as preparing pupils 'for the opportunities, responsibilities and experiences of adult life.'
[ERA (1988)]

Central amongst these must be the ability to relate to others in a way that is mutually constructive and rewarding. The capacity for cooperation is an essential ingredient for democracy.

☐ **Groupwork is one method of helping children learn these relevant skills and to become aware of how they and others behave when they are trying to operate as a group.**

Harwood (1988), Bennett and Dunne (1992) and Galton and Williamson (1992) point out that it is important to give children an understanding of different roles we take in groups at different times (e.g. clarifying ideas, organising others, playing the clown), depending on the group task and the group members.

☐ **It is essential to work with children on making explicit these basic skills of collaboration, on articulating these various roles and their feelings about the experience.**

The goals of groupwork are to help children accomplish certain learning tasks relating to the whole curriculum (eg. investigations, drama, collaborative writing, personal and social development); to extend oracy; to practise collaborative strategies; to feel good about themselves and to value others.

'I never want to work on my own again after all the fun we had in forty minutes.'

'You can say your own thing and you don't feel so shy.'

'Good fun to work with people I normally don't get on with.'

'Easier than working separately and a lot more fun.'

'Good to work with boys and girls.'

'Interesting to listen to other people's ideas.'

'We get to know people better and know how they feel about the world.'

'I think it is more educational than writing tests and listening and writing. I love lessons like this when we get together as a group and discuss.'

[Year 7 children from various schools]

III. Learning the Skills of Democracy

☐ **Groupwork in which discussion is central helps build the skills and understanding for citizenship. It is important for children to learn to tolerate difference.**

- They will hear ideas and values different from their own being expressed by their friends, and come to appreciate that people can be different and equal.

- By accepting difference in others, they can become more self-accepting of the ways in which they themselves are unique and different.

- When their own contributions are accepted, it encourages them to value the basic rights of self-expression for everyone.

- Working towards consensus (a frequent but not necessarily over-riding goal of democratic discussion), they will come to appreciate flexibility and also to recognise the need to defend certain core values such as equality and fairness.

- They will experience *power* and *powerlessness*, *fairness* and *unfairness*, *rational* and *irrational* argument, *cooperation* and *conflict* amongst others of the same age and size (roughly) which is much easier to deal with and learn from than in the authority relationships of adult-child.

- They will be able to take responsibility for their own actions as well as feeling a responsibility to their friends in the group.

IV. The Role of Self-Esteem

A healthy self-concept or sense of self-esteem is crucial for successful learning and for good relationships with others.

☐ **The small group can be an important place for children to gain confidence through having their contributions recognised and valued.**

Research over the years has shown that many children approach learning tasks (both as individuals and group-members) with an in-built fear and expectation of failure: teachers are regarded as judges whose first response will be to be critical. Investigations in the United States, Israel and Holland over the past fifteen years show *significant gains in self-esteem and performance* following structured programmes of co-operative groupwork. (Reported in Galton and Williamson (1992) inter alia.)

☐ **Self-esteem is about having an accurate inner picture of oneself, that recognises one's strengths as well as one's weaknesses — or rather, one's potential for improvement. Most of us are comfortable with self-criticism but find it difficult to acknowledge our good qualities and attributes, either to ourselves or openly to others.**

Having a positive self-concept helps children feel more confident to:

- express their ideas
- try out new ideas
- revise their ideas and work
- listen to others
- give and receive feedback — both positive and critical
- work collaboratively and constructively with others.

Self-esteem is *not* about being self-centred or self-important. It is now widely accepted that those with low self-esteem are more likely to be disruptive and attention-seeking or unhealthily withdrawn. People who cannot tolerate themselves are also less likely to tolerate others: the root of racist and sexist behaviour.

Planning and organising groupwork

The basic unit — the class — is not necessarily a group. Do the children really feel happy about being together all day? A group is more than a collection of individuals sharing space or, even, working towards some common goal. A group has an identity formed by individuals feeling a sense of membership.

Children need:

- **Affiliation** — a sense of belonging and esteem.
- **Appreciation** — experience of acceptance and praise.
- **Influence** — a sense of involvement and control over what is happening.
- **Achievement** — a feeling of getting somewhere and of accomplishment.

This relates to the child as a member of a small group, a whole class, and the wider community of the school. The creation of an environment where all feel safe and cared for and respected is essential for these things to happen. But more is required if groupwork is to be truly cooperative and purposeful.

> Initially I thought that the personality of the teacher was solely responsible for the quality of student inter-action in the classroom. I believed that if a teacher was open, honest, sensitive, understanding and willing to give students the freedom to be themselves, good group process was sure to result.
> [Gene Stanford (1977) quoted in Stanford and Stoate, (1990)]

What he, and others since, have concluded is that children need training in group skills as much as in, say, gymnastic or mathematical skills.

☐ **Children need to be taught how to collaborate and why listening carefully and courteously, taking turns, disagreeing in respectful argument, being prepared to try things out together, making mistakes and amending them, are important skills.**

> *'Good because you could communicate your point of view to other persons.'*
>
> *'I had to think hard.'*
>
> *'Sometimes I get a bit annoyed with the boys.'*
>
> *'I like working slowly step by step.'*
>
> *'You get more help if you're stuck.'*
>
> *'You can learn what other people think and you have to find a way to agree.'*
>
> *'I like little groups better than large groups.'*
>
> *'It touches you deep down and brings out your feelings.'*
>
> [Year 5 children from various schools]

I. Group tasks

Groupwork is about a collection of individuals working to achieve an outcome that can only be realised by joint effort. The outcome can be a product (eg. a science experiment, a ranking of statements about a topic, a newspaper) or it can be less tangible, such as a verbal résumé of a discussion. A 'group' can be a pair, three, four, five or six children.

☐ **Groups benefit from clearly defined tasks with the discipline of an outcome at the end of a certain period. Whether all working together or making individual contributions towards a common outcome, the children should share the planning, the presentation and the evaluation.**

Some ways to do this:

(a) The class as a whole should draw up a simple and short list of basic ground rules for groupwork, eg. taking turns talking, no grabbing of resources etc.

(b) Provide the groups with some way of recording their planning and decision making as they proceed.

(c) Assign roles within the group eg. resource distributor, scribe, reporter, envoy (i.e. the one who moves around the room for specific reasons). You can have the children pick a role- card from a pack, allow free choice, or assign the roles yourself.

(d) Assign a group observer who will report on how the group got on with its tasks. The class should all contribute to drawing up a checklist of what should be recorded by this group member.

(e) Groups without assigned roles can work well and creatively, but they should be prepared to report back to the others about what they did in their group, how they did it, and what they felt about the process.

Bennett and Dunne (1992) and the National Oracy Project, Key Stage 2 (1992) have many useful ideas for designing group tasks for the National Curriculum.

II. Equal opportunities and group formation

Children bring not only their personality 'type' and preferred thinking style into the group. They bring their gender, their cultural background, their colour, their language competence, and how these have affected their lives so far.

☐ **Collaborative work in small groups can be structured to take account of this personal 'baggage' and to help children both share the richness of their differences and also move beyond whatever limitations the experiences may have engendered.**

Some considerations:

- Are children from all social and cultural backgrounds contributing equally?

- Does the subject matter affect who contributes, who is interested, who has confidence?

- Do girls reach a consensus too quickly?

- Are girls less willing to experiment?

- Are girls taking responsibility for boys in their group?

- Do some roles tend to fall to the girls and others to the boys?

- Do boys lead, do girls defer, in mixed groups?

- Do boys tend to be competitive within a collaborative context?

- Do boys tend to see things in terms of 'right' or 'wrong' more than girls?

- Do their race or gender (or both) make some children less likely to talk?

- Do girls collaborate more readily than boys?

- Are there opportunities for peer group support for bilingual learners?

- Can bilingual children work initially in their own language? (either writing or talking). This can allow them to conceptualise at a more appropriate level than working straight into their second language.

[Based on a *Checklist for Monitoring Equal Opportunities*, Grunsell et al., in Hicks and Steiner (1989)]

The multicultural dimension of this exercise (dia-mond ranking statements about school rules) was interesting. Numan and Arfan would revert back to their mother tongue (Panjabi) when communi-cating with each other in the group. They would then express their feelings to the group in English.
[Year 3 teacher, Cleveland (1992)]

III. Getting Going in Groups

Forming Groups

(i) *Self-selecting friendship groups* can lead to greater commitment and less conflict; they can also lead to unquestioning cosiness and perpetuate the isolation of certain children.

(ii) *Random groups* are valuable in creating broader friendship groupings and can result in better classroom relationships overall.

There are a number of ways of arranging a class into random groups, for example:

☆ Number pupils in order, eg. 1, 2, 3, 4, 1, 2, 3, 4, so that all the ones go into group one, all the twos into group two and so on (random numbering).

☆ The pupils could be asked to line themselves up in age or height, after which random numbering is used. (This may help children to see that human beings can be classified in many ways.)

☆ Group according to hair or eye colour. (Ask the children how they feel about this sort of group-ing!)

☆ Put different coloured paper on the floor or in parts of the room and have the children move to their favourite colour or to the colour which matches an item of their clothing.

☆ Cut up some old Christmas/birthday cards into 3/4/5 pieces and put them in a bag or box. Each pupil picks a piece and then matches it with others, like a jigsaw, until they make the whole card. (This encourages group discussion even before the groupwork begins.)

☆ Animal Farm: Choose a number of animals — cat, dog, pig, cow, sheep — depending on how many people you want per group and make cards with each animal's name on (eg. 5 cat cards, 5 dog cards etc.). Mix them up like a pack of cards. Before giving one card to each pupil explain that once they get a card they cannot speak. On the word 'Go' the pupils must make the animal's noise and join up with others who are also mewing, barking or whatever, until they have located all their mem-bers. Rather noisy but lots of fun!

☆ Give each child the name of a fruit — oranges, peaches, pears, mangoes. Ask each child to join together with different fruits to make a fruit salad (more kinds of fruit will make larger groups).
[Brown, Barnfield and Stone (1990)]

(iii) Teacher-selected groups are very useful when you want to observe specific individuals and their progress in social and learning skills. Your purposes might be to create specific mixes of gender or language or ability. It can be useful to start discussion work on sensitive issues in single-sex groups.

There are occasions when teachers will choose to organise the class into girls' and boys' discussion groups. The issues discussed may well be identi-cal but both girls and boys sometimes need to gain clarity and strength from those who share their experiences before they can contribute fully to a mixed discussion.
[Brown, Barnfield and Stone, *op cit.*]

IV. Some responses to common problems

Poor listening and turn-taking

• Practise listening skills in pairs, eg. one child must listen to the other talk for 2 minutes about some topic such as 'My favourite T.V. programme' without inter-rupting and then précis what was said.

• Tell the children that you may ask each of them to give you a written or verbal report about what someone else has said without telling them to whom they should particularly attend.

• Give each child a small amount of 'tokens' (play-money, counters etc.) which they have to 'spend' (place on the table) each time they talk.

Conflict in the group

• Get the group to 'freeze' and to take turns to say what is going on. A child from another group can join you as impartial judge. The children can decide themselves on how to resolve their conflict.

• Restructure the task so that the group can work in a smaller unit and come together later.

The group is not taking the activity seriously

• Give the group a self-evaluation sheet to fill in and discuss their answers immediately with them. This may allow them to cool down and take responsibility for their actions.

• Change the group members.

Some children are disruptive or dominant

• Give such children the attention they may need by staying with the group for a short while. Give feedback to all the children; praise and encourage that child and then the others as well.

• Give that child a useful and specific job in the group, eg. scribe, envoy.

Some children are passive and don't participate

• As above.

• Join the group and draw that child into the discussion by referring to the skills, interests etc. you know s/he has; invite his/her comments in a direct and sensitive way.

☐ **Above all, establish clear and mutually agreed ground rules that apply to all groupwork situations.**

Selected approaches to evaluation and assessment in groups

> *'You can get to know people better.'*
>
> *'I really had a splendid time working this work.'*
>
> *'It is better working this way because you don't do it on your own.'*
>
> *'I liked doing it a lot but I don't like it if people boss you around a lot.'*
>
> *'Good because people say what they think.'*
>
> *'I hated it.'*
>
> *'You can discuss about things that we need to know.'*
>
> *'Frustrating because we argued.'*
>
> *'We didn't argue, we discussed.'*
>
> [Year 4 children from various schools]

The eight year old quoted above who, early in his autumn term, 'hated' the experience did so because he was more ready for constructive groupwork than his peers. He was frustrated because he felt a responsibility to ensure fairness.

He tried to instil a degree of discussion and democracy in decision taking.
[Year 4 Teacher, Limehouse London (1991)]

Teachers play a powerful role in the assessment process. An outsider might well misinterpret or misunderstand the child's meaning from spoken or written statements taken out of context.

This child and the others quoted throughout this section were recording their personal responses to a groupwork exercise in which they had just taken part. They had been involved in using either the Diamond Ranking or the Jigsaw Photograph procedures (Chapter Nine) in which, through discussion, they had had to arrive at a 'product' (a completed diamond) or a joint conclusion (an analysis of what the different pieces of cut-up photograph might be showing).

Through this active learning work their teachers observed and recorded oracy skills and social skills. They were able to make judgements about the development of the children's general cognitive abilities such as reasoning and analysing. They were also able to assess how well children were understanding work relating to various different subjects of the National Curriculum. Some few examples of the work covered in the forty schools are: Environmental Science, History (Invaders and Settlers, Egypt), Geography (India, local studies), English (the media).

☐ **Groups provide a coherent unit in which you can see and hear children talking, thinking and solving problems.**

The learning children can do about themselves and others using groupwork as well as about specific subject matter is vital. Through structured evaluation and reflection, they can take advantage of this awareness to enhance their skills and effectiveness. Their feedback can refer specifically to the problem, project or discussion they were working on and also to the group process itself. Their feelings about this experience and their analysis of its effectiveness are equally valid. Encourage them to be specific and concrete: even younger children can add comments as well as circling a smiling or frowning face!

Maximising the opportunities of cooperative and collaborative groupwork for evaluation and assessment

Setting the scene

Clear explanation is always important; the children get to understand what is expected of them and so are enabled to do their best. Discussion-based activities in which there will not necessarily be a right-or-wrong outcome deserve as clear instructions as, say, a science experiment. Thus your explanation will tell the children how they should go about the task, and not only what you, their teacher, want to be able to observe (eg. to hear them talking in a group about an idea and making decisions) but also what you hope *they* will get out of the experience (eg. practice in using their discussion skills, thinking something through and hearing what other people think about some question).

Deliberately talking about your intentions with the children is clearly part of the open and cooperative learning environment that world studies advocates. By doing this, you share the control of the situation which, in turn, empowers the children to own their parts in it and feel encouraged to enter fully into their task and do their best. They know what the goals are and can deliberately direct their energies to getting there. It's something being done not just *to* them, but *with* them.

The orientation of the work pushed me to give the class more control over their work (i.e. they held their own editorial meetings to examine their own work and working methods). The success of this has strongly led me to appreciate the amount of autonomy the children can exercise and how didactic I had sometimes (unnecessarily) been in my approach. Many of the things I might have said were put across very well by the children themselves.
[Manchester teacher (1991)]

Recent class research by Maurice Galton [Galton and Williamson op. cit.] confirms that children enjoy groupwork when the tasks are clearly structured and explained. Explanation means not only describing the end-product: it also means giving the children reasons why you are asking them to do the task and describing the processes that will help them along. Children like structure and purpose to their learning experiences.

Using discussion-based activity to monitor developments

Galton further concluded that of all groupwork activities, children least like to hold discussions without the teacher. *It is precisely because of this reticence and unease with communication and self-expression, that global education emphasises the value of clearly structured interactive activities.* Democratic decision making and participation rest on being able to explain and justify one's opinions and values and, equally importantly, to listen with care and attention to others.

Teachers can create 'argumentative classrooms' where there are plenty of genuine reasons for children to persuade each other... (It) is a place where children have developed an expectation that their point of view is valued, and their challenges to other points of view welcomed... A child's ability to argue and reason successfully depend less on her age, than upon the way her teacher has shaped the class's expectations... a five-year old can explore an issue... as effectively as an eleven-year old although the topics she will find interesting are likely to be different.
[Terry Phillips in D. Wray (ed.)(1990)]

World Studies teaches you that you should think what you want to think, not what other people want you to think!
[David, Year 6, Manchester]

☐ **Clear structure, obvious purpose and concrete examples make groupwork enjoyable and non-threatening to children.**

Groupwork Skills and Personal Growth

Code: C = Considerably; S = To some extent; N = Not at all

Date and Activity:

Names of Children:

Communication and Cognitive Skills					
Contributed to discussion					
Initiated discussion					
Listened to others					
Negotiated					
Explained own ideas clearly					
Justified own ideas if required to					
Questioned others' ideas					
Tolerated ideas different to own					
Supported others' ideas					
Organisational Skills					
Took decisions					
Helped prioritise tasks					
Organised others					
Accepted being organised					
Shared resources					
Accepted others' needs					
Cooperated					
Worked without teacher					
Interpersonal and Personal Relationships					
Accepted another's leadership					
Accepted group decisions					
Willing to change ideas or plans					
Used inventiveness and imagination					
Took risks in their learning					
Handled conflict constructively					
Was willing to affirm others					
Had a positive self-concept					
Accepted affirmation					

Was the groupwork worthwhile?

Date and Activity:

1. **All** / **most** / **few** of the children in the group took part.

Did any child or children particularly stand out?

What did they say or do that was significant for that child?

Anything I need or want to do about it? (e.g. praise for effort; a quiet word about listening etc?)

2. How did the children share the tasks? They organised themselves: *easily / without much difficulty / needed help / found it hard*

Did any child or children particularly stand out?

What did they say or do that was significant for that child?

Anything I need or want to do about it?

3. Were their activities and talk related to the task *exclusively / mainly / hardly at all?*

Anything I need or want to do about it?

4. Were the children interested in what they were doing?
A great deal — they really got stuck in / OK on the whole / it was a struggle.

Did any child or children particularly stand out?

What did they say or do that was significant for that child?

Anything I need or want to do about it?

5. Were there any problems with participation, e.g. withdrawal, aggressive domination, clowning, other? **Yes / some / no.**
If so, do you think this was caused by: *nature of the activity (too easy / too difficult) / the composition of the group / an 'off day' / insecurity with this way of working / something else?*

Did any child or children particularly stand out?

What did they say or do that was significant for that child?

Anything I need or want to do about it?

What could I do to improve the group skills of this particular group?

Groupwork Feedback

Name:

Please circle the answer which best fits the way you feel:

I had fun	No	A Little	Lots
Can you explain why?			

We worked well together as a group	No	OK	Very well
Can you explain why?			

I said what I wanted to say	Not at all	Sometimes	Always
Can you explain why?			

I listened to the others	Not at all	Sometimes	Always
Can you explain why?			

The others listened to me	Not at all	Sometimes	Always
Can you explain why?			

I felt embarassed to talk in the large group	Very	A little	No
Can you explain why?			

Is there anything else you would like to say about today's activity?

(Format devised by Jane Weaver: Norwich Education and Action for Development)

What do you think of it?

Your name: **The date:**

Who was in your group?

To answer the questions, please circle the number that best fits the way *you* feel:

1 = NOT AT ALL   **2 = A BIT**   **3 = ABOUT RIGHT**   **4 = A LOT**

Did you enjoy yourself?	1	2	3	4
Did you learn anything?	1	2	3	4
Do you think you worked well in the group?	1	2	3	4
Did you talk about the work?	1	2	3	4
Did you have enough time?	1	2	3	4
Would you like to do this kind of work again?	1	2	3	4

Can you explain, in a few lines, what your group did?

Can you say what you think about working in this way?

Anything else you'd like to say?

Planning learning experiences with a global dimension

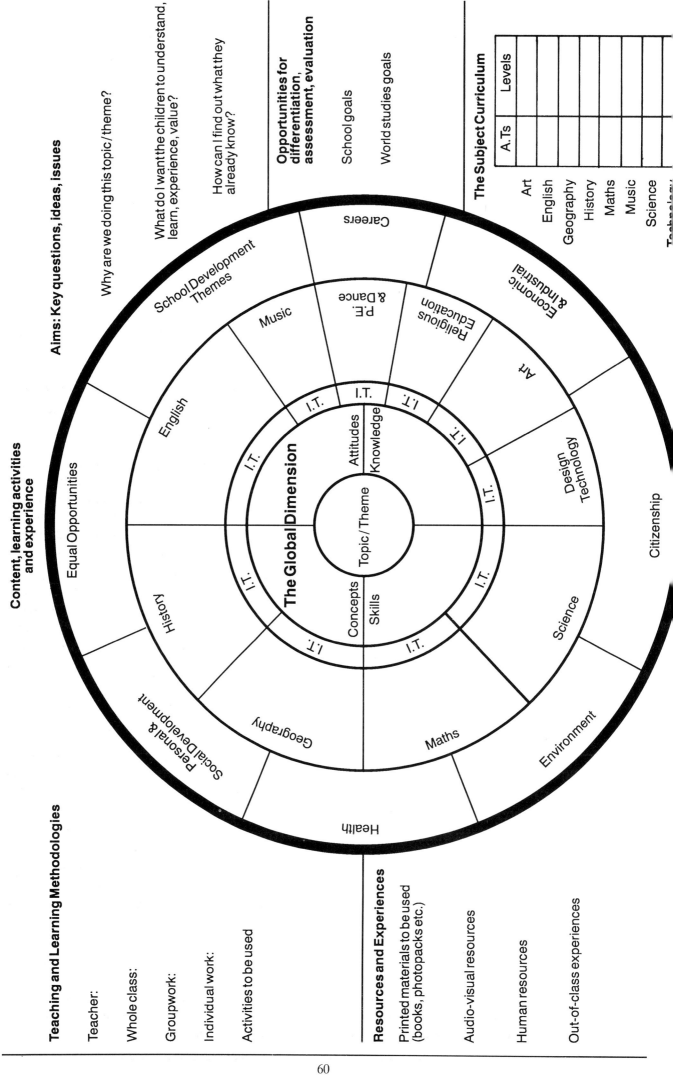

Aims: Key questions, ideas, issues

Why are we doing this topic / theme?

What do I want the children to understand, learn, experience, value?

How can I find out what they already know?

Opportunities for differentiation, assessment, evaluation

School goals

World studies goals

The Subject Curriculum

	A.Ts	Levels				
Art						
English						
Geography						
History						
Maths						
Music						
Science						

Content, learning activities and experience

Teaching and Learning Methodologies

Teacher:

Whole class:

Groupwork:

Individual work:

Activities to be used

Resources and Experiences

Printed materials to be used (books, photopacks etc.)

Audio-visual resources

Human resources

Out-of-class experiences

School Development Themes

Equal Opportunities

Personal & Social Development

Careers

Economic & Industrial

Citizenship

Environment

Health

Music

English

History

Geography

Maths

Science

Design Technology

Art

Religious Education

P.E. & Dance

The Global Dimension

Attitudes

Knowledge

Topic / Theme

Concepts

Skills

I.T.

8

Planning for Connectedness: Topic Work

Benefits

- Topic work allows you to plan for a variety of activities that engage different kinds of thinking and use the full range of cross-curricular skills (reading, writing, talking, numeracy, problem solving, collaborating with others, personal research and information technology, art and creativity).

- Topics can encompass fundamental experiences of learning — the moral and spiritual, the expressive and aesthetic.

- Topics are an unartificial and meaningful way of incorporating the dimensions of equal opportunities and life in a multicultural society and interdependent world into everyday learning. You can accomplish this by the way you design and structure work tasks, the opportunities for talk, the actual content and the resources you provide.

- The five Cross-Curricular Themes can be coherently integrated into topics closer to the children's interests.

- Key concepts such as 'Change', 'Interdependence', 'Similarities and Differences', 'Justice and Fairness' for example, recur throughout the primary stage, giving children the chance to revisit and understand them more deeply. One or more concepts can either run like threads through topics which are pegged to National Curriculum subjects, or they can themselves be the starting point for a wider, cross-subject investigation.

- Individuals can work to their own best levels on both joint and individual tasks. Your assessment can differentiate by individual outcome; *their* self-assessments and evaluation will also help them to articulate what sense they are beginning to make of concepts and knowledge.

- Planning for topic work encourages creativity and cooperation amongst the staff and between children and teachers. Getting the children to plan components of a topic will develop their investi-

gative and analytical skills. It will also involve them in their learning as active co-owners rather than passive recipients.

Some strategies and tools for planning topics from a world studies perspective

1) The **Planning Wheel** opposite allows you to see at a glance how your topic relates to all areas of the curriculum: subjects and themes, organisation of teaching and learning activities, implications for resourcing and assessment. You can identify your key aims and your objectives for bringing in the global dimension.

2) 'Food' is a classic **starting point** for a cross-curricular topic. The exemplar on page 62 is taken from '*It's Our World Too!*' *A local-global approach to environmental education at Key Stages Two and Three* [Development Education Centre, Birmingham (1992)]. This builds on concepts with a broader global perspective (eg. sustainability, interdependence).

The diagram shows the work planned for the second half-term, each 'slice' of three layers representing the key activities for one week. The teachers also prepared more detailed plans for each week, specifying activities, attainment targets, resources etc. The overall aims were to create a broad, balanced, practical activity-based project. Key Concepts rather than specific subject content (eg. The Romans) are at the heart of the planning.

The teachers who developed this plan found that it:

- ensures continuity and progression in development of ideas, knowledge and skills;

- ensures that all the work is linked by more than just a knowledge base, i.e. concepts enhance coherence;

- helps the teachers to focus on what they really want the children to learn;

- makes the weekly planning much easier, as the teacher has a structured overview of the whole. [DEC (1992)]

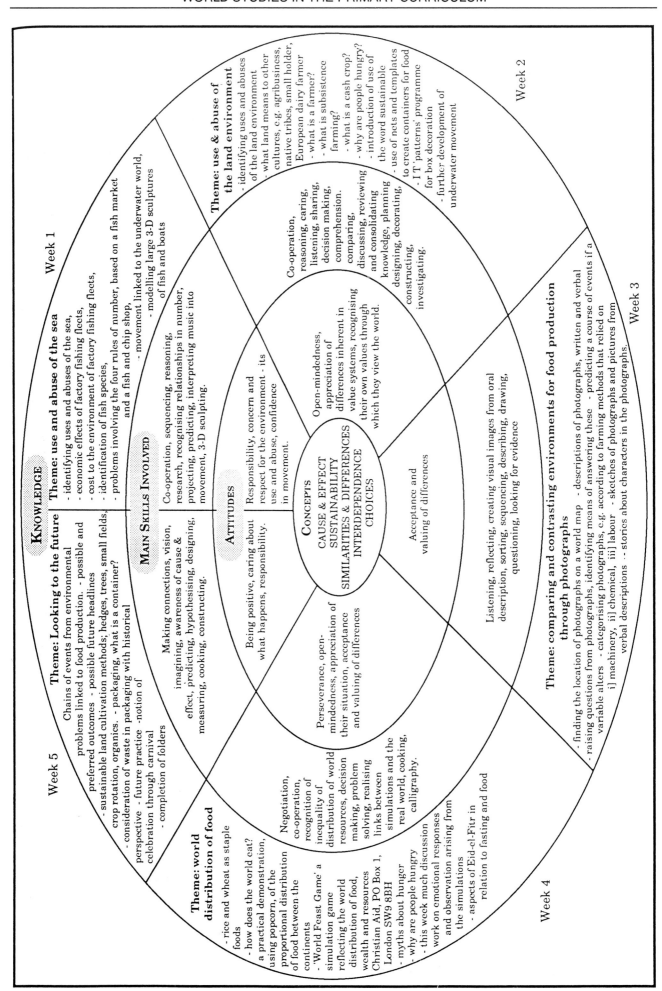

KNOWLEDGE

Week 1

Theme: use and abuse of the sea
- identifying uses and abuses of the sea,
- economic effects of factory fishing fleets,
- cost to the environment of factory fishing fleets,
- identification of fish species,
- problems involving the four rules of number, based on a fish market and a fish and chip shop,
- movement linked to the underwater world,
- modelling large 3-D sculptures of fish and boats

Week 2

Theme: use & abuse of the land environment
- identifying uses and abuses of the land environment
- what land means to other cultures, e.g. agribusiness, native tribes, small holder, European dairy farmer
  - what is a farmer?
  - what is subsistence farming?
  - what is a cash crop?
  - why are people hungry?
- introduction of use of the word sustainable
- use of nets and templates to create containers for food
- IT 'patterns' programme for box decoration
- further development of underwater movement

Week 3

MAIN SKILLS INVOLVED

Co-operation, reasoning, caring, listening, sharing, decision making, comprehension. comparing, discussing, reviewing and consolidating knowledge, planning designing, decorating, constructing, investigating.

Co-operation, sequencing, reasoning, research, recognising relationships in number, projecting, predicting, interpreting music into movement, 3-D sculpting.

ATTITUDES

Open-mindedness, appreciation of differences inherent in value systems, recognising their own values through which they view the world.

Responsibility, concern and respect for the environment - its use and abuse, confidence in movement.

CONCEPTS

CAUSE & EFFECT
SUSTAINABILITY
SIMILARITIES & DIFFERENCES
INTERDEPENDENCE
CHOICES

Acceptance and valuing of differences

Being positive, caring about what happens, responsibility.

Making connections, vision, imagining, awareness of cause & effect, predicting, hypothesising, designing, measuring, cooking, constructing.

Week 5

Theme: Looking to the future

Chains of events from environmental problems linked to food production. - possible and preferred outcomes - possible future headlines
- sustainable land cultivation methods; hedges, trees, small fields, crop rotation, organics. - packaging, what is a container?
- consideration of waste in packaging with historical perspective - future practice -notion of celebration through carnival
  - completion of folders

Theme: world distribution of food

- rice and wheat as staple foods
- how does the world eat? a practical demonstration, using popcorn, of the proportional distribution of food between the continents
- 'World Feast Game' a simulation game reflecting the world distribution of food, wealth and resources Christian Aid, PO Box 1, London SW9 8BH
- myths about hunger
- why are people hungry
- this week much discussion work on emotional responses and observation arising from the simulations
- aspects of Eid-el-Fitr in relation to fasting and food

Negotiation, co-operation, recognition of inequality of distribution of world resources, decision making, problem solving, realising links between simulations and the real world, cooking, calligraphy.

Perseverance, open-mindedness, appreciation of their situation, acceptance and valuing of differences

Week 4

Theme: comparing and contrasting environments for food production through photographs

- finding the location of photographs on a world map - descriptions of photographs, written and verbal
- raising questions from photographs, identifying means of answering these - predicting a course of events if a variable alters - categorising photographs, e.g. according to farming methods that relied on i] machinery, ii] chemical, iii] labour - sketches of photographs and pictures from verbal descriptions - stories about characters in the photographs.

Listening, reflecting, creating visual images from oral description, sorting, sequencing, describing, drawing, questioning, looking for evidence

Selected approaches to planning for assessment and evaluation

Active learning and topic work with a global perspective

Active learning and topic work assist affective and intellectual development through talk and collaboration. A more detailed description of a variety of active learning processes comes later in this chapter. The following pages look briefly at some of the key principles and methods for assessment and evaluation with a world studies perspective. These approaches are intended to supplement the many other techniques for assessment found in current publications (see Bibliography).

Core considerations

- Equal Opportunities

- The Entitlement to intellectual, social, spiritual and moral development

- The Global Dimension

- The National Curriculum

These four considerations determine how the children are organised to do the learning, which activities you use, what the basic goals are and what content you select in order to highlight the wider global dimensions. Specific activities relating to the National Curriculum and the Global Dimension are described in more detail in the activities section.

Planning for Equal Opportunities

- You can ensure that bilingual children have appropriate opportunity to work in their first language.

- You can also arrange bilingual support from adults or from other children more advanced in English.

- You can organise groupwork for peer tutoring. This has double benefits because the responsibility to explain and clarify to another (or others) also helps the 'tutor' to understand the work better.

- You can structure some groupwork activities so that each person is responsible for a concrete task that enables the group to complete its work. The feelings of inclusion and team participation build confidence.

- You can preplan the roles and tasks within the group so that all the children have genuine equality of access to all the tasks. (For example, a non-reader can take responsibility for the resources.) Plan for activities that suit different research styles; monitor the division of labour to make sure that both girls and boys undertake a fair mix of creative, mechanical and language work.

- You can plan topics so that children's different experiences and home circumstances are sensitively reflected. Do titles like 'families' or 'homes', for example, imply there is some 'normal' standard, or are they inclusive of a wide range of cultural and economic experiences?

- Do your topic titles have a wide appeal? Are they geared equally to boys' and girls' interests?

Intellectual and affective growth

This can be observed and described if you know what you hope to see and by what means you plan to collect the evidence. You can identify in advance those thinking and social skills, and attitudes towards themselves and others, which you want the children to develop. Prioritise, because you can never hope to look for and record it all!

Continuous evaluation will help you keep a record of the extent to which the tasks and resources you present are helping this to happen. In *Equal Opportunities in Schools: New Dimensions in Topic Work*, Antonouris and Wilson (1989) suggest that such evaluation should:

- be continuous and relatively frequent;

- cover the full range of all the potential learning the children could experience;

- focus sharply on a specific situation;

- be clear about criteria: these should reflect what children are genuinely capable of doing at their age and stage. The Lesson Evaluation sheet on p.44 has been found by many teachers to be a convenient framework for focusing on what learning has taken place in a specific context.

Antonouris and Wilson also suggest four criteria for assessing broad affective and intellectual development; criteria which correspond to the world studies goals of helping children become open-minded, clear thinking, sympathetic and unprejudiced. Their criteria are: *inclusiveness of thought, elaboration of response, abstractness, tentativeness and 'de-centring'*. The first three can be noted by remarking the descriptions, explanations and opinions the children offer in talk or writing. One can observe growth (or its absence) in the degree and depth of detail and in the growing sophistication of their vocabulary. Other evidence is available when children's reasoning is based not only on the concrete, immediate and personal but also on abstract generalisations. For example:

> *'We could improve our street by mending the pavements. They're dangerous to blind people.'*
> [8 year old, Stockport]

Tentativeness is not the same as indecision or lack of confidence. It is the recognition that one may not have the definitive answer; that there may be other ways of understanding a situation; that other perspectives exist. In terms of cognitive development, this is about the ability to perceive complexity. Effectively it means developing the general maturity to be able to tolerate uncertainty.

'De-centring' is an extension of tentativeness. It is a skill that is essential, on a basic level, for many learning situations (eg. drama, history, geography) and, at a deeper level, for citizenship in a multicultural society and interdependent world. It means being able to step outside one's own attitudes and values and to see other perspectives. Going one (developmental) step further, this could mean 'representing' someone else's views in a discussion. For example, in some recent work in geography, some Year 5 children were scornful of homes in a photograph of India.

> A more mature child commented: *'You'd feel differently if you lived there. It could be **your** home then and you'd be proud of it'.*
> [South Tyneside school]

Involving the children

Involving the children and planning for progression enables them to show what they already know and can do, and how they are integrating new information, skills and attitudes.

- Find out the general level of awareness before a topic through **brainstorming** (collecting ideas by allowing everyone to call out suggestions which are all listed without comment, whether negative or positive). This can be 'Everything we already know about... (topic X)', 'What we'd like to find out about...' or 'Some questions we have about...'. At the conclusion of the topic work, repeat the procedure and make comparisons. This can take the form of 'What we now know about...'.

- Individuals can make **personal lists**, eg. 'Four things I know about ...' and at a later stage add 'Four new things I know about...'. They can also reflect on what they've learned through completing sentences such as:

> *'Before we started this topic I didn't know that...'*
> *'Before we started this topic I wasn't as good at.......... as I am now'*

> *'The part I remember best is...'*
> *'The most difficult bit for me was...'*

- Children keep **individual files** of work, which they can rate for themselves. For example, they can sort these into three piles: work they're pleased with; work that's OK; work they could have done better. You can discuss samples from each category with them and share your criteria for improvement.

- **Drama and roleplay exercises** give children openings to display knowledge and attitudes. These too can be used as 'before and after' indicators. By altering the context slightly, the children can repeat a theme and show how they have integrated understanding. For example, a scenario which was first based on bullying or litter in the playground could now be set in the streets outside the school, or in an international context such as civil wars, rainforest conservation and so forth.

- **Observe** one group making a presentation (a roleplay, a poster, a verbal explanation about some finished artefact) to another group. The verbal and social behaviours of both the presenters and the audience, such as describing and questioning, can demonstrate both social and cognitive development.

- Are they comfortable arguing from different perspectives in role-plays? Does their written work show pride in presentation? Do they listen with attention to others and tolerate other points of view?

These techniques can also be used to provide insight into children's attitudes and how these are developing.

There are further suggestions and formats for assessment in the fourth chapter of this book.

Plan for progression

In his preface to two of the geography activities later in this section, Roger Wassell Smith wrote:

> One of the challenges of the National Curriculum is to cover prescribed matters while at the same time offering children opportunities to:

- engage prior knowledge with new understandings and build effectively on what they already know;

- explore information about the world without resorting to closed 'learning by rote' activities, but using activities which offer children scope for imagination and creativity.

He suggests that children can (and should) continue to work collaboratively even when progressing towards dif-

Topic planning: the global dimension

Y= directly planned for   P= potential   N= not relevant this time

	Y	P	N
It is a broad theme that permits genuine cross-curricular coverage (e.g. Food, Homes).			
It builds on students' own experiences, ideas, attitudes and values. It encourages open-mindedness.			
It shows how Britain is a multi-ethnic and multicultural society.			
By making local connections with the wider world, it promotes a world view.			
It presents positive views of black people and other ethnic groups, both in Britain and elsewhere in the world, and of women, children and people with disabilities.			
It helps children recognise and accept the merits of different points of view and ways of living.			
It includes images, examples and situations that help children recognise and challenge stereotypes.			
It presents a range of views, images and explanations of the past, present and future.			
It considers attitudes as well as developing skills and knowledge.			
It poses questions.			
It uses activity and discussion-based group learning and also involves opportunities for individual research.			
It will consider issues and have planned-in, clear strategies for dealing with controversial matters as they arise.			
The subject content is underpinned by concepts such as *change, fairness, values and beliefs, interdependence.*			
It promotes a positive and responsible attitude to the environment.			

ferent levels. You can differentiate between individuals by outcome — whether different *products* (eg. individual versions of a joint story), different verbal feedback, or by looking at an individual's input into a joint product (model, artefact or story). This is also an area where self-assessment (eg. 'I think I did better/worse/the same work as last time') or group evaluation will add to your evidence for judgement.

- Are the children clear about what is expected of them?

- Have you decided on your criteria and methods?

Some useful resources for topic work are: *Teacher Assessment: making it work for the primary school,* Primary Association (1990); *Themework,* C. McFarlane (1990); *Why on Earth: an approach to science with a global dimension at Key Stage two,* C. McFarlane et al (1991); *Equal Opportunities in Schools, new dimensions in topic work,* G. Antonouris and J. Wilson (1989); *Topic Planning and the National Curriculum,* R. Arnold ed. (1991); *Assessment Matters,* D. Balderstone and D. Lambert, Geographical Association; *Assessment in the Multi-Ethnic Classroom,* P. Keel (1993); *'Fitting it all together' Topic Work and the Primary Curriculum,* Sheffield City Council Education Department (1992). See Bibliography for full details.

9

Core Processes and Skills for Active Learning throughout the Curriculum

Affirmation Exercises

Purpose

One of the foundations of world studies is the belief that a healthy self-esteem is an essential ingredient for holding positive attitudes to people different from oneself. These activities are essential for work in equal opportunities and definitely help reduce racist and gender stereotypes. There is a well established relationship among positive self-concept, high level social skills and good performance at school. See the bibliography for resources for affirmation and conflict resolution activities. A few examples follow.

☆ Name Games

Procedure

Each student introduces themselves and states one of their attributes (eg. brown eyes), skills (I can play the piano) or likes (my favourite colour is green). The person next to them re-introduces the speaker — eg. 'This is Josh. He has brown eyes and he likes to ride his bike.' The speaker then introduces herself and is described in turn by her neighbour. The circle is complete when everyone has spoken about themselves and one other.

☆ Affirming Adjectives

Procedure

The children introduce themselves with a positive adjective. It can be alliterative, such as Joking John or Super Sanita, or describe some skill or interest eg. Footballing Amir or Dancing Rebecca.

This can also be a powerful tool for helping children to learn and pronounce non-Anglo-Saxon names. After each child has introduced him or herself, the rest of the class repeats what has just been said. They can say, for example 'Hello, Amazing Amir', or make a statement, eg. 'Sanita is Super'. Children find it difficult to be openly self-

affirming and affirming others is also unfamiliar. The circle can be a safe place for sincere positive comments to be made.

☆ 'Stocking Fillers'

Procedure

Start with small groups of four to five. Give each child an envelope and four slips of paper. The children write a positive comment about each member of their group on each slip of paper. (These could range from 'I like your jumper', to 'you are good at maths', to 'you are a nice friend'.) The children write their own names on their envelopes, which are passed around and the slips put inside. Allow them to read the contents in private.

Form the circle and ask each child to pass their envelope to their neighbour on the left. Going round the circle, each child reads aloud one of the positive statements about their neighbour. Alternatively, the children could select one for themselves and have a neighbour read it. This provides practice in affirming someone in public and also in accepting affirmation.

Discussion

These simple activities can arouse very powerful feelings. Using the 'Magic Microphone' tool (see below) helps children express them.

Communication

☆ Discussion Circles

Purpose

To provide students with the opportunity to be heard and with a clear purpose for listening. It enhances concentration, builds a positive and caring environment and increases skill and confidence in self-expression. This is a cross-curricular tool, enabling the discussion of ideas, concepts, problems or issues arising in any subject. It can help children use specialist vocabulary (eg. science, technology, geography etc.) in a familiar conversational context.

Preparation

Find a comfortable space for the circle, whether on chairs or on the floor.

Set aside a specific time (daily, weekly) and set a fixed time-limit for the discussion. Setting a clock-timer can help children use the time confidently and constructively.

Identify subjects or specific formats for the discussion. These might be: sharing news, specific feedback about a previous activity, discussing topics selected from a topic box, talking through some general concept or particular subject matter in the curriculum, doing affirmation and self-esteem work.

Procedure

There are few formal rules other than turn-taking and basic courtesy. Students should always be allowed to 'pass' if they wish. Initially, you may wish to do some warm-ups to encourage listening. For example, focus in silence for one minute on the sounds around, and then have each child share one.

This procedure is a very powerful tool in the multicultural and multi-lingual classroom. Children can bring their personal experiences of travel, festivals and cultural outings into the circle; this can both widen everyone's knowledge and give validation to these experiences. Those for whom English is a new or second language can express themselves in a safe environment.

Self-Esteem: A Classroom Affair (volumes 1 & 2) and *Esteem Builders* by Michele Borba, contain many helpful suggestions for discussion topics and variations on the circle. *Esteem Builders* is particularly relevant for KS2.

The Topic File

A shoe box with a slit cut in the top can be decorated to serve as a suggestion box. The children can post in ideas for circle time discussion, whether their own interests or newspaper clippings. They can keep a list of the topics discussed over the term. You can also have a Graffiti Board on which ideas can be written down during the week.

Extensions: Interviews and Journals

The topics discussed can be followed up with further oral work and written activities. The children can interview

each other about their opinions, using a format such as the one included below.

- The discussion topic can be the subject for their journals where they can explore it in greater privacy. They could also discuss the topic briefly with a partner, sharing what they plan to write.

- Journal writing can also be a class activity. Working in groups of four after a circle discussion, the children can reflect on the views they expressed and record them, using a 'Feedback' sheet like the one on page 70. A format such as this allows a group literally to see the range of opinions that an issue can generate. It also allows them to reflect and elaborate on their ideas and to share their evaluation of the activity.

Opportunities for global education

The discussion circle is clearly a place where children can express opinions and views about a wide range of issues, whether local to the school, neighbourhood, town or more widely global. This can be done by nominating or brainstorming a current topic for discussion and going round the circle inviting comment. It is also helpful for children if the discussion is structured. Thus you could have a list of incomplete sentences as prompts such as...

'If I were in charge, I'd...'

'My wishes for the future are...'

'Things in the news that worry me are...'

'Things in the news that interest me are...'

'I wish I could...'

Assessment Opportunities

Observation and listening: either informally or with a predetermined checklist of oracy components. Children's clarity and confidence in self-expression can be observed, as well as their use of appropriate vocabulary. The children can evaluate the activity either through on-the-spot techniques like thumbs-up/down; or on evaluation sheets. See Groupwork, earlier. They can rate their own contribution on personal profile sheets.

Written work

The journals, interview sheets and group feedback sheets will be evidence of writing skills, showing how children communicate thoughts and feelings. You can also use the discussion topic as a focus for a personal written exchange between you and individual children, writing to a few every week. This can be a useful diagnostic tool for assessment of development.

The following practical tips are taken from: Richardson (1990) *Daring to be a Teacher.*

Discussion Exercises — Some Practical Tips

Things to handle

Arrange for pupils to have things which are literally tangible — objects, pictures, slips of paper, which they can move around with their hands.

Precise task

Give precise instructions about what is to be done. For example: 'Here are pictures of six different people. Choose the two people you would most like to meet. For each of them, write down the one question you would most like to ask.'

Co-operation

Choose discussion tasks which require pupils to listen to each other and to help each other. For example, use 'jigsaw games', which can only be completed if everyone takes part.

Small groups

The smaller the group, the more pupils feel secure. Also, the more they're able to talk. Often arrange for them to work in pairs or in threes. The maximum for most group work is six.

Controversy

Choose subjects on which pupils are likely to have conflicting opinions. Or build controversy into a discussion by requiring some of the participants to play specific roles.

Nonverbal material

Use material which communicates ideas symbolically and nonverbally, rather than through words alone — photographs, cartoons, posters, statistical diagrams.

Comparing, contrasting selecting, justifying

Provide a collection of things to be compared and contrasted with each other; require people to arrange them or to select from them; and to explain their arrangement or selection.

Activity then reflection

Give pupils an activity to perform, or require them to watch an activity — for example a nonverbal game or exercise. Then invite discussion and clarification of what happened, and of how they felt, and of what can be learnt.

Not too easy, not too hard

Definitely try to stretch pupils with discussion tasks you set. But don't depress them or annoy them by providing things which are too difficult. When you fail (as you sometimes will) to get the balance right, invite discussion of how people feel.

From Richardson (1990) *Daring to be a Teacher*, Trentham Books.

JOURNAL FEEDBACK

TODAY'S TOPIC:

DATE:

TEAM MEMBERS:

WHAT WE SAID

MEMBER A:

MEMBER B:

MEMBER C:

MEMBER D:

How We Felt About This Topic:

From Borba (1989) Esteem Builders (California, Jalmar Press)

Name _____ Date _____

Your Thoughts About: _____
(Topic)

Interview several of your classmates about the daily topic. What are their thoughts and feelings? Write their names and answers in the spaces below.

From Borba (1989) Esteem Builders (California, Jalmar Press)

Name _____ Date _____

Let's Write to Each Other...

Student's Turn

Topic: _____

Dear_____,

_____

_____

_____

_____

_____

_____

_____

_____

_____

_____

_____

_____

_____

_____

_____

_____

_____

Signed _____

Teacher's Turn

Dear_____,

_____

_____

_____

_____

Signed _____

From Borba (1989) Esteem Builders (California, Jalmar Press)

☆ *Magic Microphone*

Purpose

- To help children express what they feel and think
- To value each person's reactions
- To promote listening and co-operation
- To help evaluate previous activities.

Preparation

You will need some object to serve as 'magic microphone'. and the following statements (or similar) on a large sheet, depending on the purpose of the circle.

- I was interested to hear
- I feel
- I learned that
- I was surprised to see
- Something I don't understand
- I really enjoyed
- My opinion is
- I didn't like
- Something I'd like to find out more about/I wish that
- Next time I'd

Procedure

Seat the children in a circle. Each person can speak only when they're holding the 'microphone' — which will be passed around. Allow them to think silently for a minute before beginning. Ask them to share their feelings or opinions using one of the starting points on the large sheet. Beware the influence of the first speaker! If s/he says 'I was surprised...' the odds are that everyone else will too! That's the purpose of the prompt sheet. Encourage, but don't enforce, variation. It's OK to pass. If there's time, go around a second time!

Questioning Children's Talk: the teacher's role

A minimum of direct input from the teacher during discussion activities enables the children better to explore their own ideas and values and to develop oracy and cooperation skills. The best approach is 'Hands off, stand back and let them be the stars of their own show and take things as far as they can alone!'

But with the best intentions in the world to do this, there are occasions when you'll want to and have to intervene in some way, at some point. I want to explore two reasons for teacher intervention and some appropriate strategies and techniques.

Prejudiced comments — racist, sexist, mocking disablement

These should not go unchallenged. They should be dealt with consistently and firmly, in the way that is right for the children in question, the time and the place.

Contexts and strategies

Sometimes such statements just come up in classroom or playground; sometimes they arise because of the nature of the issue being discussed or the resource being used. When you purposefully provide the opportunity for opinions to emerge, you will have your follow-up strategy in mind.

If you overhear such incidents, and the children are not aware that you have, it is valuable to remain silent and hear how they handle it themselves. You will find out what they think and how individuals react. Such comments should still not go unchallenged and need to be picked up later, either in a discussion with the children involved or as a topic that can include everyone. *It is clearly important to consider the feelings of the victim, the bystanders and the 'insulter(s)'.* You will have planned how to frame the discussion, without targeting the children involved.

- Be prepared in advance by thinking through your own 'bottom line' and how to express it to children in a calm and positive manner.

- Be familiar with school policy; what the agreed procedures and common strategies are, as well as who your allies are.

- Negotiate a code of conduct on unacceptable put-downs as part of the class 'rules' that you and the children draw up at the start of term. This will provide a relevant context to put equal opportunities issues up front.

If they know that you have overheard, you must ask the child or children concerned why they did what they did and what they meant by it. Ideally, this will be followed by a more general discussion about labelling and prejudice or by one of the other strategies suggested further on.

Your own value position can and should be clear to the children, not to influence them, but to let them know where you stand and why. This is part of the democratic classroom in which the teacher models democratic values at all levels. The fact that your position is clear contributes to creating an environment in which assumptions can be challenged safely.

Some ways to follow up:

- reading a story or poem in which an actual or imaginary victim of prejudice describes her/his feelings;

- using puppets to explore a situation of discrimination or prejudice;

- using drama or role-play similarly;

- setting individual writing tasks in which the children can describe to a friend or confide to a diary how they felt after being put down;

- holding a circle discussion around the topic 'Word Power'. (See the activities for English). You can explore which put-downs are acceptable and which are not.

As well as dealing with the issue through empathy and feelings, it is very important for the children to begin to think about the origin of prejudice against different groups. A useful focus is to ask them where *they* think the idea behind the insult or stereotype comes from. This will not only help them explore their own preconceptions, it will also provide you with the entry point to an appropriate investigation into the history of prejudice.

Using open-ended questioning purposefully to extend thinking

Contexts and strategies

When children are talking with a purpose, a wide range of learning can be monitored. For example, you could use a ranking exercise as an opportunity to see what elements in recent work the children have picked up on or really understood. It will be an occasion to hear them 'think aloud' in a cooperative context. In that case, you will want to be a non-participating observer. On the other hand, if your aim is to work on building skills, you may well want to prompt occasionally by asking them to expand on a point, or explain a bit more, or by reminding them of something *you know that they know* that can move the discussion on. (For example, 'Do you remember that film we saw last week? Does anything here remind you of that?')

Whatever the situation that prompts you to intervene, your own opinions and values really ought not to feature. Teachers can unwittingly limit the development of independent reasoning by taking too leading a role in discussion or by 'helping' when the talk seems to falter. Uncertainty is uncomfortable, as we all experience, and children are very adept at getting you to rescue them or to do the work for them!

Some strategies to help without unduly 'taking over':

- Let them know that you are confident that they will be able to handle group work on their own and that you will be available if really needed.

- Help all the children take part without turning the spotlight on specific silent individuals. Questions like 'Are there any other opinions on this?' or 'Does anyone disagree with that decision?' can provide space for them to show agreement or disagreement.

- When the students' lack of information or experience limits their thinking, you can introduce them to more information and back-up through books, stories, television programmes rather than through your own opinions.

- Ask open-ended questions (questions without a right or wrong or predetermined conclusion; questions to which you don't know the answer!) and encourage the children to express themselves fully. Use phrases such as 'Can you explain that a bit more?'

Respond to pupils' ideas by questions which ask them to clarify, develop and test them, remembering that this is a long term process. [C. Adelman (nd)]

When teachers intervene in the ways described above, they are actively promoting development. Vygotsky [Harvard University Press (1978)] defined this kind of process as assisting the learner through the 'zone of proximal development'. This is '... the distance between the child's actual developmental level as determined by independent problem solving and the level of potential development as determined through problem solving under adult guidance or in collaboration with more capable peers.' For Vygotsky, all learning is social and occurs through language.

Moving children on

Some roles for teachers in discussions	Non-Intervention	Intervention
1. Cases of moral development (racist/sexist comments etc.)	*In order to see 'where they're at', to be followed up very soon*	*If you are clearly involved*
2. To foster development; (cognitive, social and other skills)	*Avoid swamping tentative fledgling efforts*	*Prompt with examples that allow them to extend their skills, and to find out what they think by hearing themselves say it*
3. Providing an open-ended invitation to explore a new topic or idea	*Leave them to it, unless they stray wildly off course*	*Respond to questions for more information or resources, but not to opinions; prompt with open-ended questions; reminders of past experiences*
4. Observation specifically planned to evaluate teaching and assess learning	*As above*	*Put forward challenging but non-judgmental ideas; feed in resources, new information if necessary*

Developing Empathy and Enhancing Communication Skills

Roleplay and Simulation

Purpose

- To explore an issue or situation from the inside.

- To give students an opportunity to become aware of different points of view and to learn about someone else's feelings and perspectives.

- To develop communication skills, empathy and confidence.

- To encourage creative problem solving as the children experiment with different scenarios and reflect on choices and consequences.

- To deepen understanding relating to specific concepts/knowledge within the curriculum, depending on the subject focus. All subjects provide opportunities — eg. historical settings, understanding the implications of some design decision in technology, 'living' in another location, experiencing a scientific process (see Science section below), environmental issues etc.

Role-play and simulation highlight the fact that a range of choices can exist in different situations. Both are dynamic, helping children experience and deal with change in situations that mirror the complexity (and contradictions) of 'real life'.

Preparation

Role-play requires little preparation as it depends on spontaneous performance in a hypothetical situation. Both you and the children can sugest situations. You can make role cards which give a few details of the characters or work straight from a verbal introduction.

Procedure

Simulations are usually structured activities which present complex situations (such as World Trade, the siting of an airport or motorway etc.) in a simplified form. All the class take part, either in specific roles (eg. local residents, developers, government officials) or in teams that represent particular groups or countries. A wide range of prepared simulations are available in global education publications (see Bibliography). The *World Studies 8-13 Handbook* has some good suggestions for role-plays on everyday conflicts. A Trading simulation is described in greater detail in the section on Maths activities. Computer simulations allow the group to manipulate variables in several different ways, so that the consequences of choices can be compared.

You could also design your own situations. Incidents in the classroom or playground can be played out again to help the children work them through and perhaps come up with alternative ways of reacting. Groups can invent their own scenarios and characters.

It is important to make sure that no-one is excluded and that everyone takes part in some way they find comfortable, for example as an observer, who keeps track of the arguments and opinions. Younger children can play inanimate 'props'. Various warm-up activities follow which can help children overcome shyness.

Some Techniques and Tools:

 'If I were you'

Purpose

To help children become accustomed to 'being someone else'; to encourage empathy and breakdown reticence to role-play.

Procedure

In pairs, children interview each other about their likes and dislikes (food, clothing, television, books etc.), their interests, hopes and fears. It is helpful if the class collectively compile a list of questions so they agree about what is suitable. Each interviewer can select up to six questions and makes a note of the answers. This can be first done in friendship groups and repeated at some later time with others less close.

Working in small groups, each child introduces their partner to the others, *taking on their identity*. They repeat the answers to the questions as if they were the other (eg. 'My name is (other person); I live at...; my favourite food is...; the country I'd most like to visit is... and so on.

Discussion

It is important to find out how the children felt when someone else was 'being them' and how they felt taking on someone else's identity. This is a good first step in developing empathy and the notion of 'walking in someone else's shoes'.

☆ Facing Lines

Purpose

As all the children participating are involved simultaneously, this can reduce initial self-consciousness. The activity also encourages a variety of solutions to be found for the same problem.

Procedure

This can be done with part of the class observing the others in action. The children stand in two facing lines, each line with a title (eg. a number or a colour). Read a conflict scenario to the children and allow a few moments' reflection. All the children in Line A take on the same role and all in Line B take on the other side in the conflict scenario. The children must remain in their line, responding only to the person directly opposite. The action starts at your signal.

Two minutes is a good length of time. The children in the audience can be asked how many different solutions to the situation they heard. They can then be given their turn at role-playing. You will need a range of simple scenarios which can have different solutions.

Possible scenarios:

(1) Line 1 is Chris, whose ball has been burst in the playground. Line 2 is Terry whom Chris accuses of doing it.

(2) Line 1 is Robin, Line 2 is Lee. Robin has just teased Lee because Lee speaks with a different accent.

After 2 minutes the children switch roles, Line 1 becoming the character in Line 2 and vice versa.

Discussion

As role-playing can bring strong feelings and stereotypical views to the surface, it is always important to talk out how the children felt in each role and why they chose to behave as they did. The fact that each situation can have a range of responses is an important area to explore: this helps children learn to widen their expectations.

Opportunities for global education:

These techniques are particularly valuable for global education:

- They can begin to inform children about life in other countries and help them try to imagine the experiences of people in very different circumstances from their own.

- They can introduce children to complex issues in simple ways which illuminate fundamental underlying relationships, (whether social, economic or political).

- They can be an arena where gender roles are examined, as girls take on male characters and boys female ones (sometimes best done using animal fables).

- Similarly, children can 'become' members of cultural or ethnic groups different from their own.

- They encourage working in collaboration and participation.

- Ideas and fantasies about the future can be explored, helping children to widen their horizons and extend their vision.

Watchpoint:

These techniques can lead to children airing stereotypes and clichés. Challenge these without being confrontational. This can be done by freezing the action and having children play an opposite role, or by injecting some other challenge to their thinking about the situation. The children need to know that while they are in role they may take on the opinions, attitudes and values of others, which they can afterwards disown. It is very important to debrief the experience, whether you are using role-play or simulation.

Opportunities for assessment

Children bring their own experiences, attitudes and values to drama work. Thus it can be used to diagnose what they already know and where they are in their thinking, as a baseline to chart progress. Skills of working together under pressure can be extended and development (or lack of it) highlighted.

Research into the learning opportunities afforded by simulation games and role-playing has tended to focus on higher and secondary education. Taylor and Walford have suggested that simulations can help stimulate these characteristics:

- Show perseverance.

- Pursue understanding of basic ideas.

- Show readiness to modify ideas/strategies in the light of 'experience'.

- Show sensitivity to relationships between people and between ideas and to how these can change.

- Practise decision making under pressure.

- Show openness to intuitive judgements when reason is not possible or appropriate.

- Show awareness of role and group dynamics.

[Taylor and Walford, *Simulation in the Classroom* (1979)]

Planning and Evaluation: a case study

The following lesson plan and lesson evaluation are based on a simulation about development choices in an imaginary rural community. The teacher kept a record of the children's contributions and found that many of them demonstrated enhanced social and language behaviours.

World Studies Lesson Plan

Date: 1 May 1991

Objectives for this lesson:

*   *Use groupwork for cooperation and language skills.*

*   *Use role-play to develop empathy, to encourage hypothesis forming and testing, to develop insights into complex situations.*

*   *Extend geographical awareness, eg. land-use, understanding of typography.*

*   *Extend language skills: discussion, listening, description, justification of arguments.*

*   *Relate to the class topic work on 'Environment'.*

Resources used:

(a) *open-ended questionnaire to show their attitudes and understanding of environmental issues (earlier in day)*

(b) *board game 'Man and His Environment' (sic)*

Description of activity/activities used and timing:

(1) *Before going into role, the children looked at the board, (which shows an idealised rural village), discussed what they thought life would be like there, and named the village.*

(2) *Two large groups, Residents and Developers, were formed by combining two classes (Year 5s). Each main group was then subdivided into small interest groups, eg. Shopkeepers, Children, Unemployed Workers in the village; Factory/ Airport/Playground developers (about 3-4 in each group) etc.*

(3) *Groups then worked separately, exploring their own identity and interests. Gave justification for change, if developers; described pros and cons of change, if residents.*

(4) *Each of the developers presented their case. After all the presentations were finished, the residents discussed each, and voted which to accept or reject.*

(5) *Debrief and evaluate (thumbs-up/down) the activity.*

World Studies Lesson Evaluation

Date: 1 May 1991

Main activities during this lesson:

Play environmental simulation game involving children in role playing village residents or 'developers'. Whole group to give name to village and discuss their ideas of what life there is like. Small groups to discuss and then write the pros and cons of keeping things as they are or of going for various development projects.

What did the children actually do?

Talked, listened, negotiated, argued, imagined, evaluated, prepared presentations, reasoned, wrote, judged.

What did I do?

Explained, questioned, provided ideas, chivvied kids along!

What were they learning/developing further?

(a) *skills: reasoning, justifying, persuasion, cooperation, decision-making, patience, listening*

(b) *knowledge: about the development process, about democratic processes of decision making, about some environmental and ecological impacts of building in rural areas eg. pollution, animal welfare*

(c) *attitudes: empathy for different life-styles, respect for evidence, respect for environment*

(d) *concepts: change, development, actions and their consequences.*

How do I know this learning was taking place?

The nature and quality of the discussion, the voting decisions, the written comments, the degree of concentration and listening during the presentations, the general comments and the mood in the room. The quality of the listening silence.

How worthwhile was this lesson in terms of my goals? What do I intend to do next?

The children were clearly using the knowledge and insights they'd gained from the earlier topic work on 'Environment'. It was re-enforced. Enabled to engage in empathy through role-play. Key thing was feeling empowered through having personalised the situation because they could act out people trying to make change (developers) and 'citizens' making choices. Had their say (unlike real life)! Need to explore further their very stereotyped and fantasy view of rural life.

Practising Critical Thinking

☆ *Diamond Ranking*

This is a classic world studies activity. It is a powerful tool for developing language skills, clarifying ideas, concepts and values. It can be based on pictures or objects as well as words, enabling emergent readers or children still learning English to take part on equal terms. The ideas or items to be ranked can be chosen by the teacher to fit into a planned progression of work or they can be suggested by the children.

Purpose

- To enable all the children to focus on identical information at the same time.

- To give children an opportunity, within a structured situation, to think about and discuss ideas, choices, values and opinions.

- To demonstrate that whilst opinions and values are an individual matter, they can be shared with others, explained, defended or altered through discussion.

- To encourage the skills of listening, explaining, justifying, constructive criticism, and cooperation.

- To demonstrate a method of achieving consensus.

- To help children understand that a range of opinions and perspectives are possible without necessarily having 'rights and wrongs'.

- To show that everyone in a group has something to contribute.

Brainstorming

Brainstorming is one good method of generating a list of items to be ranked. Katy Benson (age 11) describes here how her class used first brainstorming and then ranking to select some priorities for improving the school quadrangle. (The children's detailed and cross-curricular project actually lead to a DOE/Inner-city Improvement Grant for the school grounds).

What a Brainstorming Session is

A brainstorming session is a time when we have one idea in mind (now it is improving the quadrangle) and we all have ideas as to how we think it should be done. Our teacher writes down our ideas on the blackboard till we either can't think of any more or the board is filled.

We then have to make a list of nine things that were on the board as individuals. The nine things were either the things we wanted to have done to the quadrangle, have improved or have removed. Then we paired up and compared our ideas. If they were the same we wrote them down and the different ones that were left had to be agreed on. It's sometimes rather difficult to agree but in the end every pair had a list of nine things that were off both our lists. Most of the lists were in the order of importance. Then we were put in fours and made another list but this time it was a 'diamond nine'.

To add to Katy's description, a brainstorm is a time for collecting ideas. It has one 'rule' only: everyone's contributions are taken down without anyone making any comment, either praise or criticism. The idea is to create a list of ideas as long as the board or the piece of paper or the time limit you set in advance, allows.

Preparation

Each pair or group of four will require nine items to rank. These can be words on the board that they copy onto slips of paper or cards already prepared in advance with words, statements or pictures, or actual manageable sized objects they are investigating.

Procedure

The children start off in **pairs** with a pre-chosen set of nine items. Their task is to arrange these in a diamond pattern with the most 'valued' item at the top and the least at the bottom.

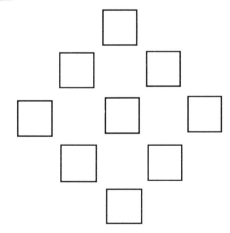

The criteria can vary, e.g. *most/least important, interesting, relevant to the investigation, favourite* and so on. It's important that they all understand the procedure and that it's clear to everyone what the purpose of the ranking is all about. When one pair have agreed their diamond ranking, they then compare their decisions with another pair. These **four** then work together to create consensus in a new diamond.

Alternatively, start with **four** children and in the second stage they work as an **eight** to decide their group diamond.

As in Katy's example, if you have a larger number of items or ideas to pare down, the children start on their own to select the nine units to be worked with. They discuss their lists with a partner, arrive at an agreed nine and rank them in a diamond formation. Then this is repeated with another couple, consolidating their two diamond nines.

Discussion

This is a crucial part of the whole process! It can focus upon the actual decisions arrived at and the similarities and differences between the two original diamonds. It is also vital to talk about how the group arrived at decisions and at consensus. Was it hard or easy? Did everyone feel that their ideas had been listened to? *Reflecting on how they felt in the group discussion and on what each child believes that s/he has learnt from the experience is an essential part of the learning process that the activity promotes. It is also part and parcel of the focus upon the development of self-esteem and regard for others.*

This activity is very language-focused. Children with less skill or experience in English can gain because the desire to express their opinions is very motivating and the structure of the activity encourages other children to listen. Several teachers in the classroom research noted that emergent English speakers would debate the issues in their first language and then share these views to their best abilities.

An activity such as this also provides them with structured support though working with a partner and using props such as photographs, objects or written statements. Being involved in action, moving their cards or pictures about, enables the children to experience a variety of possibilities and literally to see how, through their actions, they can create change.

Ranking in today's curriculum

(This is based on the 1991-2 survey of world studies practices and their role in the development of children's skills and attitudes described earlier.)

- in a local history and geography study about the factors influencing the siting of the local airport;
- during science-led topics on the environment to find out what the children thought caused the most/least harmful pollution or what fe·tures in their localities they are most concerned about;
- to find out which countries the children would most like to visit as tourists, and, a term later, which of these same places they would most like to live in;
- by ranking historical photographs, the children decided which feature of their history topic would be the starting point;
- several classes looked at their own basic needs for survival one term and, in the next, what basic amenities a town needs;
- to survey opinions about what jobs/occupations the children valued;
- to act as newspaper editors, ranking actual headlines from the press, to decide on what counts as 'newsworthiness' (and, in the process, reflecting on what is happening in the world and on how the media reports it);
- to investigate feelings, attitudes and opinions about a range of personal and social issues: gender roles in the home and wider world, the qualities of a friend, things going on in the world that they felt affected their lives;
- in a very local study of the school itself, to decide on class rules and on changes to the playground.

One Y3 class looked at a group of photographs showing daily life in school and ranked the photos by their degree of resemblance to their own situation. (From Behind the Scenes, *DEC, Birmingham.) Their teacher had hoped that they would begin to reflect more on their lives and explore the concepts of 'Similarity and difference', as they looked at and discussed the photographs (and he had intervened to help them take their time and not just rush to complete the task!):*

I recognised that by slowing the process down I had focused in on a kind of visual literacy and that the children were literally reading the photographs... Both groups (by their choices) had readily identified with certain frozen images that were part and parcel of our school as well as clearly distinguishing which things were unfamiliar. The activity definitely nurtured discussion and co-operation skills. It encouraged decision making, critical thinking and listening. However, the most important fact was that the children were requested to prioritise the photos; this catered for the need to be flexible and that ideas can be changed.

The children finally arrived at more mature and sensible decisions which leads me to believe that these kind of activities do provide a platform to openly observe children's deeper ability to arrive at consensus. Certainly the more dominant children set the ball rolling. I have also observed that bilingual children often revert to their mother tongue, to discuss things more deeply, and then share their conclusions with the others.
[Teacher, Stockton-on-Tees (1992)]

Children's views and 'choosing' strategies

What do children themselves think of this activity? Virtually all of the two hundred who used it in the recent classroom work found it fun and would do it again. *'Talking helps you understand what other people think'* (11 year old). *' I thought it was hard at first, but when we started working I found it easy'* (7 year old). *'It's better than working on my own, I don't know what to do on my own'* (9 year old).

They use a wide range of strategies, of course, to make their decisions, as well as rational discussion! Teachers reported:

- voting;
- taking turns to place items on the diamond;
- one or more people putting forward convincing arguments;
- 'dibbing';
- on one occasion when the group had reached a total impasse, they turned the photos face down, shuffled and chose that way.

The content and the material they are working on also has an impact on their willingness to engage with the process.

> *'Gradually the structure of the ranking exercise made them discuss the statements they really differed on.'*
> [Teacher, Wolverhampton].

☆ *Sorting Activities*

Purpose

- To help children recognise that there is more than one way to perceive the connections and relationships between things. The ways in which we categorise things, ideas or people can be unnecessarily limited.

- To encourage decision making skills and flexibility.

- To develop group work skills (cooperation, communication) and cognitive skills (sorting, comparing, contrasting, evaluating etc.).

Preparation

A set of objects to sort for each group taking part. These could be photographs; statements written on cards; pictures; artefacts from other places or periods of history; a variety of food, (tinned, packaged and fresh); toys; books of different sorts (preferably in more than one language).

Procedure

☆ *Objects*

Ask the children to list all the ways in which their objects are similar and also different (eg. size, shape, colour etc.). Then ask them to sort them into two groups, setting a time limit. When they've done this, ask them to try and sort them into two other, different sets. A final step would be to sort the objects into three sets: this goes beyond using simple opposites such as big/little etc.

☆ *Statements*

These can be brief statements of differing opinions about an issue, ranging from matters of immediate interest to the children (eg. how the playground space is organised; food choices at dinner; the time spent watching and choice of television programmes), to wider concerns (eg. environmental issues; predictions about the future; issues of fair trading between countries). The statements can be prepared in advance or brainstormed by the children, but they must express a range of views.

The children can sort the statements into ones they agree or disagree with; optionally they can extend the choice by adding their own.

☆ *Body sets*

This is an enjoyable game in a large space. The children move to different areas of the room, depending on the 'set' to which they think they belong. You can start on distinctly different sets of two or four characteristics and end on several sets of three, for which the choices or overlaps are more complex.

Some categories for sets of two or four: shoe colour, hair/eye colour, likes/dislikes, play an instrument/don't; born in the area/born elsewhere (this can lead to other sets showing how many different origins there are in the class).

Some categories for sets of three: Like something (e.g. foods, sports, T.V. programmes etc.) a lot/mildly/dislike; know a lot about/a bit about/nothing about; always tell the truth/OK to lie at times/not sure; like being in groups a lot/a little/never; would like to live in another country a lot/maybe/never; rather to be kind/smart/good-looking etc.

Values Clarification [Simon, Howe and Kirschenbaum] is a useful source of similar activities. See also 'Themework' [McFarlane].

☆ *Venn diagrams*

Purpose

This is a very useful device to help children recognise that most situations contain elements in common as well as offering opposite choices. It also helps them accept that uncertainty and open-mindedness are both acceptable and necessary.

Preparation

They can sort statements of various kinds: preferences, issues, attitudes and values. You can prepare these in advance or they can arise from discussion with the children.

Procedure

- For example, they can think about and brainstorm the possible consequences of events taking place now (eg. litter in the playground, environmental consequences of unchecked car exhaust pollution, deforestation, etc.). They can then sort these potential consequences into categories such as *'could happen/don't know/likely to happen'*; *'would like to see happen/can't decide/would not like to see happen'*.

- Another way of using Venns is to show overlaps and similarities. In one sector they list all the characteristics of one topic, in the other those of another, and in the centre they note the common features. Some examples: Girls can.../Boys can...; Britain has.../Country X has... (a country of origin of some of the children or their parents or a locality being studied in Geography).

- Statements about values and beliefs can also be explored in this way. The structure helps the children discuss and clarify their views. The following activity looks at children's rights and is a useful way to start a topic which addresses rights issues, human and/or animal.

Discussion

Sorting activities such as these help children to clarify and articulate their preferences and values. Further discussion is very important to pick up on issues such as the variety of opinion in the class, the complexity of issues once you look closely at them, the fact that one can hold contradictory views and so forth. If strong opposing opinions have emerged, it is important for the children in question to give each other a hearing.

☆ *Children's Rights*

Procedure

Start with a list of up to 20 statements about what the children think should and should not be allowed to happen in school. These should refer to their own and adults' behaviour, the physical condition of the school and so on. The suggestions can be both realistic and outrageous. These can be written on the board during a brainstorm and then copied out for each group onto slips of paper.

Each group will need a large sheet with a Venn diagram marked AGREE/DON'T KNOW/DIS-AGREE. The group discusses each statement and decides where to place them on the diagram. They can either put the slip into the zone they all agree on, or write a key word from it (eg. 'homework', 'no bullying'). When complete, all the groups can report back on their decisions and compile a list of the most common decisions in each category. A circle discussion can be the setting for further sharing.

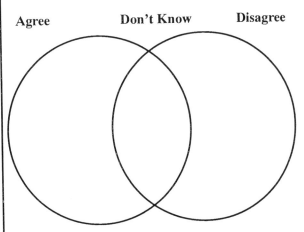

A second stage could involve the children in rewriting the ideas they placed in the NOT SURE/DIS-AGREE sectors so that they become acceptable. They could use qualifying words such as 'unless', 'usually', 'except' to make changes. For example:

'We should be allowed to say whatever we like in class... unless it insults people'.

(Drawn from an idea by Cathie Holden and Hugh Starkey, reprinted in *Global Teacher, Global Learner*, G. Pike and D. Selby. See Bibliography.)

Opportunities for global education

Recognising the complexity of issues and the range of possible decisions and choices is an essential part of developing an open mind. These activities enhance communication skills such as listening, explaining, justifying and group participation. The examples and issues you select can illustrate things going on in the world, show a variety of life-styles and be chosen so that they affirm the customs, languages and cultures of different groups in the school.

Opportunities for assessment

The development of oracy skills can be charted through observation and taping group discussions. The children should be encouraged to reflect on their experiences by writing about them in journals or specifically designed feedback forms (see examples earlier). You can monitor the children's understanding of concepts in subjects such as science, technology, geography and history, using images, statements etc. that relate to the appropriate programmes of study. For example, in any of these subjects, they could sort the factors that cause/ do not (or did not) cause something to occur, or similarities and differences.

Using photographs

Photographs are windows into the world around and into the past. Visual images are a powerful part of our culture and children need to be taught skills, akin to literacy, in order to 'read' or understand the messages images convey. They are also excellent teaching aids, stimulating the imagination, enhancing observation and descriptive skills, and conveying complex information concisely.

You can use your own photographs or those taken by the children and their families, or calendars, postcards, magazines. An increasingly wide range of photopacks (collected photographs centring on a theme with accompanying information and activity books) are available, which support work on different localities throughout the world and also themes such as gender equality, water, and so forth (see Bibliography).

If you are making your own collection, it is important to bear these considerations in mind:

*   Is the photograph interesting, showing people doing things?

*   Do they present a positive image of people from other cultures or overseas; of women, older people, children? That is, are the people shown doing things competently and with pride? Or are they shown as dependent and unhappy? If you choose to use such

images, do you plan to show a balance of positive images as well?

*   Have you included any photos which demonstrate the multicultural nature of our society?

*   Do they help raise awareness of bias and preconceptions? Will they reinforce stereotypes?

*   Do your photos show more than one aspect of a locality, eg. African countries are not all jungle and wild animals, nor are they all in the grip of famine and desertification, although these latter are serious realities. Similarity, life in the United States is not all Disneyland, skyscrapers or fields of wheat. Rural and urban poverty and homelessness exist there too.

Some photograph-based activities are outlined in the section on geography below. Photographs can also be used in the Ranking and Sorting activities described above.

Some basic steps

Purpose

*   To help children develop observation skills

*   To move beyond an unquestioning, surface reaction to images

*   To stimulate curiosity and empathy.

Preparation

Enough photographs for pairs or small groups, showing people engaged at work or play. These can be of one place or a variety of places.

Procedure

The children place the photographs in the middle of a large sheet and take turns listing everything they can see on one side of the sheet. They next write down on the other side a list of questions they would like to ask the people in the photograph if they could meet them. Two groups join together and compare pictures and questions. They can sort their questions into different groups:

*   questions they could get answers to from books (factual);

*   questions that could only be answered by the person/ people concerned (personal).

Extension

The children can write a list of the questions they think the people in the photo might like to ask *them*. These too should be a mixture of personal and factual inquiries.

Discussion

Feedback could focus on things the children saw in their photographs which interested or surprised them. Close observation can help to overcome limiting preconceptions.

☆ Jigsaw Photograph

Purpose

- To encourage observation, analysis and discussion skills

- To demonstrate how we can make assumptions based on incomplete evidence and judgements based on misconceptions and prejudice

- To learn to examine or read the components of a picture and see how pictures convey messages.

Preparation

Make a jigsaw out of a photograph by photocopying it and cutting it into 3-5 sections. Make enough photocopies for each group to have the jigsaw pieces and one intact copy.

Selecting photographs: Whether you find your photos in magazines, newspapers or calendars, or use photopacks, there are a few points to consider to help make this activity a world studies one. Some of these considerations must apply:

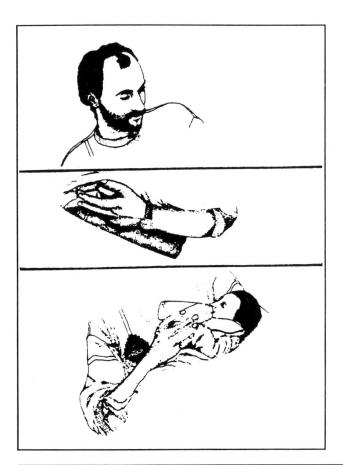

Does the photograph show:

- the multicultural nature of society?

- positive images of people from other cultures or overseas, of women, older people, children; ie. people looking happy/confident/relaxed doing things competently and with pride?

- does it help raise issues about biases and preconceptions? Will it reinforce stereotypes? Is it interesting? Does it show people doing things?

Variation

Photocopy a photo and then cut or 'crop' a small section showing part of some action, a small object etc.; it should be easily recognisable. Mount this piece on a sheet of A4 paper and copy it. Crop a larger section which includes the first bit and adds more surrounding detail. Copy in the same way. Each group will have three images to use: a small fragment; a more detailed fragment; a full picture. (You can also do this in two steps: a ready-made example can be found in *Making Global Connections,* see below.)

Procedure

The children may feel tricked! To avoid this, explain that they're going to look at a photo bit by bit to see how it works. They put the first fragment on a piece of paper and decide what they think the whole picture might be. They can jot down (suggest they take turns scribing) all the 'clues' that support this guess, eg. background, facial expressions, clothing etc. Give them another part of the photo after about 5 minutes. What do they think now? Are there more clues? Finally supply the complete picture and tell them to write their reactions, as a group, on a separate card or paper. (If using the three-step set, they can jot their comments in the space on the sheet around the fragments for steps one and two.)

A **variation** is to give each group a different segment and ask them to guess or predict what the whole picture would show. The groups can each report what they expect to see and then join their segments together to form the whole.

Discussion

The two groups can compare their guesses at each stage or each group can give a step-by-step report at the end. How far were their guesses based on stereotypes, eg. about gender or age related roles, or about other countries? You can also help them think about who took the picture and for what purpose, and whether this influences what we see, eg. compare a fashion photographer's view of a beach with a tourist's or a local resident's.

The example which follows reports the reactions of a Year 3 class.

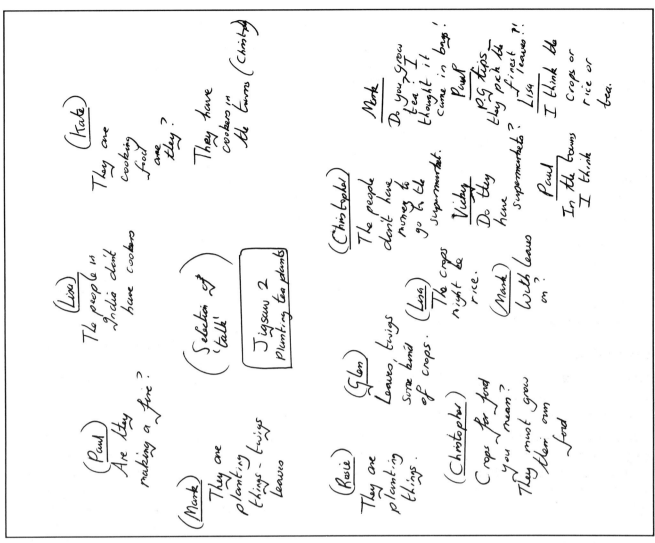

(Kate) They are cooking food are they?

They have cookers in the towns (Christy)

(Lisa) The people in India don't have cookers

(Paul) Are they making a fire?

(Mark) They are planting things - twigs leaves

(Selection of 'talk')

Jigsaw 2 Planting tea plants

(Christopher) The people don't have money to go to the supermarket.

(Vicky) Do they have supermarkets?

(Mark) With leaves on?

(Lisa) The crops right be rice.

(Glen) Leaves, twigs some kind of crops.

(Rosie) They are planting things.

(Christopher) Crops for food you mean? They must grow them own food

(Mark) Do you grow tea? I thought it come in bags!

(Paul) P.G. tips they pick the finest?!

(Lisa) I think the crops or rice or tea.

(Paul) In the towns I think

Magic Microphone Activity

Paul — I thought that the children and their families worked very hard. I didn't like them working so hard — I felt sorry for them.

Mark — I learned that people grow their own food.

Lisa — I was surprised to see that the people in the village were quite good clothes. When I saw the bare legs and feet in the jigsaw I thought the people would be scruffy and poor.

Kate — I was going to say that as well. I thought the children looked sad at first but in the other photos some of the people were laughing.

Glen — I was surprised to see the girls had to look after the baby brother and sisters. I learned quite a lot today about other people but I'm glad I am myself ('me').

Rosie — I was surprised at the tea leaves — I thought they were carrots. It was good putting the jigsaws together and guessing — I'm glad I didn't have to do any working about it!

Christopher — I was surprised to see the children working with their parents — I think the girls should spend time at school not looking after the babies. The boys should have a turn. (to Glen → "I don't mean us — I don't like babies!!!")

Vicky — It was interesting to see that the children were in charge of the little ones. I would like to do that in the morning and go to school in the afternoon.

Children from Manor Green Primary, Denton, Tameside

From: Action Aid (1991) *Chembakolli: A Village in India*

Opportunities for global education

Photograph work is a straightforward means of showing children concrete images of people and places to increase their knowledge and understanding. Children have many preconceptions about the world and positive images can correct incomplete information (eg. 'Africa is all jungle') or extend their horizons (eg. showing people in non-stereotypical gender activities). They can also learn about incomplete and biased information by posing critical questions such as — Who took this photograph? Why? What's left out? How does this image make me feel or think about the people in it?

Opportunities for assessment

Your photographs can be selected to support any subject in the curriculum. Thus in addition to developing skills of communication, children can be extending their understanding of place and their factual knowledge about specific places and how people engage with their landscape (geography). They can examine evidence about the past and gain understanding about people's lives (history); they can explore issues to do with the environment, animal and plant care ('life and living processes') in science; indeed, most topics to do with the body, hygiene, health and food, weather and its effects. Technology and art also provide learning situations in which children can use imagination and analyse form, shape and function through taking their own photographs or using prepared ones.

As in other areas, your assessments will rely predominantly upon observation, listening and recording speech, and reading the children's factual, imaginative or self-evaluative writing.

(This section on *Critical Thinking Skills: sorting and using photographs* has drawn on ideas in C. McFarlane, '*Themework: A Global Perspective*'. (See Bibliography.)

Sources for Images

Making Global Connections: A World Studies Workbook, Hicks and Steiner (a ready-make jigsaw on page 88).

Global Teacher, Global Learner, Pike and Selby (an interesting variation on pages 142-143).

Selected Photopacks (also see bibliography)

Doing Things in and about the Home, Trentham Books.

What is a Family?, Development Education Centre, Birmingham.

New Journeys: Teaching about other places — learning from Kenya and Tanzania, Development Education Centre, Birmingham.

Working Now: exploring gender roles, Development Education Centre, Birmingham.

Investigating Images: Working with Pictures on an International Theme, Development Education Project, Manchester.

Palm Grove: Zambia Pack (1992), Unicef, London.

Living and Learning in a Tanzanian Village, C. Midwinter, Development Education Project, Manchester.

Where Camels are Better than Cars, Development Education Centre, Birmingham.

Pictures of Health in a Changing World, Jenny Button, CWDE.

New Internationalist calendars and magazine.

'Free' sources such as newspapers and magazines. History, Geography textbooks, your own photographs.

LOOKING AT ARTEFACTS

When we look at an object that has been made by an artist or craftsperson, we need to look at a variety of things in order to get a better understanding of that object.

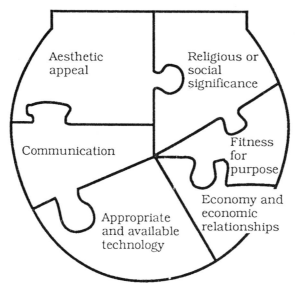

An artefact can be the amalgam or result of all or a combination of some of the above considerations. These factors will be reflected in varying degrees, depending on what the artefact is, how, where and why it was made and who made it.

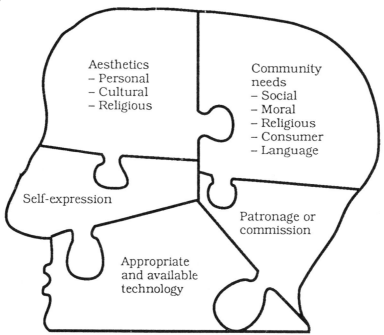

The maker brings a set of considerations to the making of an object, which may vary from person to person depending again on what, where, why and who is making the object.

'*Evaluating Artefacts*, Museum Education, Leicestershire Museums, Leicester

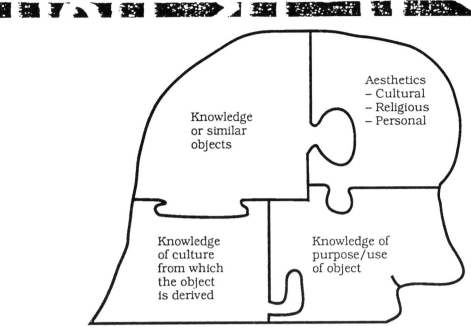

The person that looks at an artefact and attempts to evaluate it, does so using a set of considerations which may be determined by the interaction of the above factors.

In order to understand an artefact more fully, the viewer needs to attempt to empathise with the factors which contribute to the making of an object or artefact. This is of particular importance when viewing objects from other cultures to avoid culturally biased judgemental evaluations.

The object is made and shaped by the maker, and the maker has been 'shaped' or influenced by society, culture and the environment.

Society, Culture and Environment

Society

Society can be said to be any group of people living together under the same political system for the purpose of mutual benefit for economic, social or defence purposes. The political system can be a set of written laws, or an unwritten common set of social or religious codes.

Culture and Language

Culture is customs, traditions, beliefs, value systems (what is and what is not important), in fact everthing that shapes our lives. A society can be made up of different cultural groups. These groups in living together meet with each other and exchange ideas; in this way cultures change as new ideas are introduced. It can be said that a culture is not static and changes with time.

The Environment and Economic Organization

Climate, location, materials, the available technology and the economy effect the making of an object.

We should not judge other cultures from one standpoint, but we should try as far as possible to understand why those cultures operate as they do. Different groups place emphases on different things. Whereas European art is almost always on display, most African art is hidden away and only seen a few times a year. Likewise in some cultures books are valued, in other cultures the spoken word and the oral tradition of passing on information is thought to be superior.

'*Evaluating Artefacts*, Museum Education, Leicestershire Museums, Leicester

Using objects and artefacts

Handling, describing and discussing objects are excellent ways of helping children to have 'real' experiences of other cultures and of looking more closely at their own. This way of working promotes discussion and problem solving, helps develop an aesthetic sense, sensitises children to design issues and to the ways in which people make and use objects for both practical and ceremonial purposes.

It can contribute to learning experiences across the curriculum; for example, in **Maths** all the ATs to do with calculating, weighing, measuring, estimating: in **Science**, AT1 will always be relevant, and ATs 2 and 3 when investigating the basic materials of any object. Working with artefacts clearly relates to all of **Design and Technology** and in **Geography** to the understanding of places (AT1) and of how people live and work in their environments (AT4 Human Geography). In **History**, artefacts are powerful means of investigating evidence about the past and provide tangible ways for children to relate to the lives of people in the past (AT3). Discussing artefacts can develop both the aesthetic and spiritual awareness of children as they examine how and why people make things to express their relationship with the natural and spiritual sides of life.

Using objects/artefacts from other countries: some considerations

It is important that the object is placed clearly in its context — its time, culture and place. The following considerations are intended to signal sensitive areas but not to be discouraging!

- What do I know about this object? What might some of the children already know about it? How can I positively use their knowledge?

- How will I find out what impressions or preconceptions the students may already have about the country or culture in question? How can the work help them explore their preconceptions and broaden their understanding rather than reinforce any stereotypes?

- Is it useful to compare this to any similar objects familiar to the children? If so which ones and from where? Could making comparisons lead to value judgements of inferiority or superiority? Would it increase or reduce the students' prejudices or merely leave them untouched? What can or should I do about this?

- If any negative attitudes or comments do arise, what are my strategies for dealing with them?

- Does it have any special or symbolic use in its culture or place of origin? Would handling it cause offence to its makers? To anyone in the class?

Using objects/artefacts: some questions to ask the children

What is your opinion — do you like this object?

What does it feel like to the touch? Light, heavy, rough, smooth?

What does it look like? How can you describe the shape, colour, size, patterns, decorations?

If there's any writing on it, can you read it? Do you know what the language is?

Who do you think made it and how did they do it? Was it one person?

A man, woman, child? A group? A machine, by hand?

Where do you think it was made?

What do you think this object is used for now or was used for in the past?

Was it to be used by the maker personally? To be sold or exchanged?

To be used daily in an ordinary home? For special uses in the home or in a special place? To be kept and used again or thrown away?

What kind of person might use it?

What material(s) is it made of? Would they be easy or hard to get? Easy or hard for the maker to use?

Is it like anything you use in your daily life?

Could this object harm or benefit people?

What do you think and feel about it now?

The work on Artefacts is based on '*Evaluating Artefacts*', Museum Education, Leicestershire Museums, Leicester

Working across the curriculum: an exemplar

☆ *Know Your Potato*

This is both an enjoyable and powerful way to raise awareness about individual uniqueness and the power of expectations.

Purpose

- To practice and develop skills: mathematical, artistic and oral

- To look at the concepts of similarity/difference, interdependence

- To provide experience of affirmation

Preparation

Enough clean potatoes of roughly the same size for each child.

Other natural objects eg. fruit, leaves, small stones that are easily handled and similar in size and shape could also be used.

Children from Baguley Hall Primary School, Wythenshawe, Manchester

Procedure

Brainstorm everything the class can think of about potatoes. Explain that they'll have a chance to find out much more detail through using their senses. Each child picks a potato from a pile or bag. Instruct them to look at it *really* carefully for two or three minutes. A few pointers are to look at it from all angles noticing different spots of colour, blemishes etc, to rub it gently all over to get to know its shape and bumps. **The observation must take place in silence and in seriousness**. The circle is a good setting.

At the end of three minutes, put all the potatoes into a pile (two piles if the children are young and the group large). Taking it in turns, have each child go to the pile and find their own potato. (They *always* do!)

Discussion

The children always respond well. They often feel a very strong bond with 'their' potato and are pleased that they have rescued it from the pile. Discussion could focus upon their feelings during the activity itself and how they were able to identify their potato. This is an excellent means of promoting discussion about the uniqueness of each individual and how each person's individuality is denied when people are labelled and 'lumped together' in groups. The *Magic Microphone* is an ideal way to debrief this activity. (see p.73).

Gemma McElroy

Potatoes

On Friday Mrs Steiner came in to do work on Potatoes.

First we chose a potato from out of a shopping bag. After that we had to do a very close observation on the potato and we did some feeling. Then after looking at it Mrs Steiner took our potatoes and jumbled them up. Then we had to identify our potato. It was easy to find my potato because it had sort of a C shape on it. The potatoes were not all the same because they had different patterns. The measurements that I used was by putting it in scales and putting weights in it. Sometimes I put pencil crayons, or felt tips. My results were.
The potato weighs 1.50 grams.
My potato is 10cm long length ways.
My potato is 7cm width ways.
All the way round it is 20 cm

A Potato Story

I was planted under ground in Autumn, and through Winter & Spring I grew bigger & stronger. It went on to summer and I grew strong roots from my legs and I grew bigger. I was harvested and I was bathed and everything it was lovely. I was stored in a warehouse and I made lots of friends. After that I was transported to a shop. I was stored on shelves. After that lots of people looked at me and felt me then I was bought. I was taken to a have in the house there was a little girl in there.
She looked at me. She started to throw me up into the air. It was awful but her mum told her to stop it. The nice kind lady took me to the bathroom and left me in the warm sink. I really liked it. I was taken down and she peeled me It tickled me. After that she cooked me and I became a lovely roast Potato

My potato at first   How I came out as a Roast Potato

Emma Tomlinson.   A Timeline of a potato

seed

roots and shoot

roots shoot and leaves

potato roots more leaves

potato being dug up

being washed

being ate

uses of a potato.

crisps

chips

mash

boiled

shepherds pie

Alphabites

jacket

meat and potato pie

waffles

roast

Year Five children (1992) Baguley Hall Primary School, Wythenshawe, Manchester

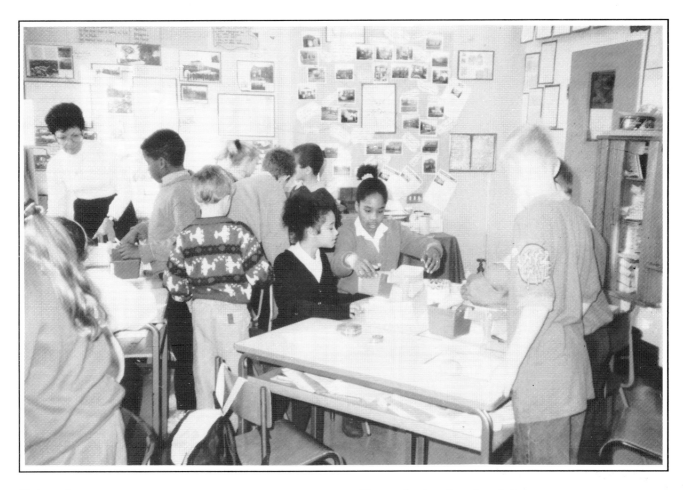

Extension

The following sequence of cross-curricular activities is suggested as an immediate follow-up. It strengthens the positive experience of affirmation.

Creating a potato profile

Have the children suggest what more they could find out about each of their potatoes: what they have in common and how they are unique.

Each child weighs, measures their own potato using a variety of apparatus. They can record these statistics and also do a careful observational sketch on a sheet labelled *My Potato.*

Compile everyone's measurements on a graph/bar chart or other appropriate format.

Either discuss together or do individual research about the life-cycle and growing of potatoes. This can be represented as a timeline (as below), or drawn/written as a story sequence illustrating each stage in the potato's life from planting and growth to harvest, transport to a shop, to the present.

Some facts about potatoes

- First brought to Europe from South America (the Andes) by the Spaniards in the 16th century.

- Introduced to North America by European settlers soon after.

- Widely adopted as a crop in the U.K.; became the major food in Ireland during the 18th century.

- Therefore the potato blight of 1845-1846 created widespread famine in Ireland, leading to disease, death and emigration, mostly to the USA.

There are recipes for potatoes in most of the cultures living in Britain. For example, **Colcannon**, a potato and cabbage dish, has links to Celtic Britain and the harvest feast of Lugnasa. **Latkes**, fried potato pancakes, are traditionally served at Chanukah, the Jewish festival of lights in December.

The planning wheel which follows on p.96 has suggestions for activities throughout the whole curriculum.

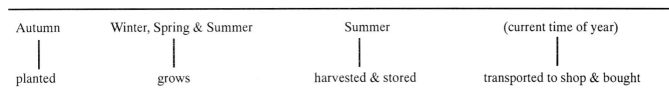

Autumn	Winter, Spring & Summer	Summer	(current time of year)
planted	grows	harvested & stored	transported to shop & bought

"KNOW YOUR POTATO"

The cross-curricular potential of active learning exercises

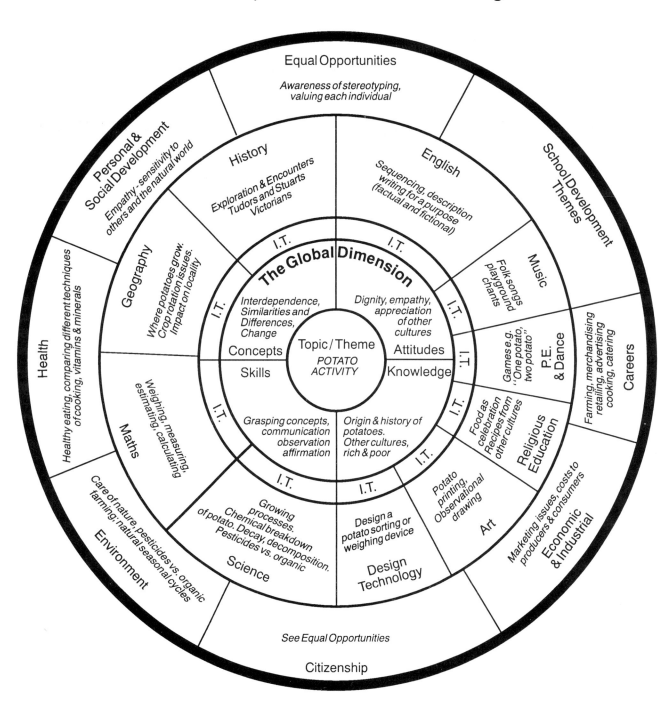

PART THREE

An Active Learning Approach to the National Curriculum

10

An Active Learning Approach to the Subjects of the National Curriculum

The following bank of activities demonstrates how you can incorporate a world studies approach into the subjects of the National Curriculum. Most of the activities have already been used successfully in age 8-13 (and younger) classrooms.

These activities are not tightly pegged to ages or levels. Experience has shown that older, more sophisticated children love the affirmation exercises and younger children respond enthusiastically to the cognitive and social demands of the more complex activities. Your skill, knowledge of the individuals in your class, and choice of resources to support the National Curriculum subjects will turn the basic 'recipe' into the correct diet for your children.

The activities focus specifically on the subject side of the Curriculum, on personal and social development, and, above all, on the dimensions of equal opportunities and education for life in a multicultural society. While world studies firmly supports a cross-curricular approach to teaching and learning, there is also a recognition that the subjects themselves require deliberate infusion with those dimensions and with the wider global perspective. Thus the five themes are not addressed specifically, although the concerns of Citizenship and Environmental Education in particular are embedded throughout.

The active learning processes and activities are based on these common goals:

1. Each one enables you to touch on one or more relevant aspects of the global dimension (see page 38).

2. They provide experiences that can teach the content, concepts and skills identified in the Attainment Targets.

3. They centre primarily on talk: either in groups or with the whole class.

4. Evaluation and assessment opportunities exist for both teacher and children. I have indicated which Attainment Targets the activities can help you plan for, however 'levels' are not indicated as the activities are intended for all children at whatever 'level'.

Differentiation will be observed through outcome; that is, the varying responses to the same task.

The National Curriculum is an evolving restructuring of education. The ATs referred to here were the ones in force in 1992-1993.

5. Whatever the specific subject, the activities are intended to offer these common experiences:

a) Build self-esteem

b) Develop cross-curricular skills (particularly communication and problem solving)

c) Reinforce core cognitive concepts.

d) Foster learning of an experiential and affective nature

e) Collaboration and cooperation in pairs, small groups and the whole class.

6. These activities are not intended to teach basic skills (eg. drawing maps, setting up experiments). I hope they will form part of your repertoire, enabling you to develop and extend skills and understanding.

List of Activities (by subject)

Art

Art is an area where self-expression and individuality are valued. It is therefore a 'useful' context in which to explore self-esteem and interpersonal relationships. These values lie at the heart of world studies. It is also ideal for positive encounters with different cultures and traditions.

The children can observe the two faces of art. It is on the one hand universal; all peoples in all places in all times have expressed themselves through a variety of artwork. It is also particular to cultures and places and reflects the spirit of the society from which it springs. Children can learn to apply their own criteria of aesthetic excellence and to value the works of the global community of artists.

☆ Portraits and Silhouettes

Purpose

- To provide opportunities for children to observe facial features carefully and to examine body shape and symmetry

- To enable experimentation with mixing colour

- To encourage cooperation, affirmation and self-esteem.

Preparation

Large sheets of paper, equivalent to a child's body length, smaller sheets, paints, brushes, pencils and crayons.

Procedure

Working in pairs, the children take turns to draw the outline of their partner's shape while s/he lies on the paper.

They next take turns at drawing *one another's* full-face portrait with as much care and attention as possible. Continuing to work collaboratively, the children help each other to mix colours to approximate to their skin tones. Each child paints in their silhouette and glues on the facial portrait done by their friend.

Variation

Using an overhead projector, cast each child's profile silhouette onto a large sheet of paper. Children take it in turn to draw round each others' silhouettes. These can then be cut out and traced onto dark paper or painted.

Discussion

This can start with how each child felt as s/he had their portrait drawn. Was it hard to sit still and be stared at? They can also describe their feelings about being the artist. A range of issues to do with similarities and differences between people, uniqueness, skin colouring etc. can be fruitfully explored.

Assessment opportunities: KS2 AT1

☆ Totems

Purpose

- To introduce children to one aspect of Native American/Canadian art

- To introduce them to the use of symbols

- To provide an opportunity for both individual curiosity and group collaboration.

Preparation

Resources: small cardboard boxes (one per group of three to four), paints, glue, loads of 'art junk' (tubes, foam scraps etc.).

Art books or history books with realistic drawings or photographs of Totem poles.

Background: Many cultures have 'totems' which are representations of plants or animals with which a group (clan, tribe) identifies. There may be some quality the totem possesses which the members of that group admire, and a totem object must not be killed or eaten. Clan totems can be seen engraved on weapons or carved on masks. Poles carved with a collection of totem symbols are specific to the Pacific Northwest of Canada and the US.

Procedure

Stage One

Explain about the use of Totems. Discuss what animals the children might choose to be, focusing on the skills and qualities the children think these animals possess. Some stereotypes may well surface eg. bad wolves, greedy pigs etc. Exploring these clichés and providing information to counteract them is an effective way to highlight the dangers of stereotyping. Various story-books, as well as natural history books, can be used to support this preliminary work.

Stage Two

The children work in groups of three or four, and select an animal *all* the group agree they would like as their totem. Allow sufficient time for this discussion. Each group explains to the others what they have chosen and why.

Stage Three

Give each group a box (the sizes can vary). The children choose one colour to paint the box. While it is drying they can plan and design how they will make the face of their totem. This can be done in several ways.

Basic: They draw the animal's face and colour it on a sheet of paper equal to one side of the box. They can use various 'art junk' like cardboard rolls, fabric etc. to create eyes, noses, beaks etc. that protrude. The drawing and features are glued onto one side of the box.

Advanced: Each group has a large piece of card or stiff paper. Fold this in half and draw the outline of the profile (ear, forehead, nose/beak/snout etc.) from edge to edge. Cut around the outline taking care to leave a join at the front between the two symmetrical sides. This totem sheet can then be spread flat and colourfully decorated. When it and the box are dry, staple the totem to the box so that it protrudes at the front.

If the box is too large for one sheet of paper, the face can be divided to fit two sheets, as long as the nose/beak/snout is made of one sheet.

Stage Four

All the boxes are stacked on top of each other in decreasing size. They can be joined together more securely by cutting holes in the boxes, top and bottom, and stacking them on a long tube such as a used carpet roll. Ingenuity will find other ways of securing them!

Discussion

This can focus on the feelings experienced during the group work and on how the children evaluate their finished totems. Do they feel that the class or 'tribe' totem has a more powerful impact than the single box? Do they think that the totem pole says something interesting about them as a class?

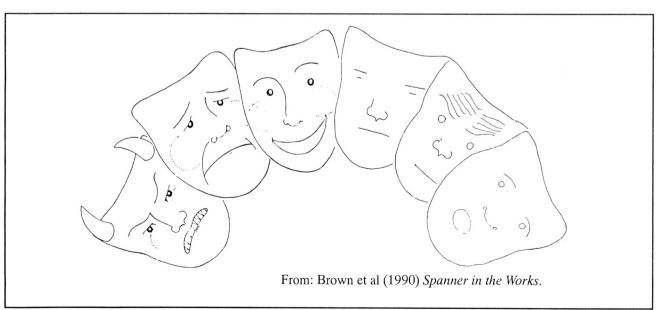

From: Brown et al (1990) *Spanner in the Works.*

Extension

The children can make individual masks of a small character or animal they identify with. Masks can also be made to represent emotions. The children can be encouraged to attempt subtlety and to represent as wide a range of moods as possible: for example, not just 'happy' but 'thrilled', 'excited', 'pleased', 'joyful' etc.

Assessment opportunities: KS2 AT1; AT2

☆ *Co-operative Shapes*

Purpose

* To work collaboratively on creating a pattern that is satisfying for all the participants

* To help children focus consciously on the process of collaboration and co-operation.

Preparation

Plain A3 paper, a variety of smaller pieces of coloured paper and scissors, enough for each child.

Procedure

Each child cuts one piece of coloured paper into a 'soft', curvy shape and the other into a 'hard', jagged, spiky shape. They then arrange these two shapes on the A3 sheet to make a pattern. When everyone is finished —and you can set a time limit—the children join in twos and, placing their two sheets side by side, agree a joint pattern for their four shapes. Next two pairs join and repeat the process. The final combination is two fours (eight shapes to form a pattern).

Discussion

The children can describe their feelings at the various stages as they had to create and then 'destroy' their patterns. They can also describe the outcomes: what did they think of the various patterns they had helped form? Can they find words to explain what combinations of shape, colour and size pleased (or displeased) them the most?

Assessment opportunities: KS2 AT1

This activity is based on 'The Co-operative Art Game' described in *Making Global Connections*, Hicks and Steiner eds.

English

At the heart of the objectives of world studies are the skills, values and attitudes of clear and confident communication, based on mutual attention and respect. The 'Basic Processes' section suggests a wide variety of techniques to get children talking, thinking, feeling and then expressing further these thoughts and feelings. Earlier I suggested that the skills of oracy linked with the ability to cooperate are the foundations of citizenship.

Through oral work, children can learn to listen and take turns, clarify their ideas and explain and justify them to others, negotiate and come to recognise the difference between fact, opinion, hearsay and fantasy (see pp.67-89).

The English curriculum is also a powerful tool for promoting equal opportunities. The skills of literacy, spelling, writing and speaking English fluently are the entitlement of all children. Meaningful contexts for exploring ideas and opinions will give speakers of other languages the incentive to develop a competence in English to match their cognitive levels. Similarly, reading literature produced by all of Britain's different cultures will inevitably make it a truly global experience!

The activities in this section explore words and meanings and the way the world enters into children's minds through the public media. If schools are to play a role in preparing children for life, they cannot ignore the power to shape 'minds and hearts' which these media so clearly possess.

☆ *Word Power (1)*

Purpose

- To give children opportunities to see the power of language
- To provide practice in using positive ways of communicating

Preparation

Up to ten cards showing different negative statements. The following are only suggestions: you may want to use ones more commonly heard in your setting!

- Shut up!
- You're thick!
- Stop copying from me!
- Don't be a stiff! (i.e. a swot or snob)
- You're well tight!
- You got told! (i.e. 'ha, ha you were wrong')

Copies of the **Word Power** sheet for each small group.

Procedure

One child passes out the cards to the group. As each statement is read out, the group brainstorm alternative and *positive* ways of saying the same thing. They decide on the alternative they like best and write it on the sheet.

Variation

The children themselves suggest a list of put-downs and insults. Each child writes down the insults they most hate and these are put anonymously into a box. *This format may encourage the children to come forward with sexist or racist insults they have suffered.* If such comments do emerge, you might want to bring them up in the context of the circle discussion at the end of the activity.

You can select items yourself for the groups to work on, or you can read out the cards and discover the ten to which most children relate. Alternatively the class could brainstorm a list.

Discussion

Insults to do with size, colour, shape, family are common in the playground and cause considerable pain. This exercise provides a safe context for the issue of destructive language to be addressed. As in all feedbacks, no one need contribute if they don't want to. Focusing on how the group worked on the task can be a safe beginning, leading on to more personal reactions and experiences of insults. If racist or sexist issues have surfaced, this is a good opportunity to discuss the harm they do and the pain they cause.

Extension

The children compile a collection of positive statements (words, phrases or whole sentences) that could 'put a smile on someone's face'. These can be written on cards and stored for use at various times.

For example, they could be used as a circle-time activity. Pass the box around the circle. Each child draws out a positive statement and reads it to her/his neighbour. (The statements will need to be general enough to apply to anyone). The child receiving the positive comment should be encouraged to respond with some kind of acknowledgement.

Assessment opportunities: AT 1, AT 2, 3, 4, 5

These activities are drawn from '*Esteem Builders*', by Michele Borba (1989).

Word Power

Team Name: _____ Date: _____

DIRECTIONS: Choose one member to be the dealer and pass out all the cards. Moving clockwise, each team member reads one put-down message to the group. After each reading, the team brainstorms builder-upper statements that could be said instead. Now choose the team's best answer and write both the put-down and builder-upper statement on your worksheet. Go on to the next card.

Put-Down Statement	Builder-Upper Statement
1.	
2.	
3.	
4.	
5.	
6.	
7.	
8.	
9.	
10.	

Remember: You can change a put-down to a builder-upper by...
1. Starting the message with an "I."
2. Telling the person how you feel ("I'm angry...").
3. Telling the person what he or she did that made you feel that way ("I'm angry because you took my pencil").

 "You're a dummy Tommy!"   "I'm angry because you kicked me!"

From: Borba (1989)*Esteem Builders* (California, Jalmar Press)

☆ *Word Power (2)*

Purpose

- To give children opportunities to see the power of language
- To discuss the meaning of certain concepts and terms relating to the values of human rights
- To provide a meaningful context for writing

Preparation

Sufficient copies of the poem by Martin Luther King (on right) for each small group.

Procedure

Read the poem aloud yourself or have a child read it. The different statements should be explained and discussed in ways you think appropriate to the age, stage, and awareness of your class.

Ask the children to make a list of words that describe things they would wish to see changed in the world.

Discussion

It is important to explore some of the more complex issues raised by this writing with the children in ways appropriate to their age. For example, should any words be banned? Is 'removing words from dictionaries' the same as censorship? This in turn can highlight issues to do with freedom of speech and how this human right is denied to many throughout the world.

Extension

The children can write similar statements or poems as a collective or individual task. They can find out more about Martin Luther King and also about the different situations he mentions in this writing.

Assessment opportunities: AT1, AT2, AT4, AT5

One day...

Youngsters will learn words they will not understand.

Children from India will ask:
What is hunger?
Children from Alabama will ask:
What is racial segregation?
Children from Hiroshima will ask:
What is the atomic bomb?
Children at school will ask:
What is war?

You will answer them.
You will tell them:

These words are not used any more,
Like stage coaches, galleys or slavery.

Words no longer meaningful.

That is why they have been removed from dictionaries.

Martin Luther King

Becoming skilled media users: some activities for listening, viewing and analysing the printed page

The precise impact television has on children's emotions, attitudes and behaviour is not quantifiable. What repeated research and common sense observation tell us is that it *does* have an influence. For example, an investigation into what six to nine year olds understood of what they watched regularly was undertaken during the period of the Gulf War. Amongst other findings, children seem to decide on 'goodies' and 'baddies' in drama programmes on the basis of physical characteristics rather than attending to the plot details. In fact, these details are often misconstrued or ignored and interpretations are made 'to fit the children's own world.' Many treated the War like another soap opera, apparently ignorant of the fact that what they were seeing was real. ['Children, Television and Morality', Anne Sheppard, University of Leeds, reported in the *Times Educational Supplement* (May 1992)].

Other research has shown how hard it is to budge negative images of the South or Third World. The television has been a powerful instrument in alerting us to famine, war and injustice. Yet it has equally perpetuated stereotypes of dependency and passivity. Even with powerful counter-images like the ones presented in 'Comic Relief' films or other positive documentaries, children's expectations continue to be of disaster and inferiority. Such positive pictures are often interpreted in an ethnocentric, even colonialist manner, as in the old Ladybird books: 'They're O.K. because we helped'.

The media can create, reaffirm or challenge stereotypes. This can have real implications for the children's own lives, now and as adults. It touches all aspects of equal opportunities in our own society, i.e. gender role expectations, race relations, attitudes to disablement, as well as the attitudes children develop towards other nationalities and to sensitive issues like the environment. The skills of critical viewing, reading and interpretation are essential.

Listening skills

☆ *Broken telephone (a familiar favourite)*

Purpose

- To encourage children to listen carefully

- To demonstrate how easily information can be distorted and how personal interpretation of inaccurate information can be misleading

Preparation

- Work in small groups of 6-8.

- Write a one-sentence message (either simple or complex) on a slip of paper.

Procedure

'Phone' the message to the first child who then whispers it to the second. Each child passes the message s/he has heard onto their neighbour, as along a telephone line. You can allow one repeat the first time you play this, if you feel this is necessary.

☆ 'Reports from the field'

(This reflects the often circuitous route news takes as it travels from an onlooker at the 'scene' to a reporter and on to the news desk of studio or newspaper).

Preparation

A short description (about five sentences) of an event, including such details as names, distances, quantities, colours etc. It can concern something familiar to the children or some imaginary 'newsworthy' happening.

Procedure

* Organise the children into groups of 4-6 (the younger the class the smaller), giving each child a number or letter. For older children, it is helpful if there can be a clear corner in the room for a group of six to sit.

* Set the scene by telling the class that they are going to be reporters passing a story on from the place it happened back to the news desk.

* Assemble all the 'A's' from the groups. If you can, go outside the classroom and read the 'News flash' once only: this can also be done by a good reader.

* **Younger children**: Each A returns to the group and gives them the report. The rest then each write down what they think they were told.

* **Older children**: The 'B's then join the 'A' from their group and are told the story. The 'A' group of children return to the classroom or move to another corner, where they all sit together. The 'C's are told the story by the 'B's, who then sit together and so on until each child has taken part. When everyone has heard the story, reassemble the class and have the last listener in each group repeat it.

It helps to separate the team members after each telling although, if your space is inflexible or limited, you can insist on silence in each group until all have heard the tale. Alternatively, each child can join a different group from the one they started with and reassemble at the end, although this might reinforce competition between the groups, which is not the point of the exercise!

Variations

One group prepares a Newsflash to tell another.
One group watches a short television clip, of news or fiction, and passes on the details in the same way to members of their group.

Discussion

This can focus on how inaccuracies enter into information. The children can compare their experiences and make suggestions about how to improve their listening.

Assessment opportunities: AT1

☆ Becoming a skilled viewer

Purpose

* To provide practice in attentive television viewing

* To demonstrate how different people can 'see' things differently

* To illustrate the influence of our preconceptions and expectations on what we see

* To teach children about television techniques of presentation and editing

Preparation

Pre-record Newsround or a regular TV news bulletin. Some of the following procedures can also be used with taped radio news.

Procedure (and Variations)

1. **Prediction**: Select one item from the bulletin and ask the class what they would expect to see on the news about that subject. List all their brainstormed ideas on the board. Look at the clip and compare the predictions.

Discussion

The circle is ideal for feedback and the activities following. The children can report their reactions using sentence stems such as 'I was (not) surprised to see...' 'I learned that...' etc.

Issues they can discuss might include: how far were their predictions accurate? Do they think that this is because television uses certain 'stock' techniques or because the episode could *only* be shown in this way?

2. **Sequencing and timing:** Give the class a list of the various items contained in the news bulletin and tell them how long it is overall. (This can also be done with the radio news). Ask them to guess the order in which these will be shown and the time allocated to each. They can do this collectively as above or write their predictions down privately and check them at the end. Alternatively, they can discuss this in pairs and compile an agreed list. This pair can then compare their predictions with another after the viewing.

Variation

Use the local news.

Discussion

Do the children think there's a reason for the order of the news items? Why do some come before others? Is there a pattern in the way the news is presented? What makes a story newsworthy? They can also discuss what kinds of stories do *not* get reported. What is the difference between matters of local or national interest?

Even quite young children can do these prediction exercises.

3. **Observation and attention**: The students watch or listen to a news bulletin without any prior discussion. They then write down or talk about all the different items, trying, if possible, to list them in the correct order.

Each child tries to remember a detail that they think no one else will have noticed. Working in a small group, they ask each other questions to see if others spotted it (eg. 'What's the first thing that happened after the plane took off?').

Extension

Older children can be introduced to the language of film. You can explain terms like 'close-up', 'cutting', 'fade out' etc. They can watch for these and note down how often each is used. They can also look for some of the other camera techniques employed to catch our attention. For example, how are any people being 'framed'? Are they in the middle, to the edge, the left, right, the background, the foreground? Does the framing have any impact on how we react to them? How can we tell who is considered to be important or unimportant in a story?

Groups can design the presentation of a news item. They can prepare a 'story board' showing the sequence of the shots and the kinds of camera technique used for each one. If your school has a video camera they could actually set up and film an imaginary documentary or news item.

Assessment opportunities: AT1

Many excellent ideas for investigating the media can be found in '*Watching the World*', Cathy Midwinter, Manchester Development Education Project (1988).

☆ *Press Portraits*

While few primary age children actually read newspapers, they can still become aware of the impact the press has on public opinion and how it both reflects and creates attitudes. Sometimes the reporting of local events can reveal this to them: one Y5 class in Moss Side, Manchester was so incensed at the sensational and negative way that their community was depicted in a national newspaper that they invited the journalists to come and defend themselves. Children can also become aware of the ways in which the different communities living in this country are described. Does the press convey negative images of black people, of the Afro-Caribbean, Chinese, Jewish and Moslem communities? Are they represented as an integral part of this country or as exotic outsiders?

The print media, such as newspapers and magazines, can also show the children the connections between their community, country and the wider world. What are the images given of our European partners? Of people in other parts of the world, North or South?

☆ *Making Connections with the Wider World*

Purpose

• To trace the connections between their local community and country with the wider world

• To become familiar with the layout and writing style of newspapers

Preparation

Copies of local papers, national papers and one week's television listings magazines. A large world map.

Procedure

Each small group has one or more of the above. They cut out all the references to places outside the UK. This can be stories about events outside the UK, advertisements for items from abroad (food, clothing etc.), programmes about other countries (made there or here), and so on. Make a list of all the places mentioned. The clippings can be sorted into piles according to the type of outside link they represent (people, goods, trade connections, political connections etc). For younger children you can cut out and make copies of a selection of items in advance which they can then sort into the different categories.

The places mentioned are marked on the map. It is particularly important to do this with items cut from the local papers.

Discussion

The *circle format*, with children reporting back about what surprised them, what they learned, etc is an effective way of highlighting the way in which we are interlinked with all parts of the globe. Some other issues to explore with older children could be what impressions of other places the images convey. They could list the types of adjectives used and decide if these convey the full picture of the place(s).

Extension

The children can find out more about the goods from other countries sold in their locality. They could conduct an 'environmental audit' finding out about the raw materials used, the work conditions and pay of those producing them.

Assessment opportunities: AT1, AT2

☆ *A Message to Mars*

Purpose

- To become familiar with the layout and writing style of newspapers

- To explore how stereotypes are created and communicated

Preparation

Copies of a range of different national and local papers, tabloids and broadsheets.

Procedure

The task is to create a paper that would give a visiting Martian a picture of the world as it is today. The children must decide what image of the world they want to convey and cut out the articles and pictures that they agree best carry that message. Each group has a selection of newspapers to cut up to create a composite paper.

The clippings are pasted together into a newspaper, along with additional articles written by the children. Alternatively, they can make a poster of the clippings and add a few brief explanations.

Younger children can work with a selection of positive pictures as well as more serious descriptions of issues that you have prepared for them. They choose the ones they would show the Martian.

Each group displays and explains the newspaper they have created.

Discussion

The groups can explain what kind of world they were 'showing 'the Martian. Were they influenced by what the newspapers had to offer or is this their own opinion? Do we have access to any alternative perspectives on how the world works?

Extension

The children can produce their own school newspaper. This is in fact what the class referred to above did, following their own experiences of having their community described in the press. Try to establish semi-realistic conditions: i.e. allot only short periods of time for the children to work towards some goal, whether it is a report of some incident in the school, an interview with some member of the staff (from playground supervisor to head teacher), drawing cartoons or the design of the layout and so forth.

Assessment opportunities: AT1, AT2, AT3, AT4, AT5

There are many good ideas for media work with a global dimension in the other activity books in the bibliography.

Geography

Geography is clearly a key area where children can study the world and develop a truly global perspective. They can make local/global links by seeing how their locality connects to others more distant. They will start  to understand the ways in which these places and the people who live there share common needs and experiences with themselves. They can also start to appreciate how distinctive life-styles and cultures have developed in response to the basic environments which geographical forces have created.

The study of geography calls for the skills of investigation and enquiry and above all for an open mind and a frame of reference which is sensitive to different perspectives. Children should not only be learning about *life* in differing localities: they should also be learning *why* people make the choices they do and the local and international forces and structures that influence these personal and national decisions. Even very young children can comprehend that a child their age living in a 'locality in an economically developing country' will have similar basic needs and can begin to investigate the economic and cultural links between the two places.

Geography provides an ideal context in which certain basic concepts and themes can be explored in ways appropriate to the children's age and stage eg. migration and population movement and settlement; comparative development; sustainable growth; protecting the environment. Our own localities also reflect these issues.

> Of all the words that have been used to help clarify the meaning of the curriculum in recent years, the one that stands out for me is entitlement. Children are entitled to know more about the wider world and the National Curriculum for primary school children offers a good (though limited) deal in this respect... It does at least attempt to ensure that children will learn something about other people and places, and will thereby discover something about alternatives to their way of life. It literally extends their horizons.
> [Patrick Wiegand, *Places in the Primary School*, (1992)]

A Sense of Place

ATs 2, 4 and 5 all require children to show an understanding of how the places people inhabit affect the way they live and the choices they can make. Many studies of children's attitudes to other countries, both in Europe and other regions, show that they combine understandable ignorance with negative stereotypes based on media images and societal prejudices. Starting from a base of positive curiosity about distant places, children can investigate the lives of people who live there in a more open-minded way.

Photographs are an excellent way of gaining access to places you can't actually visit, whether another country or another county. Using a range of photographs, from the school's locality and from more distant places, can help the children explore some of the key notions of human geography. There are many good sources of photographs offering positive images of economically developing localities (see bibliography).

The general introduction to the activity section earlier makes some suggestions about using photographs to stimulate thought and discussion. These questions can be asked about each image, whether it is local or distant:

- *Where is this place?*
- *What is this place like?*
- *Why is it the way it is?*
- *How is this place connected to other places?*
- *How is this place special to the people who live here?*
- *What would it feel like to live in this place?*
- *How is it similar to our own locality and how is it different?*
- *How is this place changing?*
- *How could this place be improved?*

(Based on Michael Storm's work)

The following two activities focus particularly upon helping children develop an understanding of the concept of 'place' and the similar ways people respond to their differing environments. They also help show that images can be interpreted very differently, depending upon your point of departure.

☆ *A Sense of Place*

Purpose

- To help children explore the concept of 'place' and how people are attached to a wide variety of places
- To make a survey of the variety of places visited by or lived in by the members of the class
- To develop skills of close observation of photographs

Preparation

A piece of A4 paper for every child. Pictures of a place and a person special to them (brought in by each child). These can be family photographs or pictures from other sources of someone the child would like to meet. A list of questions is written on the board.

Procedure

The children divide their paper into two equal columns heading one PERSON and the other PLACE. They write down the following information:

PERSON column:

> *who* — (friend, relative, someone they'd like to meet?)
> *where* s/he comes from
> *when* the photo was taken and under what circumstances
> something about *how they feel* about the person

PLACE column:

> *where* it was taken
> *why* it is special or interesting to the child
> some *information* the child knows about the place
> *how* the people in the photograph got there
> *why they're there* (e.g. holiday, live there, work there?)

They place or stick the photograph in the middle of the other side of the paper.

Working in small groups, the children take turns to study each other's photos carefully. In the blank space surrounding the picture, they write down any questions they would like to have answered. They might try to guess where and why it was taken, who took it and so on.

When all the photos have been looked at in this way, each child reads out the information on the back and answers any other questions that have been asked. Each group lists all the different places their photographs show. Finally compile a class list.

Extension

The places visited can be located on maps and further research done about each.

Discussion

This activity gives children a meaningful purpose to learn to observe images closely. They will be able to share their experiences of being in places outside their everyday locality and to articulate some ideas about the differences and similarities between places. It is possible that they might voice negative generalisations about places (eg. 'the food is awful and everyone there eats weird things!') based on their actual experience or on adult comments. These can provide opportunities to explore the nature of stereotyping, and of ways in which *different* need not mean *worse than*. Ask the children to imagine changing roles with someone their age in the other country and to make generalisations about Britain (eg. 'it always rains', 'they only eat fish and chips' etc)!

Assessment opportunities: AT2

☆ *'Spot the Myth'*

Purpose

- To raise awareness that photographs can represent both positive or negative pictures of a place and that our opinions and judgements about places are influenced by these images

Preparation

A variety of images of your own local area (from newspapers, tourist information, postcards, home photos) and from another place (locality, region, or country). See the bibliography for a list of photopacks. Sort these pictures into a variety of sets, eg. city/town scenes, people at work, at play, etc.

Stickers of three different colours or coloured pencils/crayons.

Procedure

This activity has two stages. It is probably preferable to have small groups (about half the class) involved at any time.

- Mount the pictures on large sheets of paper and display them so that they can be easily looked at. Work with those of the school's locality first.

- Each child puts a red mark or sticker next to the picture they think really shows what their area is like; a brown mark next to the one that only gives a partially accurate image and a green mark next to the photo they think is an unfair or inaccurate image or one that they don't like. Working in pairs, they look at each other's choices, each explaining and justifying their own.

- Give small groups a selection of photographs from another locality. Ask them to mark these in the same way. If you have sorted the photos into sets such as urban/rural; work/play etc., ensure that each group has a variety of sets. It is better not to identify the place until they have all seen a range and discussed which they feel represent fair (or unfair) images.

Discussion

There are bound to be a wide range of reactions to all the images on display and children may have quite opposite opinions. Explaining their views is an excellent way for children to develop an awareness of how subjectivity influences judgement. In the debriefing it is also useful to discuss whether photos can give us an unrealistic or biased image of a place; how the images we see on television (news or documentary) are selective and can also be inaccurate.

Extension

The children can sort mixed sets of local and 'distant' photographs into pairs or sets to highlight a variety of themes, (e.g. work/play, similarities/differences between two images etc.).

Using a jigsaw or other cropping exercise on some of these pictures shows how selective editing influences our perceptions.

(See pages 85-88 for further procedures).

Assessment opportunities: AT2

This activity is based on 'Spot the myth' in *'It's our world too'*, Birmingham DEC.

Children from Claremont Junior School, Manchester

Working with maps in the world studies classroom

☆ *Making Mental Maps*

Purpose

- To give children experience in recognising and drawing maps of the world

- To provide opportunities for collaborative work

- To develop agreed criteria for assessing the children's work

Preparation

Large sheets of paper, lengths of cotton, fine string or thin chain. Scissors. Glue or tape.

Procedure

Stage one: Conceal all maps and globes in the room. Draw, freehand, your own mental map of the world on the board. Discuss it with the students, getting them to point out any errors they think you've made. *This helps establish a climate in which making mistakes is seen as part of the process of learning.* Their ideas can be checked afterwards in an atlas.

Stage two: Remove or cover up your map.
Groups of three to four children use string, cotton or chain to make a joint outline of their mental map of the world on a very large sheet of paper. When they have all agreed on their outline, they fix it to the paper and fill in the names of places, features etc, which they know.

These should be compared with the projections in atlases and published maps. It is very important that they get to look at alternative projections (eg. Gall, Peters, Mercator, Winkel). This will help them to understand the complexity of making accurate representations, and the different interpretations which can be made of even 'fixed' realities. Looking at world maps in which Europe is not central is also a good way of demonstrating this.

Extension

All the maps the children have drawn are examined and scored by the groups. After comparing their scores, each group must explain their 'marking' criteria. *One class realised that they had all started from different points: some went for neatness, others accuracy, others colourfulness and yet others humour!* This can be a very valuable exercise to give children skills in self-assessment and help them to understand the assessment process generally. It will show how judgements can be made on the basis of a range of criteria, so that different 'performances' can be evaluated on both generally agreed and also individual merits.

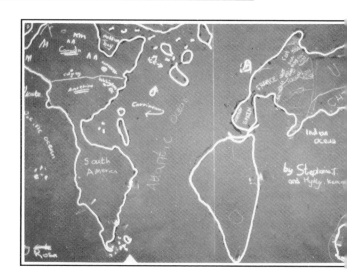

Discussion

Feedback can relate to the group process itself as the children will have had to negotiate a common map. To extend their geographical understanding more widely, you can discuss the 'rightness' and 'wrongness' of different projections. It is important to stress, however, that while the proportions and placing of the different features of the planet are fixed, they can never be truly represented on a world map, but only on a globe.

Assessment opportunities: AT1

This activity and 'Ellie off the Bridge' which follows were written by Roger Wassell Smith, Chair of Humanities, School of Education, Exeter University. He has also written the activities found in the recent Pictorial Charts publication *'Map of the World'*, (1992).

☆ *Ellie off the Bridge*

Purpose

- To give children opportunities to use map conventions (eg. symbols for recurrent features, keys to decode symbols)

- To provide children with a meaningful reason to create their own maps: to tell a story and to represent a sequence of features on a journey

- To enhance cooperative and collaborative skills

- To provide an incentive for children to engage in learning about a variety of localities.

Preparation

One sheet of A3 sketch paper and one large sheet of paper per group of two or three.

One or more copies of the story.

Procedure

Prepare the children for careful listening: they will need to remember the details of the place where the story takes place. Read the story once and briefly discuss what they can remember about the setting. Have each group make a rough sketch map, annotated to show the events in the story (eg. falling off the bridge, catching the driftwood etc.). It is important to emphasise that this is a rough draft.

Allow the children to check the accuracy of these maps, either by reading the story aloud again, or by giving a copy to each group to read for themselves.

The details can now be amended on this draft. Before drawing their finished map, the children should decide how the story ends and add to their draft map any new details created.

They now draw their final, completed map of the journey, consistent with their version of how the story ends.

Variation

A wide range of settings for the basic story can be used.

- For younger children, stories such as *Rosie's Walk* (P. Hutchins) or *The Cow Who Fell into the Canal* (Spier & Krasilovsky) will help them visualise features. You will, of course, stop reading before the end!

- You can use the familiar features of your own neighbourhood, city or town.

- To set the scenario in the context of an economically developing locality, use the features and vocabulary of that area. You can either devise your own story, with a danger situation to suit the locality (e.g. floods, desert sand storms, mountain trails etc.) or use a story book. For example, *Angry River* (R. Bond, Antelope) describes a young girl's adventures during a flood in Bangladesh.

- You can also create an international context which calls for use of the atlas, globe and world map. An example follows.

Discussion

The nature of the story you use will influence the discussion. This activity offers opportunities to get feedback from the children on group process and their use of geographical techniques. It can be a powerful incentive to engage in learning about distant localities and can also provide space for stereotypes to be aired.

Assessment opportunities: AT1

Ellie off the Bridge

Ellie and friends were out for a walk one rainy afternoon. They were crossing the bridge over the flooded river when the side suddenly gave way and Ellie fell in.

When I hit the water there was a moment of panic. It felt like my whole body had gone numb. Underwater it was dark and threatening. But I struggled back to the surface — gasping for breath. In the distance I could hear Sally shouting from the foot-bridge: 'Ellie! Ellie!'

There was all kinds of junk bobbing along beside me in the cold, brown, treacly water. The pine trees of the woods on both banks felt like two green walls fencing me in.

I tried swimming but it was taking all my energy just to keep my head above the water which was sweeping me swiftly along. I remembered hearing Mrs. Wellsbury, our swimming instructor, telling us once that if we ever fell in the first thing to do was to kick off our shoes, and get rid of any bulky clothing. Easier said than done!

After a lot of struggle I got rid of my coat and my shoes. This was the point where the two rivers join together. The banks looked even further away now, and then there was a horrible crack on the back of my head and I was under again. Up I came spluttering and hurting and crying. I had bumped into one of the columns of the railway bridge. 'Last bridge before the sea', I remember thinking to myself, and then there was another, softer thump on the head and I was under for a third time.

This time I came up in a tree — well, most of one — that was being swept along in the flood; but at least now I had something to hold on to.

I remember thinking how furious my Mum would be about my coat and shoes. And about messing around on the foot-bridge.

Then I caught sight of Sally again for a second, tearing down the footpath that runs along the far bank. It seemed miles away. She looked tiny and hopeless. I saw her turn off the path and go running across the field to Crab Lane. I could see Mr. Gordon's house up on the hill at the top of the lane, and my hopes rose.

Looking over to the other side I could see Pines Farm, and the woods up on the slopes above it. And up beyond the woods, the houses of the village with the church spire sticking up. I had never seen it before from the middle of the river and it looked a bit odd! I thought for a moment of all the times I'd walked up through those woods from the bridge. Walking home.

I could see the big old oak just where the path goes into the woods near the farm. I couldn't climb that tree until I was seven. It's the best view of the valley, and you can see the bridge, Halsley on the other side, with the big old mill below it on the bank, the weir... I'd forgotten about the weir!

International Context

On the Trail of the Smugglers

Jo had followed the smugglers' trail from Africa into Europe. The ivory had now reached a capital — the major port on the Eastern Banks of the Bosphorus where the Black Sea joins the Mediterranean. Jo found a way into the warehouse, and soon located the crates that friends had secretly marked. Now they were labelled for export to other European capitals: Berlin, Vienna, Madrid, London and Prague. Jo had to find out if these deliveries could be made by sea, or if some would be flown out. Using a phone in the corner, Jo told her controller of these destinations. Friends in Europe would follow the illegal trade and find out who was behind it. Where would the ivory go next?

Suddenly, a bright light was shone on Jo. It was impossible to tell who held the torch but the voice spoke perfect English: 'As you like following our cargo so much, perhaps we should find you a box so you can travel with it too'...

☆ *Co-operative Maps*

Purpose

- To enable children to use and extend their knowledge of the world map by completing five copies of the map in silence

- To provide a meaningful exercise in cooperation and collaboration

- To enhance cognitive skills such as shape and spatial perception

- To provide diagnostic opportunities to observe the above

- To develop an understanding of empathy.

Preparation

Make enough copies of the maps in Figure 1 for each group of five children to have a complete set of five. Cut up each map along the lines indicated and put the pieces, according to their letter, into envelopes marked A-E. Each group will need a complete set of five envelopes with the map pieces in each one.

Procedure

You might want to try out the basic process first with squares, cut-up faces or an actual jigsaw. Some ideas for this follow.

Explain that the purpose of the activity is for each member of the group to make a complete and correct map of the world using jigsaw pieces. It would be useful to have written the rules on a sheet or on the board so that you and the children can refer to them as the exercise proceeds. The rules are:

1. No one is to talk during the activity or make any kind of communication or signal to anyone else in the group.

2. No one must take a piece of the jigsaw from anyone.

3. You can pass pieces.

4. You can stop at any time.

Give each child an envelope and make sure that they all start at the same time. It can be useful to assign a child to each group to act as observer, who will report back at the end about what went on in the group and to remind them of the rules if they forget in the heat of the moment! This can be done if there are an unequal number of children or as a standard part of the exercise.

This activity ends when all the groups have completed their maps.

Discussion

Debriefing the children's feelings at the end is essential and the circle-discussion form is ideal for this. This is a classic exercise in learning cooperation and can produce strong feelings of frustration, irritation and elation. Realising that groupwork rather than competition will achieve each individual's goal may not be an obvious conclusion at first.

Some other issues you can explore are the children's thoughts about the rules, about non-verbal communication, about empathy and interdependence. What did they feel about other members of their group who were finding the task more difficult or easier than they? Are there other occasions they can think of where group collaboration helps each person achieve what they want for themselves?

If there were observers, they can also report. Encourage them to describe what they saw happening without criticising the other children.

Extensions

This activity also provides an excellent opportunity to introduce the children to the different ways the world has been drawn over the years. The Gall, Mercator, Eckert IV, Winkel and Mollweide projections follow (Figure 2). You can use the markings on the set of five maps which follow (Peters' projection) as a template. Looking at these different projections will help children to understand how all projections are essentially inaccurate. They can also discuss whether they feel that the size of a place, as shown on the map, affects their view of its significance.

Variations

Older children might enjoy trying maps which place Australasia or North and South America in the centre.

The original of this exercise requires the completion of five equal squares, as in Figure 1. A number of other shape variations are available in *Global Teacher, Global Learner.* A further interesting variation, in which the task is to make five complete sentences, is found in *Creative Conflict Resolution. Coping with Conflict* shows how to use an actual jigsaw.

Assessment opportunities: AT2

Figure 1

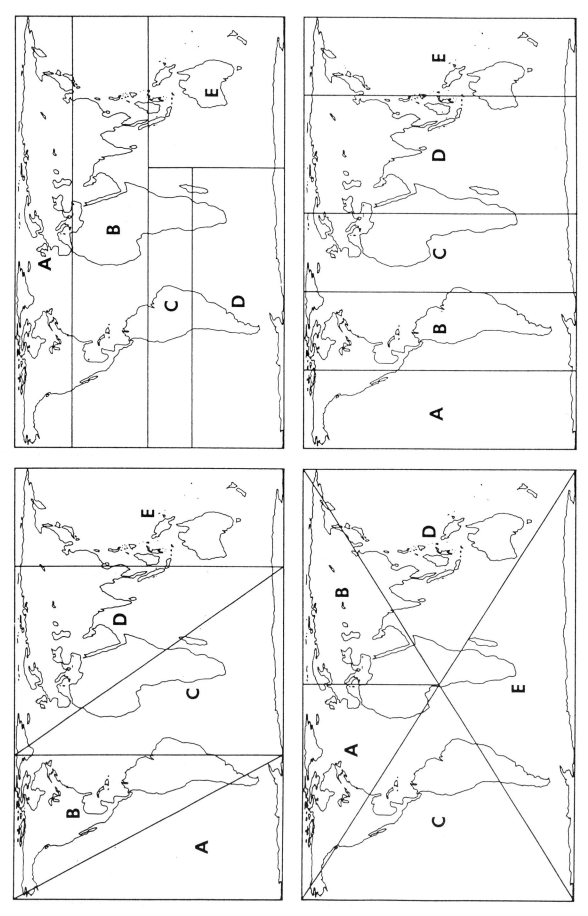

From: Fisher & Hicks (1985) *World Studies 8-13: A Teacher's Handbook* (Edinburgh, Oliver & Boyd). (Figure 1)

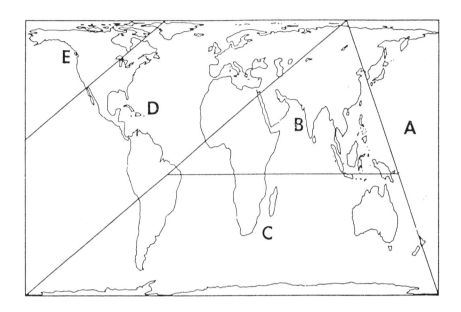

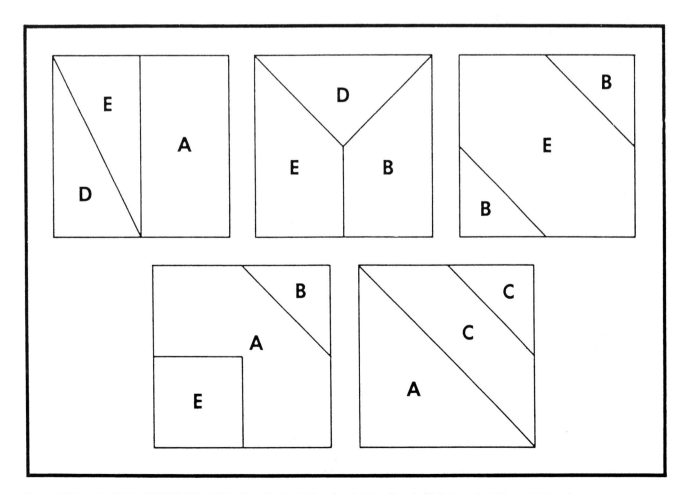

From: Fisher & Hicks (1985) *World Studies 8-13: A Teacher's Handbook* (Edinburgh, Oliver & Boyd).

Figure 2

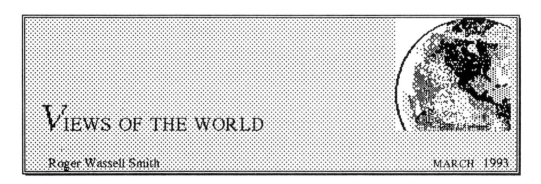

Children and adults assume that world maps are 'true' views of the world in all respects. They are not. Relative size and location, as well as distances, are adjusted in order to make the impossible task of peeling an orange and laying its skin out flat achievable. So world maps are rather unreliable witnesses, actually offering partial views of the world, without appearing to do so. Hence they can be misleading. Only the globe avoids this partiality.

Discovering that there are different maps of the world is an important stage in children's understanding about representation and about viewpoint. All world maps are implicitly biased. They are centred on the part of the world the cartographer thinks it is important to show. So Map One, which is from the People's Republic of China, looks strange to European eyes more accustomed to Map Three which places Britain and the EC firmly centre stage. In looking for differences between the maps, children will identify this issue of how the maps are centred and often suggest that people will draw world maps with their own country close to the middle.

They will also notice that different map projections change the size of landmasses. This is very significant: children, quite logically, can view the size of a country as a measure of its importance. So Map Three reassures them of the importance of their part of the world: it is central. It is Eurocentric showing the rest of the world in relation to this region. This map also emphasises the significance of Europe in fact, the whole Northern hemisphere by greatly exaggerating its size relative to the, apparently, less significant South.

For a more realistic and balanced view, see Maps One, Four and Five. These are **equal area** projections, i.e. they neither exaggerate nor diminish area and significance. This is also technically important as most tasks for which children will use a world map will involve area, e.g. of rain forests or ice-caps. If an equal area projection is not used, the forests will shrink as the ice grows. It will be inaccurate and a lie.

And as Map One and Two illustrate, seeing the world flattened out as we in Europe do, makes us forget that the former USSR and North America are such close neighbours, while Map One,Four,and Five include the world's sixth largest continent, which is completely absent from the others!

MAPS
1. A view from China
2. North Polar Projection
3. Mercator-Europe centred
4.Winkel's equal area projection
5.Eckert IV-an equal area projection

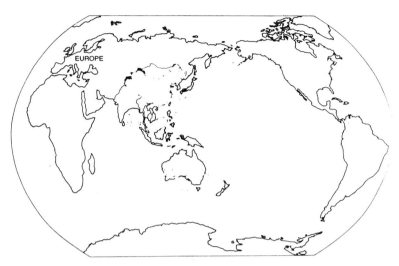

1. *A view from China*

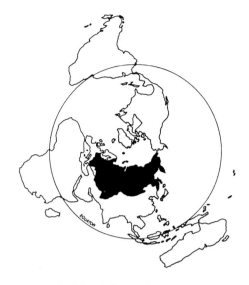

2. *North Polar Projection*

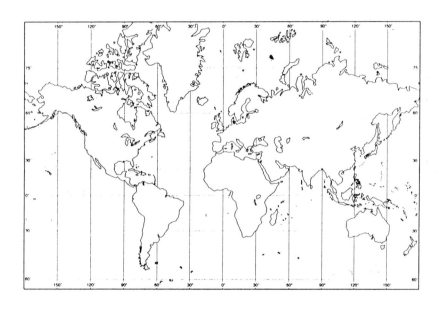

3. *Mercator-Europe centred*

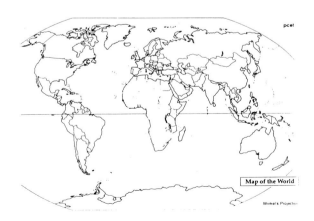

4. *Winkel's equal area projection*

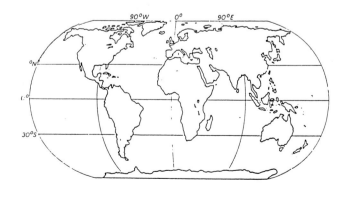

5. *Eckert IV — an equal area projection*

History

A global approach to the study of history is straightforward. Only in emphasis does it differ from the objectives described in the *Non-Statutory Guidance* to the History Orders (NCC 1991). It is about looking at the story of people's lives and at the public actions of governments and countries with a sensitivity to the many sides of human affairs. The skills and the stance identified earlier in the Geography section are vital for understanding History equally: skills of investigation and enquiry, an open mind and a frame of reference which is sensitive to different perspectives.

The intellectual skills which lie at the heart of 'training the mind by disciplined study' (*Non-Statutory Guidance*, 1991) are those skills of engaging with evidence and with an awareness of potential partiality and bias. The purposes of developing 'a sense of identity through learning about the development of Britain, Europe and the world' and of 'understanding other countries and cultures' (*ibid.*) lie at the heart of world studies.

The difference in emphasis comes perhaps in a wider definition of national identity. Whose story is being told, and whose missed out? Do the lives of ordinary people — men, women and children — figure as 'real' history? Can children understand that the actions and decisions of ordinary people such as themselves are the engines that drive the wagons of history as much as the doings of more 'glamorous' individuals and powerful groups? Are connections being made that can affirm the cultural identities of children from all the groups in contemporary Britain? Learning history is also one way of gaining a sense of the future and of the roles we can play to shape it. Children can come to grasp that we are always in the process of 'making history'. Our present was our forebears' 'future', for which they too had hopes, concerns and plans. They can start to comprehend 'causes and consequences' in the widest sense, if they can be taught in a way that enables them to perceive that actions generally arise from values and choices.

Invaders, Settlers and Native Peoples

The following activities explore some key issues of human rights and justice, raised when one group invades or takes over another's country or territory. While the first focuses upon what happened between the Spaniards under Colum-

bus and the Tainos people (*Explorations and Encounters*), the format can be applied to any episode in the History Study units in which one group has invaded the territory of another (eg. *Invaders* and *Settlers*; exploration and empire during *Tudor and Stuart times*; *Ships and seafarers*; episodes of invasion and conquest in non-European societies, *Supplementary Unit C*).

☆ *The Greedy Guest*

Purpose

- To give the children an opportunity to explore some of the moral dimensions of conquest

- To provide a meaningful context in which to learn some of the facts of the historic episode

- To use an interactive, cooperative activity to develop empathy.

Preparation

Write out the following two sets of statements on large cards or on the board, so that they can be visible to everyone taking part. Do not show the 'B' statements until you have completed your discussion of the 'A' ones.

Set A:

1. A visitor arrives in your home

2. You give this visitor lots of nice food and drink

3. The visitor sees some roses in your neighbour's garden

4. The visitor asks you for these roses

5. You ask your neighbours if you can have some roses and they give you some for your visitor

6. In the middle of the night you see your guest digging up your neighbour's rose bushes.......

Set B:

1. Columbus and his men arrive

2. The people give the Spaniards food, fresh water and shelter

3. Columbus sees some people wearing gold jewellery

4. Columbus asks for some gold

5. The people give Columbus some gold

6. He and his men then demand more and force the people to get it

7. Anyone refusing has a limb chopped off...

Procedure

- In a preliminary discussion share some ideas about what the children would do if a visitor from another country came to their house as a guest. How would they look after them? How would they expect their guest to behave? A follow-up to illustrate this situation and the next could include some work in drama or art.

- Display and discuss the sentences in Set A with the whole class. Working in pairs or small groups, the children complete the scenario by writing, taping or drawing 'what happened next'. The groups or pairs then share stories in turns with the others. You can also explore issues of conflict resolution through this activity.

- Display the statements of Set B to show the children what happened when Columbus came to the Caribbean. How does this compare with what they thought was appropriate behaviour for guests and hosts?

This activity is taken from *The Great Wave 1492-1992*, an activity pack for KS2 about encounter and resistance. It was written and published jointly by education workers from CAFOD, Christian Aid, Oxfam and Save the Children, 1992.

☆ *Invaders and Settled Peoples*

Role-play and drama are also powerful learning tools for studying these themes.

Scenario one

- Make a square on the floor out of several sheets of newspaper. A group of children must work together to stay standing on this, their 'land'. You remove pieces of paper a bit at a time, explaining that you are doing this for the sake of progress. The group continue to try to stand on this diminishing space until it becomes impossible.

- Alternatively, you can use either paper or a mat. Another group tries to pull the paper or mat out from under those standing on it (with the basic rule of no violence on either side!).

- Discussion can focus on the feelings the students experienced either 'defending' the land or 'conquering' it. The first option has the added dimension of power and powerlessness, as you are clearly an authority they couldn't fight back against. The children who did not take part should be invited to share their opinions as well; what would they have done in the same situation?

Scenario two

- Demonstrating graphically the destruction of indigenous peoples can help children understand the impact of invaders, whether the Spaniards, or the British in Australia, or other European nations in North and South America. Working in a clear open space, the children stand well apart with their eyes shut. Tell them to sit down silently if they feel a touch on the shoulder. Either you or another child should move through the group touching four out of five of the children (only a fifth should be left standing). This represents the devastating depopulation of aboriginal peoples.

Those left standing can express their feelings at seeing their family, friends and neighbours killed.

Assessment opportunities: AT1, AT2

☆ *The Thoughtful Timetraveller*

In this activity, BENIN is used as an examplar case study. The interactive process and the use of artefacts and other evidence can be applied to other Study Units. This is an extended activity that can take place in several stages or in one go.

Purpose

- To introduce children to a range of historical concepts such as chronology and time, interpretation of primary and secondary sources, similarities and differences between past and present

- To develop critical thinking about handling evidence

- To introduce them to Benin as a place in West Africa and to snap-shots of certain features of life in Benin in the 16th century AD.

Preparation

- Copies of the Time Traveller computer console (or use a computer)

- Sets of visual evidence (e.g. appropriate artefacts such as cloth and pottery; carvings, maps, books etc. You will find some useful suggestions about using artefacts on pp.90-92.)

Procedure

Explain to the children that they will begin to find out about a place called Benin by 'visiting' it in a Time Travel Machine. They will need to programme the computer which controls this machine.

Stage One

Before going on a trip through time, it is important to discuss some of the practical and moral implications. This helps develop a historical imagination and the sense that all peoples and places are *not* alike, although they are similar in many ways. You can hold a general discussion, compile a brainstorm list or ask small groups to come up with three problems each. Some points to consider are:

- Will we be able to speak the language and make ourselves understood? (NB. even if we speak the language used there now, language changes through time; words change their meaning.)

- Will our sudden appearance alarm the people of that time? Why?

  — clothes
  — hairstyles
  — speech
  — belongings (eg. pens, watches)

- We might introduce germs/viruses for which they have no defences. We might encounter illnesses unknown to us. We might not understand what we see. We might be:

  — puzzled
  — angry
  — afraid
  — confused

So might they.

- We might be in danger and need to get away fast.

- What will happen if we interfere with these people? If we stop something happening, what could be the consequences centuries later?

Discuss some possible 'solutions'.

Stage Two

- Programme the time machine by marking and colouring the 'Time Sensor' appropriately. Have the children mark on the timeline the point to which they want to return (now) and where they want to get to (in this case, 1542). Fill in the other boxes as appropriate.

- When 'programming' is complete, ask them to close their eyes, explaining that time travel is very fast and makes you dizzy. Then they can visualise your descriptions and enter imaginatively into the activity. You can also ask them which way the clock is going to be moving!

All hands on the Start button,
Count-down... Press...
[Talk them back.]
The machine moves slowly at first... back to this morning... breakfast time, people going to school and work, traffic jams... getting dark... last night... tea time yesterday... what are they eating, watching on TV, playing...
Then a bigger jump... a week ago, a month ago...
Then twenty or more years ago... if we had time we could find their mums and dads — how old would they be?
Then very, very fast... the clock is spinning... light, dark, light, dark...
Slowing down...
Press STOP, open eyes. We're there...
Benin, 1542 (or where and whenever).

Stage Three

All the groups have three tasks: to go out and 'explore', to gather information and to look, observe, try to interpret and make sense of things.

Each group is sent to a different table: these are the SCENES of life they are seeing. They find visual evidence such as objects, representing people's lives, and source materials, representing people talking to us. They have ten or fifteen minutes to look, talk, think and note down some questions. They will also decide what kind of report to bring back to our own time. They may want to photograph or sketch the 'evidence'.

Assemble and reverse the process of time travel.

Don't get back too late... or early... you might be back before you've started, whilst they're still doing something else!

Discussion

- What have they found out about Benin?

- What questions have they got?

- They can begin to map out what they need to know and how to find it out.

- How can they check the accuracy of the conclusions they drew from the evidence they handled?

Concluding comments

The groups could have been given some, but not much, information on key areas to work on, to arouse interest and curiosity.

eg.

the Oba	a European traveller's
Benin City	descriptions
a village	examples of
a house	bronzes or
a market	ivories etc.

Assessment opportunities

This activity will be enabling children to think about **AT3**; about sources, whether they're helpful (or not), interpreting them, hypothesising, testing ideas, reporting.

Differentiation can be remarked by observing how the children handled the artefacts. Some may only be able to cope with one item, others several, some with different **types** of sources.

This comes from *Fitting it all together: Topic work and the Primary Curriculum,* Sheffield City Council Education Department 1992. Activity devised by Di Durie and Mike Morton-Thorpe.

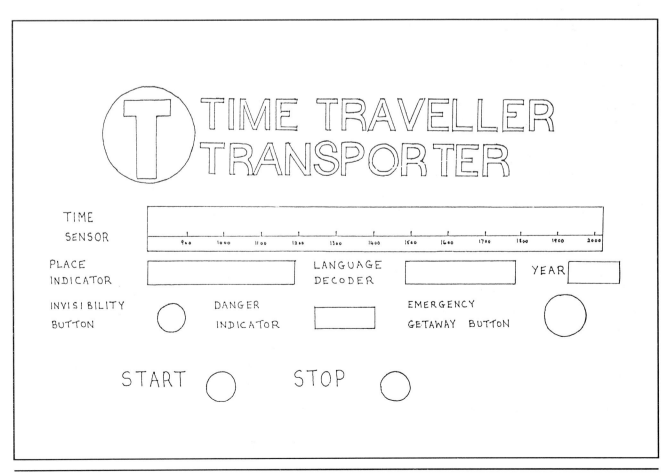

☆ *The Flood*

Purpose

- To provide an opportunity for children to assess their own personal values

- To give them an insight into other people's values and priorities

- To create a meaningful context for children to investigate living conditions in periods contained in the CSUs (1, 2, 3, 4) and the Supplementary Units

Preparation

Make sure all the children can see a copy of the following list:

1. a photo of your favourite relative (*or pop/sporting star if you think that would work better with your class*)

2. something you've been working on for a while, like a model or drawing or jigsaw or sewing

3. the latest computer game

4. a CD player/tape recorder

5. some CDs/tapes

6. your favourite jumper

7. a toy you've borrowed from a friend

8. a TV

9. a watch

10. your parents' favourite ornament

11. some jewellery

12. a valuable carpet

13. your new trainers

14. your pet

15. a religious book/object of importance to your family

Procedure

Stage one: After going over the list with the class, ask each child to write down the five things they would save in a flood. They can only have five minutes in which to make their decisions.

Stage two: Form the children into groups of five and give them fifteen minutes (at most you can set a shorter limit.) to agree a common list of five items they all agree to save.

Stage three: Each child chooses one item on their group's list and explains to the class why they had decided this was an important thing to save. Help them keep this very brief, taking at most a minute each.

Variation

The class can generate its own list by brainstorming all the objects found in their living room or bedrooms. *It is important to ensure that some personal items are included as well as 'gadgets' and furniture.* Ask them to decide individually what they would save in a sudden flash flood. Then proceed as above.

Discussion

The children can compare the kinds of choices the groups made. The group process itself is very important to debrief: did the personal nature of the choices affect the group decisions? Was it hard to arrive at consensus? Did they share common values, wanting to save the same kinds of things? What would life be like without some of the items on the list?

Extension

Discuss either of the lists used in the flood exercise and decide which of these items could be found in the home of a child of their age, living in the period you are studying. They could also try to guess what would have been saved in a flood. It is important to discuss the fact that values are formed both by personal preferences and by generally accepted cultural or religious beliefs. Thus people in the past might not have identical values although we can imagine certain common human needs and wants.

Alternatively, the students can compile a list for the past without referring to the one in the flood exercise and then compare it afterwards to those items.

Assessment opportunities: AT1

Mathematics

Mathematics develops vital skills which enable children to understand the everyday working of the world at both personal and global levels. In the classroom it can help re-enforce some of the issues world studies addresses: for example, the development of thinking skills, and, in particular, problem solving, both in groups and individually.

Multicultural understanding and equal opportunities can also be enhanced. Looking at the different number systems developed in different places and times can help children better understand the concept of basic human needs and achievements. This is as important for children in all-white schools as in schools with a culturally diverse intake.

Maths offers great potential to create an equal opportunities classroom. Equal access to mathematical experiences, including IT, can be given to all, irrespective of first language, gender, race, or special needs of a physical or educational nature. Children with a first language other than English can engage in mathematical processes on an equal footing. Activities can be structured to help all children attain their maximum potential. Maths displays can be labelled in all the languages of the school. Keeping recent research in mind, activities that appeal to both girls and boys can be planned consciously. Resources you use are also powerful contributions to modelling equal opportunities. They should include images of different cultural backgrounds and life-styles, and positive and confident images of people who are often portrayed in a subordinate way (ie. women, girls, disabled and black people generally).

☆ A Helping Hand

(A) Purpose

- For children to engage in a number of mathematical activities involving body shape.

- For children to gain deeper understanding of the concept of *similarity and difference* and the attitudes of *curiosity, dignity and empathy.*

Preparation

Paper as required.

Procedure

Using their hands as the basic unit, the children can do a number of measuring and calculating exercises. A few examples are:

a. Trace around one another's hands (left and right) on squared paper and cut out the outlines. Compare the area both by counting squares and by comparing the cut-out shapes.

b. The shapes can be used to investigate symmetry.

c. Survey the incidence of right and left-handedness. The children can try a range of activities (eg. writing, eating, brushing teeth, catching and throwing a ball) to determine if they really favour one side. This can be recorded in Venn diagrams. Survey other classes and the children's families: does 'handedness' run in families?

d. The children can investigate in groups how many different ways they can use their hands as 'counting machines'.

e. Explore pattern by designing hand-painting patterns based on the symmetrical design of Hindu and Sikh Mendhi patterns.

Discussion

These activities can be starting points for discussion about the similarities and differences between the children themselves, and all people more generally. Looking at the many counting systems based on hands which have been developed around the world both humanises mathematics and provides an opportunity to see what other cultures have developed. (*The Story of Mathematics,* A Ross, A & C Black 1984 is a valuable resource.) You can clearly follow your survey of right and left handedness with discussion about discrimination and prejudice based on physical discrimination.

Assessment Opportunities AT1, AT2, AT3, AT4, AT5

(B) Purpose

- For children to use prediction and probability

- To provide an opportunity to explore trust as well as decision-making.

Preparation

Paper and pencils for 'scoring'. A copy of the scoresheet.

Procedure

Two children sit facing each other with their hands under the table. A third child acts as umpire. On the signal of 'one, two, three, *now!*' both children place their right hand above the table as either a closed fist or open palm. This

IF	STUDENT A	STUDENT B
✋🖐 (two fists)	1	1
🖐🖐 (two palms)	2	2
✋🖐 (fist and palm)	FIST 4 AND PALM 0	

is repeated five times, scoring each round in the following way.

It is helpful to avoid words like 'win' and 'lose' although the children may well use them!

Extension

This can be done in pairs or small groups. The 'strategy' for each round can be decided collectively, with one representative from each group putting out their hand.

Classroom experience has shown different gender behaviours, with girls being more prepared to chance their palms. Therefore a variety of groupings: girls and girls; boys and boys; mixed pairs; girl pairs and boy pairs, might provide a range of outcomes which can lead to fruitful discussion.

Discussion

Was the activity seen as a contest to be won or as a problem to be solved in cooperation with the other person? While 'two palms' is clearly the best outcome, it requires trust in the other person. Did the groups generally agree on their strategy? Were some children more willing to take risks and opt for the trust choice?

The activity illustrates some fundamental dilemmas which even young children can grasp.

Assessment opportunities: AT1, AT2, AT5

This activity is drawn from *Learning for Change*, R. Richardson, World Studies Trust 1979. Both this and the 'Market Game' have been adapted to National Curriculum Maths by Ann Livesey at Baguley Hall Primary School, Manchester.

Children from Baguley Hall Primary School, Wythenshawe, Manchester.

☆ Making, Buying and Selling: the Market Game

Purpose

- To provide an opportunity for children to explore some basic economic concepts as well as concepts such as justice/injustice and interdependence

- To create a meaningful context for a variety of mathematical activities

- To encourage collaborative and cooperative group-work.

Preparation

Resources: pencils, white paper, coloured sticky paper, scissors, units of paper currency, four different templates made of card (enough for each group to have a set).

- Templates: a car, a TV set, a TV screen, a star smaller than an A4 sheet. The car should be roughly twice the area of the template for the TV set.

- A copy of the buying list, the selling list and the rules for each group. These can also be written up large and prominently displayed.

Procedure

- Divide the children into groups of four to five. Appoint two or three children to be the suppliers and buyers in the Market Place. You may wish to do this yourself or involve another adult or older children.

- Give each group thirty units of currency, a buying list, a selling list, a set of rules and discuss these carefully with them.

Buying List		Selling List	
Templates	4 units	TV white	1 unit
Scissors	3 units	TV white with	
Pencils	3 units	Coloured screen	2 units
Coloured paper	2 units	White car	3 units
White paper	1 unit	White car with coloured star on bonnet	4 units

Rules

i. Five minutes discussion time in the group

ii. Twenty five minutes buying, making and selling. You can only buy or sell in the market place (you can reduce or extend this time to suit your class).

iii. The winning team is the one with the most 'wealth' — this will be worked out from the prices above.

iv. All supplies must be bought from the market place.

The children then buy their supplies and make and sell their goods. At the end of the playing period, have each group report how much wealth they have and how many (if any) unsold goods. You can decide whether or not to take these into account and whether to subtract them from the total earned.

Variations

Once the children are familiar with the procedure, it is important to repeat the 'game' using one or more of the following variations. They can highlight the underlying inequalities in the world market system very effectively and also extend the levels of maths work covered. You can combine any number of variations.

i. Start with groups of unequal size.

ii. Have groups of unequal size, but weigh the advantage towards the smaller groups. (Some ideas for unequal weighting follow.)

iii. Unequal starts: two groups can buy their raw materials for 4/3/2/1 units; two buy them for 6/5/4/3 units and two groups must pay 10/8/6/4. Thus they each get a different price list in their instructions.

iv. Change the rules and/or values halfway through. Some possibilities are:

a. announce a fall in the price of cars because of over-production;

b. towards the middle of the time, tell the richest two groups secretly that no more cars are needed;

c. change the value of the star: because it is worth more, the sticky paper becomes more expensive;

d. change the price levels differentially; make the raw 'materials' cheaper for the group with most money, more expensive for the poorest, keeping it the same for the others;

e. alter the size required for one or more of the templates, making the old ones obsolete. Give detailed measurements for the increase/decrease in size and 'sell' the rulers and card needed to make them. (This is equivalent to new technology coming out.) The 'buyers' in the market place must be very strict about accurate measurements. This 'new technology' can be relatively expensive and you can charge everyone the same amount or load the price in favour of the richest groups.

f. get the groups to produce 3D objects.

g. restrict the number of tools (eg. pencils, scissors, rulers) so that groups have to trade with each other to buy or 'hire' them.

Discussion

Even the basic game will produce winners and losers, and it is important that the children both express their feeling and analyse some of the 'causes'. Discussion can focus on the experience of the group process (how well they felt the group got on with the tasks required; what strategies they think they used etc.); it should also explore their feelings about the experience as a whole. You can follow this up with further work on world trade. The *World Studies 8-13 Handbook* provides examples of the banana and coffee trades. Oxfam and Christian Aid also produce very up-to-date school resources about these issues.

The environmental impact of using raw materials can also be discussed and what we do with 'obsolete' or worn out goods.

Possible Extensions

Recording

The children can keep a tally of how much they spend on their item; of the items made; of the items sold. This information can be presented in a variety of ways, including a database.

Number

Given more unit of currently and higher prices, the children can use harder mental calculations (eg. two digit numbers, fractions etc.)

Practical Tasks

Altering the size of the templates or introducing new items of a specific size (eg. a circular one with a given radius; a rectangular one of a specific area etc.) will involve higher spatial and measurement skills. They can also construct cubes and make more complex stars using compasses.

Assessment Opportunities: AT1, AT2, AT3

This activity has been adapted from *Learning for Change in World Society* (see Bibliography). There are other games which reproduce the global inequalities of distribution of resources. *The Trading Game* published by Christian Aid is the inspiration for the basic market place concept: it is based on teams of unequal sizes with unequal starting resources, which represent the real conditions in the world.

Religious Education

Religious Education and world studies intersect at many points. They ask many of the same questions... Who am I? Why is there injustice and suffering in the world? What is my purpose in life? Their common concerns are personal development, an embracing set of values, empathy with others different from oneself, developing a sense of community and connectedness with the natural world, celebrating its diversity and beauty.

Global education stands for a fundamentally broad, humanistic perspective in which questions of faith and belief in a divine creator are private and individual matters. It is founded on notions of tolerance and respect for difference and also on a deep commitment to justice and equality. World studies learning can be one of the influences that leads young people and adults to choose involvement and action in the world. Therefore both its core beliefs and classroom processes can support the programmes of religious education.

Whilst each locality designs its own programme, every Agreed Syllabus must look widely at the traditions, practices and beliefs of *all* people in this country. It must go beyond basic information about customs and traditions to consider wider aspects of morality.

Attitudes in Religious Education

Certain attitudes are generally encouraged in religious education. These include, for example, curiosity, self-confidence and self-esteem, respect for the views and ways of life of others, open-mindedness, critical ability and consideration for others. [From *Starting Out with the National Curriculum: An introduction to the National Curriculum and Religious Education.* N.C.C. York (1992)]

Yet schools can go beyond this. They can be places where the seeds of spirituality are nurtured, helping to nourish a sense of beauty and awe, an attachment to the natural world and to other people. Seeking this wider connection will contribute to children's development as responsible and caring individuals.

Many of the activities in this book can strengthen the understandings implicit in RE. For example the simpler version of '**Web of Life**' described in the science section can have a powerful impact if you can actually do it

outdoors. It can follow a '**Woodland Walk**' such as the one described in *Making Global Connections* (Hicks and Steiner, eds.) where the children have been 'collecting' smells, sounds, touches and sights in a wooded area. The '**Seed Visualisation**' will also help sensitise children to the world around them. Similarly, the affirmation exercises, name games and portrait/silhouettes build up community, self-esteem and mutual respect. Values and beliefs of other cultures can be followed up in the history activities and in the Native American totem work.

The activities below are not about multi-faith R.E. as there are many excellent resources to support this. They focus instead on experiences to do with affirmation and valuing others, values clarification and opening the spirit to the wider world.

Opportunities for assessment

RE can create a clearing in the curriculum where judicious observation and listening can reveal children's moral development and their deepening awareness of the world around them. The comments they make and the questions they ask can show if insight and sensitivity to others and themselves are increasing. These developments occur in leaps and bounds, rather than in some linear model of steady progression. RE is an ideal opportunity for affective experiences that release the child's deeper sensibilities.

Empathy with others is a quality that can be developed through stories and experiences in RE. As they develop, children can begin to understand that it is possible to imagine what another person might feel in a situation. One goal of RE (and History and Drama) is to lead children to that understanding whilst at the same time encouraging each child to value and trust their own personal responses. You can see evidence of growth by observing children at work and play and attending to their conversations and written work.

Pupil's Spiritual and Moral Development: Guidance

Observation of lessons and other aspects of the school's work should enable inspectors to judge:

- whether the quality of relationships is such that pupils feel free to express and explore their views openly and honestly, and are willing to listen to opinions which they may not share;

- whether pupils are developing their own personal values and are learning to appreciate the beliefs and values of others;

- whether there is an ethos which values imagination, inspiration and contemplation, and encourages pupils to ask questions about meaning and purpose;

- whether religious education provides a necessary context and vocabulary for spiritual and moral development.
  [*Inspectors' Handbook* (DFE 1992)]

☆ *Life's Journey*

Purpose

- To help children recognise their own and other people's positive qualities.

- To introduce the concept, common to many religions of 'life as a journey' .

Preparation

None

Procedure

- Sit in a circle

- Discuss what kinds of skills and qualities would be useful if you were setting out on a big adventure (eg. being brave, riding a bike; etc.). You can elaborate on the 'life as a journey' theme as appropriate to your class.

- Ask each child to think about something *they're* good at or some quality they have.

- Starting with yourself, each person makes this statement: 'In the suitcase for this journey I will put...' ('being patient', 'being a good friend','helping people'). The purpose is to acknowledge some personal strength or ability.

☆ *Choosing and Valuing*

Purpose

- To help children articulate their values

- To provide an opportunity for them to become aware of the similarities and differences between themselves and others.

- To illustrate the ways in which unequal wealth can affect the quality of life.

Preparation

Resources: One copy per child of the list of 'values'. Use the one following or devise your own with the children. For younger children you might want to use more easily recognisable images (eg. a house, an aeroplane, money etc.).

Paper money and one pair of dice for each group of four.

Procedure

Stage One

After reading over and discussing the list with the whole class, ask each child to put a tick next to the FIVE items that are most important to them and to cross out the FIVE that matter least to them. If you're using a shorter list, reduce this number so that there are always a few choices 'spare'.

- Children join in pairs and tell each other their choices, explaining their reasons if they can. They can change their minds if they wish and make different choices at this point.

- In groups of three pairs, children decide on a list of eight items they all agree on. They record this with tally marks on an unmarked 'values' sheet.

- Collect these in for future reference.

- You can end the values exercise at this point and discuss in a circle the children's choices and their reasons. The structured format of the 'Magic Microphone' will give each child an opportunity to explain what matters most to them.

Stage Two

This can follow immediately or be postponed to another day, adapting the basic procedure as you judge best.

Preparation

Collate the different groups' values sheets onto one large sheet , ranking the choices from most to least 'popular'. Assign a 'price' to each.

Procedure

Give each child play money amounting to £100. Joining in groups of four, the children roll dice once each to earn more money. Each dot is equivalent to £10 and a seven or more earns an extra roll (this is like getting an 'inheritance').

When they have their 'wealth', hold an auction in which the children can buy items from the value sheet. You act as auctioneer and keep a record of the price bid for each and the highest bidder.

The activity ends when the items have all been 'bought'.

Discussion

This stage provides an opportunity for children to move beyond expressing preferences and values. They can recognise that choices can have costs and that not everyone has equal means to get what they want. They can look at the impact of unequal amounts of money on individuals' ability to attain their goals.

- Do the financial resources you start with affect your chances to learn or train for the skills you need for a career?

- Do all children in our country have the same opportunities? What about other countries and their peoples?

It is also essential to air the feelings they had during the auction.

List of Values

1. happy family life

2. great skill at sports

3. great skill in art

4. lots of friends

5. no discrimination because of skin colour, sex, physical abilities

6. safe streets

7. chance to go on interesting holidays wherever you want

8. ability to help others

9. lots of money

10. success in school

11. success in your job

12. good looks

13. ability to change the world into a better place

14. chance to have exciting adventures

15. good health

16. musical talent

17.

18.

☆ *Other Stories, Other Lives*

Purpose

- To inform children about lives and beliefs different to their own

- To explore core concepts of justice and fairness

- To develop empathy with ordinary people who are committed to transforming their lives and working in the community.

Preparation

Resources: 'Stories' about people in developing countries of the South. Oxfam and Christian Aid publish regular newsletters with positive images and accounts of people's lives, like the example in Figure 3. 'Here I Am' (CAFOD) is an activity pack for primary schools based on a series of recent case studies. Other Aid Agencies (eg. ActionAid, UNICEF) also produce useful resources. The local or national press tend to focus on 'disasters' and are not informative about positive attainments. Children will be inspired to hear about people who do not give up despite obstacles, difficulties and even danger to their lives.

Procedure

Read or tell the children the story you have chosen.

Discussion

Working in pairs, the children tell their partner something about the story that made them feel good; something that made them feel bad; something they'd do if the story were about them; something they could do now to let others know about the person/people in the story.

Finish in a circle. Each child uses one word to describe the person/people in the story and repeats one of the four statements above.

(This activity is drawn from *Open Minds to Equality*, N. Schniedewind and E. Davidson, 1983)

Figure 3

Oxfam News   Summer 1992

by Neil
MacDonald

VALERIA GARCIA does not think of herself as an environmental activist. In La Bandera, a slum area of Santiago, Chile, where she lives with her husband and children, things green are a long way down her list of priorities. Yet for 11 years Valeria has coordinated a health campaign that would impress environmentalists the world over.

Whole families in Valeria's neighbourhood often live in one-roomed shacks with no sewage disposal or garbage collection. "We don't eat well, we live in bad houses, we don't have water. That's why people get ill. It's not just bad luck that people suffer; there are reasons," she says, angry at what she sees around her and the lack of action by the authorities.

Many of the problems people face in La Bandera are caused by poverty and in Chile that is a direct result of 'live-for-today' economic policies that have mortgaged the country's resources and the lives of its people in the drive for export earnings.

Valeria is a member of a group called Llareta, named after a flower that blooms without water in the desert. Supported by the Oxfam-funded 'Popular Education in Health', Llareta are trying to improve the slums by making people aware of the health risks that surround them. The most recent campaign was to clean up the garbage.

"There were enormous amounts of it, filling up the green space," said Valeria. "We took photos

"So why do I laugh, if there are so many problems? Becasue I like to live, and have hopes for something better."
Valeria Garcia

Slums, often on squatted land without services, are home to increasing numbers of Chile's 86 per cent urban population.

of the garbage piles, with a note of where they were. Then we went to people's houses and showed them the photos asking: 'How can you live like this, in such an unhealthy environment?', and they'd say, 'Oh, where's that?' and we'd say, 'Right there, at the end of your street.' They were living in a garbage dump and had stopped noticing it.

"When we showed people, they started to take notice. We collected signatures and sent them to the Ministry of Health. The mayor moved the garbage. We painted the walls saying, 'Thank you neighbour. Your signature helped to get the garbage moved.' People were really impressed."

Valeria's work has cost her dear. Her husband is unemployed and finding work to support her family has to compete with Llareta and her own ambitions. She wants to go to university, but hardly has time to study.

Valeria believes that a clean healthy environment will not be achieved unless the needs of the people are taken into account by the authorities. "I continue struggling because I believe in a different future. Not for me, but for my children, so they can have milk and butter and meat and eggs. It makes me indignant, it makes me furious to think they could have a future without these things." ✦

Clean streets

From: Oxfam News, Summer 1992

☆ *Earth Visualisation*

Purpose

- To enable children to experience feelings of connection to the Earth and to other people

- To help them develop skills and abilities of relaxed concentration

- To create a shared experience of quiet reflection and inner peace

Preparation

Resources: Visualisation below. Paper, crayons, soft music (optional).

This visualisation, like the 'Seed Visualisation' on p.140, can be done by the children sitting in their seats or lying on the floor. The chief requirements are a relaxed body and mind and stillness. This may well be unusual for many children and you can build up to more sustained visualisations with practice.

Some ways to build up the skills and appropriate atmosphere

- When you read stories aloud, encourage the children to sit with eyes closed in a relaxed position.

- Help the children relax by focussing on their breathing. Count aloud from one to four as they breathe in through their noses and again out through their mouths. Move on to doing this with eyes shut, hands loose in their laps.

To set the scene, you can pin up the quotations on page 136 some days before the visual sation. Alternatively, they can be used later (or not at all) to reinforce the children's own feelings and images. *Don't just do something, sit there* by Mary Stone is an excellent sourcebook of preliminary exercises and visualisations.

Procedure

Once the children are relaxed, read the following slowly. You may want to play some soft background music.

We are going on a journey to see our planet Earth... As you breathe slowly, imagine yourself slowly floating upwards... You move magically through the air, like a feather being blown upwards on a gentle breeze... You are rising over our town... Can you see the buildings, the roads, the parks?... Can you see our school and your home?... What are the colours of the streets and roads?... You look at the patterns they make... As you move higher, you can see that our country is an island... a green island set in a dark grey sea... You are moving even higher... As you float in the

sky, you are passing over all the lands and oceans of the world... You see herds of animals roaming over vast green plains... You see tall mountains white with snow... You see dark green forests and golden brown deserts... You see tall buildings in cities sparkling in the sunlight... You see the grey, green, blue waters of the many oceans and little boats moving slowly on the surface...

You rise higher still... Now you are floating alone above the Earth... It is like a great blue and green marble... Can you see the swirling clouds as they dance across the surface?... Can you hear the noises of the world?... What can you hear?... Remember the sounds for when you return... Imagine that you could pick up and hold planet Earth in your hands... What would it feel like?... How would you take care of it?... Hold in your memory what the earth in your hands felt like...

Long pause.

Now we will come back to our classroom... We move downwards through the gentle clouds... We pass through places where it is dark night and all the world below is asleep... We move on towards the morning... Can you see the animals and people below you starting to wake up?... Now we are coming closer to our own school... Look down at the familiar streets and playground... What colours can you see?... Soon you will be back in your classroom. When we return remember what you felt as you floated above the Earth... Remember what you felt as you held the round world in you hands...

Two minute pause.

Slowly bring yourself back to this room... Notice your quiet still breathing... Slowly open your eyes.

Follow-up

Ideally a creative activity — art, dance — should follow, to help the children express their personal responses.

Later discussion can use the *'Magic Microphone'* technique to debrief what the children 'noticed' and felt during the experience. You can invite their comments about the visualisation and how you read it.

An excellent source for developing spirituality and awareness is *Values and Visions: Spiritual Development and Global Awareness in the Primary School*, G. Lamont, Manchester Development Education Project, 1993). See Bibliography.

Seeing the Earth from afar

The first day or so we all pointed to our countries. The third or fourth day we were pointing to our continents. By the fifth day we were aware of only one earth.

Sultan Bin Salmo al-San, Astronaut

You can't imagine how many borders and boundaries you cross, again and again and again, and you don't even see them... the thing is a whole and it's so beautiful.

Russel Schweikart, Astronaut

*If the Earth
were only a few feet in
diameter, floating a few feet above
a field somewhere, people would come
from everywhere to marvel at it. People would
walk around it, marveling at its big pools of water,
its little pools and the water flowing between the pools.
People would marvel at the bumps on it, and the holes in it,
and they would marvel at the very thin layer of gas surrounding
it and the water suspended in the gas. The people would marvel
at the creatures walking around the surface of the ball, and at the
creatures in the water. The people would declare it as sacred because
it was the only one, and they would protect it so that it would not be
hurt. The ball would be the greatest wonder known, and people
would come to pray to it, to be healed, to gain knowledge,
to know beauty and to wonder how it could be.
People would love it and defend it with their
lives, because they would somehow
know that their lives, their own
roundness, could be nothing
without it. If the Earth
were only a few feet
in diameter.*

Miriam Therese MacGillis,
Genesis Farm, New Jersey

*To see the Earth
as it truly is
small and blue and beautiful
in that eternal silence
where it floats
is to see ourselves
as riders on the Earth
altogether.*

Archibald MacLeish,
American Poet.

Looking at the Earth from afar you realize it is too small for conflict and just big enough for cooperation.

Yuri Gagarin, Cosmonaut

Science

World studies and school science have much in common: the learner is at the centre of the process; work is activity-based, centred on forming and testing hypotheses, enquiry, investigating and questioning 'evidence'. Children can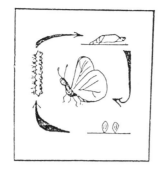
learn to be open-minded to a variety of perspectives, challenging their own assumptions through discussion with others and through using the principles of fair testing. Both promote collaboration and cooperation through group work.

Two powerful concepts underpin understanding in both areas: *Interdependence*, defining how all systems —plant, animal, physical and human, are interconnected and *Fairness* which entails starting from the basis of treating all people and all evidence equally, of not drawing conclusions based on prejudiced opinions.

> Although attitudes are not specified as targets to be assessed in the National Curriculum, this does not imply that they are a feature of pupils' development that can be neglected. Pupils' attitudes affect the willingness of individuals to take part incertain activities, and the way they respond to persons, objects or situations. Willing participation is an important ingredient of effective learning. The following attitudes and personal qualities are important at all stages of science education:
>
> * curiosity
> * respect for evidence
> * willingness to tolerate uncertainty
> * perseverance
> * creativity and inventiveness
> * sensitivity to the living and non-living environment
> * co-operation with others
>
> (*Science in the National Curriculum, Non-statutory Guidelines* 1989)

Opportunities for Equal Opportunities and Global Education

Children can have preconceptions about science that limit their own participation and confidence and which perpetuate stereotypes:

* science is what is done by white men in white coats in special locations like laboratories

* all the great 'breakthroughs', discoveries and inventions have been made by white men, working on their own.

National Curriculum Science is about children learning that 'science' is concerned with understanding the natural processes around them. It is a method of observation and asking questions that anyone can do. They can learn to distinguish between *technological science* which does rely on expensive instruments and specialised environments, and *scientific process* applied to common human situations: an everyday human activity.

Like all human experiences, scientific activities take place in a social, moral, economic and political context. They are neither neutral nor unaffected by the cultural values of those involved. The results of such activities can be benign or destructive and whilst children must be encouraged to pursue truth 'purely', there is, in the end, no such thing as 'pure' science without consequences for life on the planet.

'Global issues' can often be understood to mean 'problems' and, as such, are thought by teachers to be unsuitable for children. It is true that environmental degradation, poverty, injustice and racism are serious concerns. But we can look at this a different way. According to the dictionary, an issue can be 'a question awaiting decision or ripe for action'. The content of science work can easily foster a more positive and optimistic attitude if the materials we use and the examples children see show images of people positively engaged in actions to improve their own lives. This more positive and open-ended perspective can help children gain the conviction that we can change things through our choices and actions.

In the context of the classroom, these considerations can be addressed in ways appropriate to the children and to the positive principles of scientific process.

Incorporating the children's own experiences will bring a range of backgrounds and values into the classroom — whether based on class or culture — touching issues such as food, health, experiences of living overseas and so forth. This can help broaden the students' views and enable them to observe similarities and differences at close range.

Examples and resources can be used to:

* create a multicultural context (e.g. topics such as food, celebrations, ourselves etc.);

* explore common human needs and the variety of ways they are met (topics such as weather, shelter, energy, water);

* illustrate life in other countries (as above);

* raise awareness of global issues and the interconnectedness of life (e.g. environment, interdependence, unequal expectations of life);

- develop empathy and respect for different cultures, beliefs and lifestyles;

- enable the children to learn about and from the ingenuity of people in less technologically based communities

Some useful resources for this approach can be found in *'Why on Earth?' an approach to science with a global dimension at Key Stage 2* (Development Education Centre, 1991); *Science in Primary Schools: the multicultural dimension,* (A. Peacock, 1991) and *Race, Equality and Science Teaching* (S. Thorpe, ed., 1991).

Science activities

The following activities have been chosen to illustrate a few of the meeting points between the science curriculum and world studies. World studies processes are used to trigger scientific thinking and learning; scientific contexts are used to increase understanding of world studies concepts and values.

☆ *Ourselves and others*

Purpose

- To explore the similarities and differences amongst the children in the class in an affirming and positive way

- To give the children experience in posing scientific questions for themselves and setting up fair tests

Preparation

Resources (e.g. paper, crayons, measuring instruments etc.) as required by the children's questions.

Procedure

- Working in small groups, ask the children what they could do to find out how many ways the people in the class are alike. Encourage the groups to make as many suggestions as they can.

- Compile a list of their suggestions. *It is better not to discuss the children's actual common characteristics until they have worked on the first question, so that what they decide to look for is not influenced or predetermined.*

All groups can work through all the suggested procedures or each group can concentrate on one. Display the results in whatever forms suit the exercises.

Variation

Repeat the activity, but this time generating ways of finding the differences.

Discussion

Themes to do with gender, colour, size, shape and disability are bound to surface and can be dealt with through sensitive discussion. Children can discuss what importance they themselves attach to physical differences and what importance they think should be attached. (It would be interesting to see whether they go beyond physical characteristics in their investigation).

Assessment opportunities: AT1, AT2

Left: (From: Brown et al (1990) *Spanner in the Works*, Trentham Books).

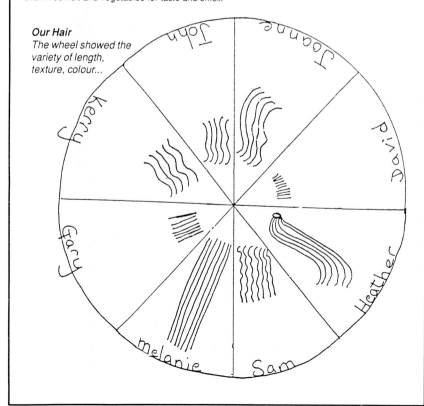

MYSELF

LOOKING AT SIMILARITIES AND DIFFERENCE

The children, aged three and four years, have been looking at themselves and other children, making comparisons and looking at differences and similarities.

They started off by looking in mirrors and making drawings of themselves. They examined eye and hair colours, height, size of hands and feet, gender, different types of families, different areas they lived in.

They examined the senses and discovered more similarities. They paid particular attention to smell, touch and taste.

They compared their drawings, paintings, computer work, woodwork and pottery. Blindfolded, they handled specimens of stones, twigs and leaves, and categorised them as rough or smooth. They examined fruit and vegetables for taste and smell.

Our Hair
The wheel showed the variety of length, texture, colour...

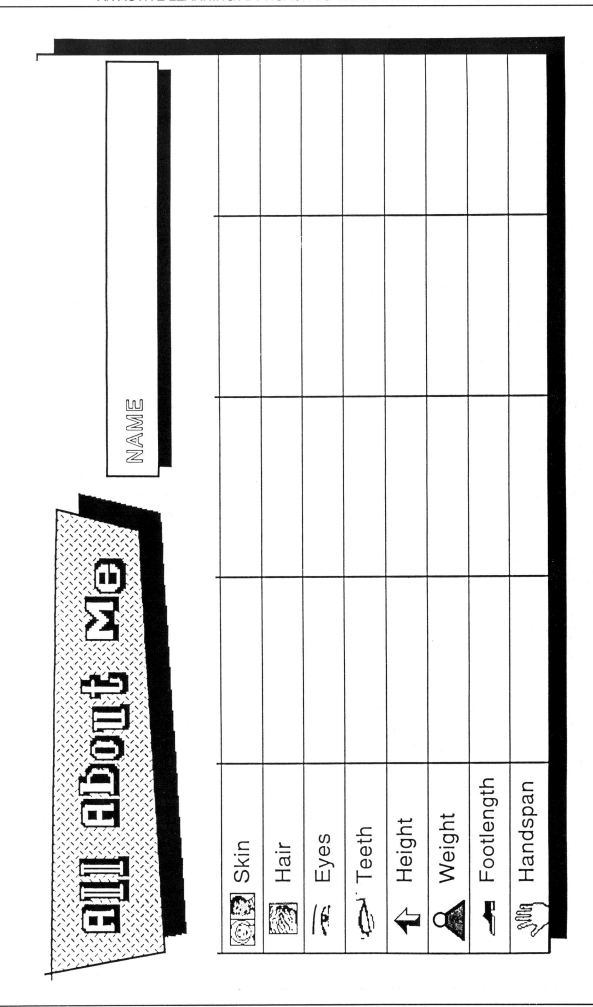

NAME

All About Me

	Skin	Hair	Eyes	Teeth	Height	Weight	Footlength	Handspan

☆ *Seed Visualisation*

Purpose

- To develop empathy, imagination and sensitivity to all living things

- To encourage observation skills

- To address the concepts of similarity/difference; interdependence

- To provide experience of activities associated with AT 1 (Investigation) and AT 2 (Life and Living Processes)

Preparation

- A quiet place where the children can all lie down without touching. Alternatively, they can sit in their chairs, eyes closed, feet firmly on the ground.

- This visualisation or guided fantasy will be most effective if the children have some previous experience of shared silence, either through relaxation exercises, music or drama work. Some simpler exercises include: imagine being clouds, or waves, or rain, or butterflies moving from flower to flower. (See also the *Earth Visualisation* in the RE section where there are further suggestions for 'warm-ups'.)

Procedure

The children lie or sit in a comfortable position. Ask them to close their eyes and to picture in their minds the scenes you are going to describe to them. Read the visualisation clearly and quietly, with frequent pauses to allow the children to create their mental images. It should take about ten minutes.

Discussion

Whilst sharing the visualisations aloud is important, it is a very personal experience and should remain voluntary. They can write about or draw it, but there need not be any tangible outcome.

Some questions to guide the discussion might include: what it felt like to be underground, what it felt like to be growing, what the person who tended them did for them, what they looked like as plant, whether they most enjoyed being a seed or a plant or both, what things they had done to care for their plant in the garden.

Extension

This exercise should be followed up by actually planting seeds and observing them growing. The children can chart and record the process, comparing what they observe with

---

Imagine you are a seed, a beautiful seed....What colour would you like to be?... What shape would you be — round?... oval?... in a thick skin?... What size would you be?...

Now imagine that someone picks you up very gently in their hand... They put you in a special spot in the earth... It's a very soft warm and safe place... Now you are deep in the earth waiting to grow...

The person who loves you comes every day to care for you ... That person gives you water... makes sure that no weeds grow and take your food and light away from you... sometimes you hear soft, kind words.

When you are ready and the time is right, you begin to grow... You feel yourself pushing out of your seed coat, because it's too small for you now... You begin to grow, up out of the warm, dark earth... At first you grow slowly, pushing through the soft soil... then you grow more quickly...

Finally you begin to push your way up into the sunlight and air... As you grow, you become a very special plant, strong and healthy... What do you look like?... Are you tall?... short?... somewhere in-between?... Do you grow straight up?... Do you bend sideways?... Do you curl around something nearby?... What colours are you?... Do you have leaves?... What size and shape are they?... Is your stem smooth?... Does it have little hairs on it?... Do you have flowers?... Do you have any scent?... Are you close to other plants or do you grow on your own?... Do any animals come near to you? If they do, what are they and what do they do?... Do any people come near to you?...

Now imagine that a beautiful garden has grown up all around you, full of other plants, all different and all beautiful... There's a path running through this garden, and it leads right up to you...

The time has come to step outside your plant and to take a good, long look at it... Keep its picture clearly in your mind... What does your plant need to keep on growing and being special ?... Imagine yourself looking after it, caring for it and giving it all it needs... Now you can walk down the path... it leads straight to this classroom and you know that you can go back to the garden anytime you wish to see your plant and look after it... Now it's time to come back to this room, so follow the path until you are here... When you get here, open your eyes.

pictures in books, other plants in their environment and plants grown for particular purposes, e.g. potatoes, tea. (See also **Know your potato** in the earlier part of this book).

At some later stage, repeat the seed visualisation, amending it as you think appropriate. Feedback can show any development in the children's understanding of the growth process and also in empathy.

The **Seed Visualisation** activity is drawn from *Learning Together* by Susan Fountain, pages 27-28. (See bibliography).

Assessment opportunities: AT1, AT2

☆ *A Web of Life*

Purpose

- To develop empathy, imagination and sensitivity to all living things

- To develop cooperation and communication skills

- To address the concept of interdependence

- To provide experience of activities associated with AT (Investigation) and AT 2 (Life and Living Processes)

Preparation

A large space where the children can easily move about, a species role card for each child and a large ball of string or wool cut approximately into metre lengths. Each child will need the number of lengths indicated on their role card. There are sixteen species so some duplication will be necessary but increase the plant layer first, so that there are always more trees and insects than foxes or owls. There will be only one sun!

Procedure

The children take up position, with the sun in the centre of the room and the trees placed around it. The other children should be spread around the room at equal distances from each other. Starting with the sun, the children hand one end of string to the species they give energy to, reading out the appropriate statement on the card; eg. *I am a caterpillar. I give my energy to small birds, snakes and shrews.* They will receive pieces of string from those to whom they are connected. Each card states the number of pieces of the web each child will collect. The sun alone will not be given any string.(The diagram on page 142 shows the different connections that will be made).

Once the food web is completed, have each child read out her/his card, starting with the sun. When they have finished, allow a few moments of silence. You might want to play some background music that creates a quiet mood.

At this point, you or one of the children representing a forester enter and 'chop' down a tree (not the one connected to the insects). The tree sits down and all those connected to the tree do so as well. Next, those connected to them sit down and so on until the web has been destroyed. A farmer then enters and 'sprays' pesticide on the insects. Those children holding strings connected to the insects are also affected. Finally chop down the remaining tree.

Variation

Create your own web by having the children themselves name the different parts of the ecosystem. Stand in a circle and start by asking them to name a plant that grows in the area. Hand the end of a ball of string or wool to one child who represents that plant. Continue to create your web by asking the children to name the things the plant will need to grow (e.g.. sun, clean air, water, soil etc.). For greatest effect, hand out the string so that a real crisscross web is created. Carry on asking for the other living things that are connected to the first plant (e.g. insects, fungi), then move onto the larger animals and birds. Continue in this way until the web contains a full ecosystem. Break the web as in the exercise above. Natural forces such as fire and wind can also be used, and it is also vital to find a way of showing the impact of human actions on this system. Rather than sitting down, the children can tug on the string connecting them to the affected member of the system.

Discussion

It will be effective to debrief this activity using the structure of the '*Magic Microphone*'. As this is both an affective and informational exercise, the question stems can be a mixture of 'I felt...' and 'I learned...' type statements. In discussing the role of people in destroying the web, it is important that the complexities of the issues are not over-simplified. Can the children suggest any ways to minimise the ecological impact of human behaviour?

Extension

Using the diagram the children can write about the inter-connections. They can also draw their own, based on the web procedure.

This exercise can be linked to scientific investigations by visits to woodland sites and observation of life chains in the school grounds. The different species observed can be named and sorted. They can also consider the impact of pollution (acid rain, litter) on the chain (e.g. PoS AT 2).

The activity can be repeated at another, later stage, amending it as you think appropriate. Feedback can show any development in the children's understanding of the processes involved, in empathy and in critical thinking in relation to issues of environmental damage.

This activity is drawn from *Tomorrow's Woods*, S. Lyle & M. Roberts (See bibliography). Also useful is *Sharing Nature with Children*, J. Cornell, and *Windows to Nature*, M. Masheder.

Assessment opportunities: AT1, AT2

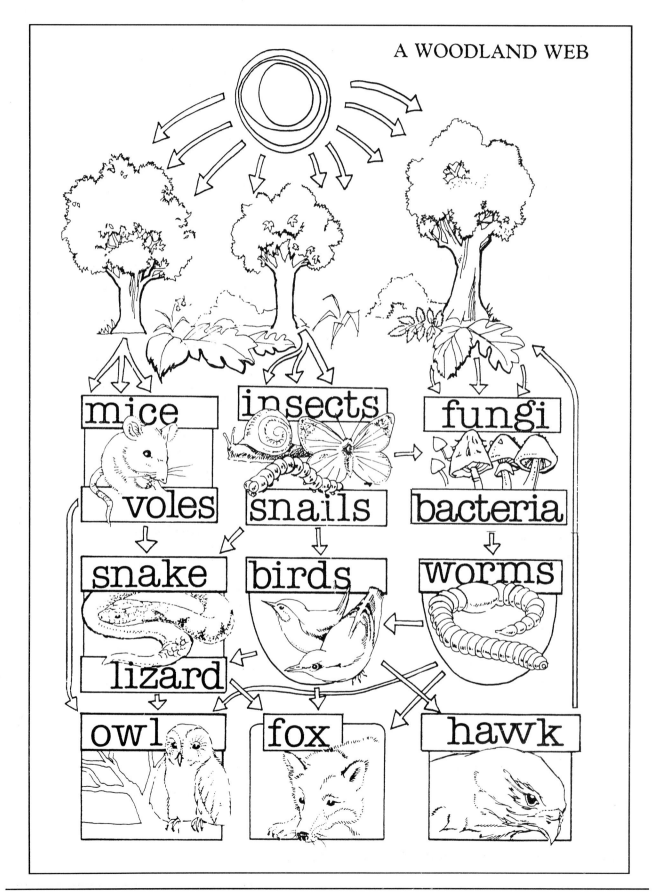

A WOODLAND WEB

Collect 2 pieces of string.

I am a **TREE**.
I get my energy from the sun and the soil.
I give my energy to the mice and voles.

Collect 3 pieces of string.

I am a **SNAKE**.
I get my energy from mice, insects and small birds.
I give my energy to owls and foxes.

Collect 3 pieces of string.

I am a **CATERPILLAR**.
I get my energy from trees.
I give my energy to small birds, snakes and shrews.

Collect 2 pieces of string.

I am a **FOX**.
I get my energy from mice, worms, small birds and lizards.
I give my energy to the fungi and bacteria when I die.

Collect 3 pieces of string.

I am a **SHREW**.
I get my energy from insects worms, and caterpillars.
I give my energy to owls, foxes and snakes.

Collect 3 pieces of string.

I am a **VOLE**.
I get my energy from roots and shoots from trees in woodlands.
I give my energy to owls, foxes and snakes.

Collect 3 pieces of string.

I am the **SUN**.
I am the source of energy for all living things.
I give my energy to the green plants.

Collect 2 pieces of string.

I am an **OWL**.
I get my energy from worms, lizards and mice.
I give my energy to the fungi and bacteria when I die.

Collect 3 pieces of string.

I am a **SMALL BIRD**.
I get my energy from worms, insects and caterpillars.
I give my energy to the fox, snake and sparrowhawk.

Collect 3 pieces of string.

I am a **WOODMOUSE**.
I get my energy from seeds and fruits from trees in the woodland.
I give my energy to owls, foxes and snakes.

Collect 3 pieces of string.

I am a **FUNGUS**.
I get my energy from the wood and leaves and remains of animals.
I give my energy to insects, mice and worms.

Collect 2 pieces of string.

I am a **LIZARD**.
I get my energy from insects, worms and slugs.
I give my energy to foxes and owls.

Collect 1 piece of string.

I am **BACTERIA**.
I get my energy from plants and dead animals.
I give my energy to the soil and the plants and insects within it.

Collect 3 pieces of string.

I am a **TREE**.
I get my energy from the sun and the soil.
I give my energy to worms, caterpillars and insects.

Collect 4 pieces of string.

I am a **WORM**.
I get my energy from the leaves and plant remains. I give my energy to small birds, foxes, owls and lizards.

Collect 4 pieces of string.

I am an **INSECT**.
I get my energy from the leaves and fruits in the woodland.
I give my energy to small birds, shrews, lizards and snakes.

Collect 2 pieces of string.

I am a **SPARROWHAWK**.
I get my energy from small birds.
I give my energy to fungi and bacteria when I die.

Collect 2 pieces of string.

I am a **TREE**.
I get my energy from the sun and soil.
I give my energy to the fungi and bacteria.

From: Lyle and Roberts, *Tomorrow's Woods*, Greenlight Publications.

Technology

This is a fruitful area in which children can exercise individual skill and also interact creatively and cooperatively in collaborative groups. They can also begin to understand how the world around them works. As well as investigating the implications of technological developments, students can come to appreciate the diversity and resourcefulness of different solutions to meeting basic human needs. This corresponds to the world studies perspective on science; children need to appreciate that a technological response to meeting needs does not necessarily entail 'high-tec' machinery.

It is also an area with great potential for equal opportunities. Girls can gain experience and confidence in their abilities in this sphere so that neither they nor boys see it as only a male domain. They can also encounter some of the global dimensions implicit in this field: for example, how a technological response is not confined to the modern, European world; how access to resources has a powerful impact upon the choices and opportunities people have to solve their problems. They can realise that people take part in shaping the processes that affect our lives and change them. The continuous impact of people's actions upon the whole environment of human life is made clearer. The observations made in the science section are also valid for work in and about technology.

On-line with the World

Pupils at the Önnered School in Gothenburg have friends all over the world. This is because the school computer is coupled to CAMPUS, a computer data-base in England, and can make contact with over 7,000 schools in over 40 different countries. CAMPUS has facilities for electronic mail, sending messages, data-search and for participating in computer-conferences. Messages can be sent in English, French or Swedish.

Broadening perspectives and better understanding

We found that pupils obtained a wider perspective on themselves and the world around them. They came in contact with information in meaningful contexts instead of as atomistic 'school knowledge'. Learning and understanding became easier for them.

What is CAMPUS for?

Our pupils get letters each week from other youngsters in their own age-group (10-16). The letters can be about all sorts of things: pupils in New Zealand asked our pupils if they could find out which New Zealand fruits are on sale in local stores in Sweden. This particular letter enabled us to raise questions about climate, agriculture, freight, trade in New Zealand, and the politics of pricing for Swedish and imported goods.

Our pupils also send messages via the computer. They wonder, for example, if other children are troubled by the same things they are. They send questionnaires and a host of other items.

Current affairs issues are also 'discussed' via the computer. Political geography lessons are enriched by 'fresh news' from all over the world, day in and day out. This may be about anything from racism to national conflict to natural disasters.

Pupil interest

I can recommend CAMPUS, or something similar, wholeheartedly for any school. Pupils enjoy working with computers and these also help to make the learning more meaningful for them. Most importantly, however, internationalisation aims are fulfilled as pupils are able to see the perspective that children from other countries have on the world.

Ingrid Sanderoth, Önneredsskolan, Göteborg, Sweden [quoted in Oscarsson (1992)]

☆ *Technology which changed the world*

Purpose

- To give children information about some basic technological processes and the impact these have had.

- To extend their awareness about non-European contributions to human development

Preparation

Make enough copies of pages 146, 147, 148 (words and pictures) for each group of five to have a set. Cut them into cards. You can enlarge the text on page 146.

Give each group their own copy of the instruction sheet or display it on a large sheet.

Explain the terms BC and AD if necessary, so that they can complete the timeline.

Procedure

The children follow the steps on the instruction sheet, first matching the drawings correctly with their write-up and then placing the pairs into chronological order.

Variation

For younger children, you can make simplified cards conveying the information in a very basic way and help them fill in the details at a later time.

> eg. MAGNETIC COMPASS
> WHEN: About 270 A.D.
> WHERE: China
> USE: To help you find your direction by showing you where North, South, West and East are.

Extension

- The children can situate the picture cards on a world map identifying the place where the technology is thought to have originated. Each group can research into one of these technologies in greater detail.

- Place the cards on a timeline chart

- The groups can diamond rank the twelve items, extending the second and fourth row of the diamond to three and the middle row to four. They could also rank the top two, followed by two rows of four, and then the two 'least' important. The criteria could be 'most benefited people'; 'most changed the world'; or criteria chosen by the children themselves.

- Each group can choose the *three* they feel most benefited people or changed the world and explain their choices to the rest of the class. You can make a class list of the 'top ten' in a number of ways:

a) compile a list by writing down each group's three choices, then vote on each one individually;

b) give each choice a point every time it is mentioned by a group, then rank on the basis of most/least mentions.

- Ask the students to imagine life without one of the processes on the list. They could write about this individually or present a sketch in a group.

- Groups can design an 'intelligent machine' system.

Discussion

Which processes were not in any group's top three? Did certain features predominate —eg. machines which are more familiar to the children? Was there any pattern amongst those they could imagine living without?

Using the circle feedback technique, find out what most/least surprised them about the places of origin and the time scale in relation to the present.

Assessment opportunities: AT1

This activity has been adapted from one developed by the Scottish Development Education Centre, Moray House College of Education, Edinburgh.

Instruction Sheet

1. **Spread all the cards with the drawings on them in the middle of the table so that everyone can see them.**

2. **Shuffle all the remaining cards and share them out in your group.**

3. **Each person takes a turn to read a card.**

4. **After a card has been read out, decide as a group which drawing goes with it. Put the card with its matching drawing.**

5. **Once the cards have all been matched, put in them in order to show when each one was developed. Start with the earliest and end with the future.**

Magnetic Compass

The compass is an instrument which is used to show direction. The first evidence of a magnetic compass being used is in China about 270 AD. This compass had a magnetic arm which pointed north as long as it could swing freely. This meant that sailors and other travellers could go long distances without getting lost.

Printing

Stamps and seals which left marks on wet clay had been used in ancient Babylon (Syria, Iran) about 1750 BC, but the first real printing process was invented by the Chinese in about 500 AD. They did this by carving words or pictures onto blocks made of wood, clay or ivory. The carved block was then covered in ink and a piece of paper was pressed against the block. This meant that books could be made quite easily. Before this they had been handwritten, making them very rare and expensive.

Intelligent machines

Some scientists think that the next big breakthrough will be machines that can think for themselves. At present all machines, including the 'robots' that make cars, have to be programmed or given instructions by people. If machines could think for themselves, we might see buses without drivers and aeroplanes without pilots.

Pottery

Pottery making began in different parts of the world at different times. It was probably first done by forming a round base of clay, then adding thin rounds and smoothing them inside and outside. The pot would then be hardened in the sun or baked on an open fire. Pots could be used to store food and water. This helped people survive in the winter, and dry or rainy seasons.

Silicon Chip

The silicon chip was invented in the USA in 1947. Silicon crystals are removed from sand. These are then cut by diamond saws into round chips less than ½ mm thick. Each chip is about the size of your thumb nail. A system of electrical circuits made up of hundreds of tiny on-off switches is printed onto each chip. Each of these switches is the width of a hair. Silicon chips are used to control the electrical supply in many products. Almost all new electronic products like videos, personal stereos and computers use them, making them smaller, cheaper and faster.

Steam Engine

The first practical steam engine was designed by Thomas Newcomen in the UK in 1711 AD. When water boils it expands and changes into steam; this releases energy which can make machinery go. Soon steam engines were being used to power machinery in factories, boats and trains. The introduction of steam meant that quicker and cheaper transport was possible and better machines for factories and mines.

Making Stone Tools

Two and a half million years ago people in East Africa learned how to make stone tools. They chipped a point on a stone, by using another one as a hammer. With tools they were able to make things from bark, hide and reeds, so that it was easier to make clothing and shelter. They could cut up food which made it easier to store and carry. All this made it possible for people to travel more freely, leading eventually to travel north into the colder lands of Europe.

Making Fire

It is not known for certain when people first used fire. The remains have been discovered in China of people who used fire 1.7 million years ago. They used it for heating, cooking and clearing large areas of land. We think there are three different ways people could have learned to use fire: they could have struck a spark from a flintstone, or rubbed two sticks together or kept alight a natural fire which had been started by lightening.

Making Grindstones

The first grindstones discovered were used about 10,000 years ago in the area of the Aegean Sea coast land between Egypt to Turkey. People made flour by rubbing wild grass seeds between two grindstones. Later they improved the process by using wind or water power to make the two stones move. Once people could make food in this way, they no longer had to depend mainly on hunting for their food.

Internal Combustion Engine

The first practical internal combustion engine was built in Belgium in 1860 AD. This kind of engine is small and efficient. Fuel such as coal, gas or petrol is burned inside the metal engine releasing hot gas. The gases expand, forcing parts of the engine (a piston, for example) to move. This produces the power to drive wheels or machinery. This lead to the invention of machines such as cars.

Paper

The first paper was made in China about 90 AD. Before this time people had written, drawn or carved information onto wooden blocks, silk or natural fibres such as papyrus. Paper was first made by soaking plant fibres that were stretched on a flat mould. The water was drained off and the wet fibres pressed flat. When dry the result was a firm, flat sheet of paper.

Wheel

The first evidence we have of wheels being used for transport is about 5000 years ago in the area of present day Iraq. Before that, it was used by potters to improve the making of clay pots. Soon wheels were added to carts. At first they were solid wooden disks but around 2700 BC spoked wheels were introduced. This made it much easier to move large loads and travel longer distances. Before the use of the wheel, people had used sledges to pull heavy objects.

Designs for meeting needs: an equal start for everyone?

Activity from *Technology: Who Needs It?*

Topic Aim and Strands

Aim: To give children experience of the technological process.
Strands: Planning, Making, Evaluating, Presenting.

Activity: Special needs and technology

After working through several structured problem-solving tasks which reinforce the technological process give a pair of children this less structured task.

Tell each pair that a new pupil who is in a wheelchair is joining the school.
Their task is to:

*   walk around the school and playground and list possible difficulties which the new pupil will face.
*   list some possible solutions to these difficulties.
*   choose one of their solutions and show how it would solve the difficulty which the new pupil would otherwise face.

Assessment criteria

*   Do the children follow the process of planning, designing, testing, evaluating, re-designing and re-testing?
*   Does their solution solve the problem?
*   Does their model work?
*   How do the pair feel about their solution to the problem?

How am I going to gather this information?

eg. By observation, by taping the pair's discussion, by discussing with pairs once the task is completed, by asking pairs to keep a written record of what they did, by testing the final model, by asking the class to judge which pair has produced the best solution to the problem, by using a tick sheet of assessment points.

From: Najda et al (1992) *A Global Approach to Environmental Studies in the Scottish Curriculum* (Edinburgh, Scottish DEC).

☆ *Designs for meeting needs: an equal start for everyone?*

Purpose

- To give children a purpose to work collaboratively designing and making a device to repel birds from crops

- To create a situation in which they will experience the impact of unequal distribution of resources and see the effect this can have on opportunity and choice.

Preparation

A variety of construction materials: string, thread or yarn, wire, coat-hangers, dowel rods (or some form of small wooden peg), paper (tissue, construction paper, other kinds), aluminium foil, milk bottle tops, other kinds of bottle tops, toilet paper rolls, toothpicks etc. Also (if available and appropriate) natural objects such as branches and pine cones. Scissors, wire cutters, rulers, crayons, glue, sellotape.

Procedure

- The children work in five equal-sized groups. You can also alter group sizes to create imbalances, although this will intensify the potential frustration of the exercise.

- Set the class the problem of designing a 'bird-scarer': a mobile hanging device that produces a noise to deter birds from a field or garden. They can use only the resources you give them, but need not use them all. Distribute the resources in the following way:

Group 1: one coat hanger (or a small amount of wire), a spool of thread (or fair amount of twine etc.), one A4 sheet of tinfoil, one A4 sheet of coloured paper, 4 toothpicks, a few bottle tops

Group 2: three coat hangers (or some wire), two dowel rods, five A4 sheets of coloured paper, two A4 sheets of tinfoil, assorted colours of yarn, a spool of thread, six toothpicks, some bottle tops

Group 3: three coat hangers (or wire), three dowel rods, seven sheet of coloured paper, three A4 sheets of tinfoil, scissors, glue, two spools of thread, some toothpicks, some bottle tops

Group 4: three coat hangers (or wire), three dowel rods, yarn, thread, lots of different paper (coloured, tinfoil, tissue), sellotape, toothpicks, some bottle tops, crayons, odds and ends e.g. small bells or things capable of making sounds etc., scissors, wirecutters (if necessary)

Group 5: some of everything, but less than Group 4.

Stage one: allow the work to go on for up to 45 minutes, depending, of course, on the age and stage of the class. For younger children reduce both the timespan and the materials. Try to observe group processes and responses. If the students complain about the distribution, your role is to remain matter of fact and encouraging, but you cannot help out.

Stage two: When the allotted time is up, the children can go around and look at each others' products. Next have a group spokesperson describe and explain how each device works and the design decisions they took. You can 'judge' the products, making sure that a group that started with the best resources 'wins'.

Discussion

It is essential to debrief the experience. Using a circle feedback technique you can focus on how the children felt during the exercise, particularly when they saw how other groups were getting on. This is as vital for those with a lot of resources as for those with less. How did they feel about being judged? Was the work hard, easy, frustrating? Do they think that everyone can do equally well even though they don't have the same amount of resources (or money or power)? Other points can be explored such as the impact that unequal resources have on people's potential to improve their lives, both in our society and elsewhere. Discuss why you set up the activity in the way you did.

Assessment opportunities: AT1, AT2, AT3

This activity is based on an idea in *Open Minds to Equality: A Sourcebook of Learning Activities to promote Race, Sex, Class and Age Equity,* Schneidewind and Davidson (1983).

Bibliography

Resources for classroom activities

Ashmore, B. et al *Questioning Tourism: a teaching pack for Key Stages two and three.* Commonwealth Institute, Focus for Change and Oxfam Education.

Association for Science Education and Nature Conservancy Council (1990) *Opening Doors for Science: some aspects of environmental education and science in the National Curriculum for 5-16.* Hatfield.

Barnfield, M. et al (1991) *Why on Earth? An approach to science with a global dimension at Key Stage Two.* Birmingham: Development Education Centre.

Borba M. and C. (1978) *Self-Esteem. A Classroom Affair: Volume l.* California: Jalmar Press.

Borba, M. and C. (1982) *Self-Esteem. A Classroom Affair: Volume 2.* California: Jalmar Press.

Borba, M. (1989) *Esteem-Builders.* California: Jalmar Press.

Brent LEA (1990) *'l can do that'* London: London Borough of Brent.

Brent LEA (1991) *'I can do that two'* London: London Borough of Brent.

Brown, C. Barnfield J. and Stone, M. (1990) *Spanner in the Works: education for racial equality and social justice in white schools.* Stoke-on-Trent: Trentham Books.

Brown, J. and Lucas, V. (1991) *Teacher Relief: an interactive video pack.* London: Charity Projects for Comic Relief.

Catling, S. (1992) *Placing Places.* Geographical Association.

Cooke D. et al. (1985) *Teaching Development Issues. Books 1-7 Perceptions, Colonialism, Food, Health, Work, Population, Aid and Development.* Manchester Development Education Project.

Cornell, J.B. (1984) *Sharing Nature with Children.* Watford: Exley Publications.

Davies, M. (1989) *Get the Picture: developing visual literacy in the infant classroom.* Birmingham: Development Education Centre.

Development Education Centre: *It's Our World Too! A local-global approach to earth education at Key Stages two and three.* Birmingham: Development Education Centre.

De Vesey, C. (1990) *Shared Learning. An active approach to the infant curriculum.* Birmingham: Development Education Centre.

Epstein, D. and Sealey, A. (1990) *Where it Really Matters: developing anti-racist education in predominantly all-white schools.* Birmingham: Development Education Centre.

Fisher, S. and Hicks, D. (1985) *World Studies 8-13. A Teacher's Handbook.* Edinburgh: Oliver and Boyd.

Fountain, S. (1990) *Learning Together. Global Education 4-7.* Stanley Thornes Publishers Ltd. with World Wide Fund for Nature (WWF) and the Centre for Global Education.

Fyson, N. L. (1984) *The Development Puzzle.* London: Hodder and Stoughton with Centre for World Development.

Grieg, S., Pike, G. and Selby, D. (1987) *Earthrights: Education as if the Planet Really Mattered.* World Wide Fund for Nature.

Hicks, D. and Steiner, M. (1989) *Making Global Connections: A World Studies Workbook.* Edinburgh and New York: Oliver and Boyd.

Hicks, D. (1993) *Education for the Future. A practical curriculum guide.* WWF/Southgate.

Huckle, J. et al. () *What We Consume: ten handbooks for schools.* Richmond Press for the WWF.

Kneidler, W.J. (1984) *Creative Conflict Resolution: activities for keeping peace in the classroom.* London: Scot, Foreman.

Lyle, S. and Roberts, M. *Tomorrow's Woods: An active learning pack for 8-13 year olds.* Carmarthen, Wales: Greenlight Publications.

McFarlane, C. (1986) *Hidden Messages? Activities for exploring bias.* Birmingham: Development Education Centre.

McFarlane, C. (1991) *Themework: A Global Perspective in the Primary Curriculum in the 90s.* Birmingham: Development Education Centre

McFarlane, C. and Sinclair, S. (1986) *A Sense of School: an active learning approach to inservice.* Birmingham: Development Education Centre.

Masheder, M. (1986) *Let's cooperate; activities and ideas for parents and teachers of young children.* Peace Education Project.

Masheder, M. (1991) *Windows to Nature.* World Wildlife Fund.

Morgan, W. (1992) *Geography National Curriculum: Planning for Key Stage two.* Sheffield Geographical Association.

Nicholas, F.M. (1988) *Coping with Conflict: A resource book for the middle years.* Cambridge: LDA.

Orlick, T. (1979) *The Cooperative Sports and Games Book.* London: Writers and Readers.

Pike, G. and Selby, D. (1988) *Global Teacher, Global Learner.* London: Hodder and Stoughton.

Prutzman, P., Burger, M.L., Bodenhamer, G. and Stern, L. (1978) *The Friendly Classroom for a Small Planet.* New Jersey: Avery Publishing Group.

Richardson, R. (1977) *Learning for Change in World Society: Reflections, Activities, Resources.* London: World Studies Project.

Schneidewind, N. and Davidson, E. (1983) *Open Minds to Equality. A sourcebook of learning activities to promote race, sex, class and age equality.* New Jersey: Prentice Hall.

Simon, S., Howe, L. and Kirschenbaum, H. (1972) *Values Clarification: A handbook of practical strategies for teachers and students.* New York: Dodd, Mead and Co.

Sylvester, R. (1991) *Start with a Story. Supporting young children's exploration of issues.* Birmingham: Development Education Centre.

Whitaker, P. (1984) *'The Learning Process'. World Studies Journal* vol. 5 no. 2.

Wilkinson, A. (1985) *It's Not Fair! A handbook on world development for youth groups.* Christian Aid.

Photopacks

'A Tale of Two Cities': Photographs and activities about London and Calcutta for Key Stage two. WW Fund and Birmingham DEC (1992).

'Behind the Scenes: Exploring the hidden curriculum. McFarlane, C. Birmingham: Development Education Centre (1988).

'Chembakolli: a village in India'. London: Action Aid (1991).

Doing Things in and about the Home. Stoke-on-Trent: Trentham Books (1985)

'Doorways' Taylor, B., International Year of Shelter for the Homeless and Save the Children (1987)

'Investigating Images. Working with Pictures on an International Theme Manchester: Development Education Project

'Living and Learning in a Tanzanian Village. A Child's Perspective: photopack and activities for the primary classroom. Midwinter, C. and Dodgson, R.; Manchester: Development Education Project (1992).

'New Journeys. Teaching about other places - learning from Kenya and Tanzania.' McFarlane, C. et al.; Birmingham: Development Education Centre (1991).

'Palm grove: Zambia pack'. UNICEF, London 1992

'Photo Opportunities. A Practical Guide to activities using photographs in the primary classroom Oxford: Oxfam Education (1991).

'Pictures of Health in a Changing World Button, J.; London: CWDE (1990).

'What is a Family? Birmingham: DEC (1990).

'Where camels are better than cars' McFarlane, C. et al.; Birmingham: DEC (1993).

"Working Now: exploring gender roles' Birmingham: DEC (1990).

Assessment

Association for Science Education (1990) *Teacher Assessment. Making it work for the primary school.* Association for Science Education.

Balderstone, D. and Lambert, D. (eds.) (1992) *Assessment Matters.* Sheffield: Geographical Association.

Black, H.D. and Dockerell, W.B. (1980) 'Assessment in the Affective Domain: do we, can we, should we?' *British Educational Research Journal* vol. 6, no. 2

Chatwin, R. (1990) 'Can we use Assessment to Improve Multiracial primary schools?' *Multiracial Education Review* Winter 1990-91.

Clemson, D. and W. (1991) *The Really Practical Guide to Primary Assessment.* Stanley Thornes Ltd

Gipps, C. (1990) *Assessment: a teacher's guide to the issues.* London: Hodder and Stoughton

Gronlund, N.E. (1985) *Stating Objectives for Classroom Instruction.* New York: MacMillan

Harvey, J. and Freedman, E. for the S.E.A.C. (1990) *Records of Achievement in Primary Schools.* H.M.S.O.

Horne, S.E. (1980) 'Behavioural Objectives in the Affective Domain: a new model'. *British Educational Research Journal* vol. 6, no. 2.

Krathnohl, D.R., Bloom, B.S. and Masia, B.B. (1964) *Taxonomy of Educational Objectives. The Classification of Educational Goals. Handbook II: Affective Domain.* London: Longmans.

Manchester LEA (1990) *A Practical Manual for Profiling for Children of Primary School Age in Manchester Schools.* Manchester LEA.

Murphy, P. and Moon, B. (eds.) (1989) *Developments in Learning and Assessment.* Oxford University Press.

Ponting, D. (1990) 'Assessment through classroom observation', *The Curriculum Journal* vol. 1, no. 2, September 1990.

School Examinations and Assessment Council (1989) *A Guide to Teacher Assessment: Pack A , Teacher Assessment in the Classroom.* London: Heinemann Educational.

School Examinations and Assessment Council (1989) *A Guide to Teacher Assessment.: Pack B, Teacher Assessment in the School.* London: Heinemann Educational. School Examinations and Assessment Council (1989) *A Guide to Teacher Assessment: Pack C -—A Sourcebook of Teacher Assessment.* London: Heinemann Educational.

School Examinations and Assessment Council (1991) *Teacher Assessment in Practice. Key Stage three.* London: Heinemann Educational.

Teaching, Learning and Social Relationships in Classrooms and Schools

Adelman, C. et al. (1981) *Implementing the Principles of Inquiry/Discovery Teaching: some hypotheses* Ford Teaching Project Unit 3. University of East Anglia.

Alexander, R., Rose, J. and Woodhead, C. (1991) *Curriculum Organisation and Classroom Practice in Primary Schools.* London: DES.

Alexander, R. (1992) *Policy and Practice in Primary Education* London: Routledge.

Buck, M. and Inman, S. (1992) *Whole School Provision for Personal and Social Development* London: Goldsmith's College.

Epstein, D. (1993) *Changing Classroom Cultures: antiracism, politics and schools.* Stoke on Trent: Trentham Books

Fisher, R. (1991) *Teaching Juniors.* Oxford: Basil Blackwell.

Galton, M (1989) *Teaching in the Primary School.* London: David Fulton.

Klein, G. (1993) *Education towards Race Equality.* London: Cassell

Kutnick, P.J. (1988) *Relationships in the Primary School Classroom.* Paul Chapman.

Mortimer, P. et al. (1987) *School Matters: The Junior Years.* Open Books.

Pinder, R. (1987) *Why don't teachers teach like they used to?* Hilary Shipman

Pollard, A. and Tann S. (1987) *Reflective Teaching in the Primary School.* London: Cassell.

Rogers, C. and Kutnick, P. (eds.) (1990) *The Social Psychology of the Primary School.* London: Routledge.

Ross, C. and Ryan, A. (1990) *Can I Stay In Today Miss?: Improving the school playground.* Stoke on Trent: Trentham Books

Rowland, S. (1984) *The Enquiring Classroom. an introduction to children's Learning.* Falmer.

Troyna, B. and Hatcher, R. (1992) *Racism in children's lives: a study of mainly white primary schools.* London: Routledge

Vygotsky, L.S. (1978) *Mind in Society.* Harvard: Harvard University Press.

Wood, D. (1988) *How Children Think and Learn.* Oxford: Basil Blackwell

Cooperative Groupwork

Bennett, N. and Cass, A. (1988) 'The Effects of Group Composition on Group Interactive Processes and Pupil Understanding.' *British Educational Research Journal* vol. 15 no.1

Bennett, N. and Dunne, E. (1992) *Managing classroom groups.* Hemel Hempstead: Simon and Schuster.

Biott, C. (1984) *Getting on without the teacher : Primary school pupils in cooperative groups.* Collaborative Research Paper 1, Sunderland Polytechnic Centre for Education Research and Development

Cowie, H. and Rudduck, H. (1988) *Learning Together — Working Together* Vol.1, *Cooperative Groupwork. an Overview.* Cooperative Groupwork Project University of Sheffield and B.P. Educational Service.

Dunne, E. and Bennett, N. (1990) *Talking and Learning in Groups.* MacMillan.

Education Department of Western Australia (1987) *Small Groupwork in the Classroom.* Language and Learning Project, Curriculum Branch: Education Department of Western Australia.

Galton, M. and Williamson, J. (1992) *Groupwork in the Primary Classroom.* London: Routledge.

Hopper, B. (1987) 'Cooperative Learning: An Overview. *Human relations in Education, issue 7.*

Johnson, D.W. and Johnson, R.T. (1975) *Learning Together and Alone. Cooperation, Competition and individualisation* New Jersey: Prentice Hall.

Lee, V. (ed.) (1990) *Children's Learning in School.* Oxford University Press and Hodder & Stoughton .

Stanford, G. and Stoate, P. (British Edition) (1990) *Developing Effective Classroom Groups.* Bristol: Acora Books.

Unesco (1977) 'Group Techniques in Education'. *Educational Studies and Documents Issue 24.*

Education Theory and Moral Education

Blyth, A. (ed.) (1988) *Informal Primary Education Today.* Falmer.

Bruner, J.S. (1968)*Towards a Theory of instruction.* New York: Norton *(inter alia)*

Donaldson, M. (1978) *Children's Minds.* London: Fontana.

Elliott, J. and Adelman, C. (1982) *The Innovation Process in the Classroom.* Ford Teaching Project

Elliott, J. and Pring, R. (eds.) (1975) *Social Education and Social Understanding .* London: University of London Press.

Gilligan, C. (1982) *In a Different Voice* London: Harvard University Press

Heaslip, P, Hurst, V. and Joseph, J. (eds.) (1991) *First Things First. Educating Your Child, a guide for parents and governors.* Early Years Curriculum Group.

Kohlberg, L. (1981) *Essays on Moral Development. Volume one — the Philosophy of Moral Development.* San Francisco: Harper and Row.

Kohlberg, L (1981) *Essays on Moral Development. Volume two — the Psychology of Moral Development.* San Francisco: Harper and Row.

Krathwohl, D., Bloom, B. and Masia, B. (1964) *Taxonomy of Educational Objectives.* London: Longman.

McPheil, P., Middleton, D. and Ingram, D. (1978) *Moral Education in the Middle Years.* London: Longmans for the Schools Council for Moral Education 8-13 Project.

Moral Education Resource Centre (1982) *Moral Values: Classroom Practice and School Planning.* St Martin's College, Lancaster.

Nodding, N. (1984) *Caring: a feminine approach to Ethics and Moral Education.* Berkeley: University of California Press.

Piaget, J. (1977) *The Moral Judgement of the Child.* London: Penguin.

Pollard, A. (1988) Purposes of Education. *Cambridge Journal of Education* vol. 17 no. 3.

Reardon, B. (1991) 'Feminist Pedagogy and Peace Studies'. Peace Education Programme, Teachers College Columbia.

Rogers, C. (1983) *Freedom to Learn for the 1980s* Columbus: Chas E. Merrill.

Simon, S., Howe, L. and Kirschenbaum , H. (1972) *Values Clarification. A Handbook of Practical Strategies for Teachers and Students.* New York: Dodd, Mead and Co.

Taba, H. (1982) *Curriculum Development, Theory and Practice.* New York: Harcourt, Brace and Walls

Evaluation

Cherryholmes, C. (1966) 'Some Current Research on the Effectiveness of Educational Simulations: Implications for Alternative Strategies' *The American Behavioural Scientist* October 1966.

Davison and Gordon (1978) *Games and Simulations in Action.* Woburn Press.

Feuerstein, M.T. (1990) *Partners in Evaluation.* London: MacMillan.

House, E. (ed.) (1986) *New Directions in Educational Evaluation.* Falmer.

Institute for the Study and Treatment of Delinquency (1989) *Conflict Management the Classroom: a study* Kingston Polytechnic Faculty of Education for the Kingston Friends Workshop Group

Marsden, D. and Oakley, P. (eds.) (1990) *Evaluating Social Development Projects. Development Guidelines 5.* Oxfam.

Morris, M and Twitchen, R. (1990) *Evaluating Flexible Learning. A Users Guide.* NFER. and TVEI .

Parlett, M. and Hamilton, D. (1972) *Evaluation as Illumination.* Edinburgh.

Reason, P. and Rowan, J . (eds.) (1981) *Human Inquiry: A sourcebook of New Paradigm Research.* Chichester: Wiley.

Ruddock, R (1981) *A Consideration of Principles and Methods* Manchester Monographs 18. Manchester University Press.

Sims, D. and Storey, S. (1990) *Development of Performance Indicators and Evaluation Methodologies for Flexible Learning* NFER.

Stenhouse L. and Verma, G. (1981) 'Educational Procedures and Attitudinal Objectives'. *Journal of Curriculum Studies* vol.13

Straughan, R. and Wrigley, J. (eds) (1980) *Values and Evaluation in Education.* London: Harper and Row.

Torney-Purta, J. (ed .) (1986) *Evaluating Global Education: sample instruments for assessing programs, materials and learning.* New York: Global Perspectives in Education Inc.

Torney, Purta, J. (1989) 'Issues of Evaluation' in Hicks, D. and Steiner, M. (eds.) *Making Global Connections. A World Studies Workbook.* Edinburgh: Oliver and Boyd.

Experiential and Active Learning

Boocock, S. and Schild, E.O. (eds.) (1968) *Simulation Games in Learning* Chicago

Brandes, D. and Ginnis, P. (1986) *A Guide to Student-Centred Learning* Oxford: Basil Blackwell.

CNAA/Oxford Centre for Staff Development (1991) *Improving Student Learning* Oxford Polytechnic.

Harwood, D. (1991) *Guidelines for debriefing Active Learning* University of Warwick (unpublished paper).

Jelfs, M (revised by Merritt, S.) (1982) *Manual For Action* , Action Resources Group.

Kolb, D.A. (1984) *Experiential Learning, Experience as the Source of Learning and Development* New Jersey: Prentice Hall.

Taylor, J. and Walford, R. (1972) *Simulation in the Classroom* Penguin.

Thayer, L. (ed) (1973) *Affective Education: Strategies for Experiential Learning* California: University Associates Inc.

Warner Weil, S. and McGill, I . (eds.) (1989) *Making Sense of Experiential Learning.* Oxford University Press and Society for Research into Higher Education.

National Curriculum

Clemson, D. and W. (1991) *The Really Practical Guide to the National Curriculum,* S. Thorne Ltd.

Department for Education *Curriculum Documents: Statutory and non-Statutory Guidance. By subject: Art, English, Geography, History, Maths, Music, Science, Technology*

Manchester LEA (1991) *Implementing the Whole Curriculum. Cross-Curricular Themes, Skills and Dimensions. Six folders.* Manchester LEA.

National Curriculum Council (1992) *Starting Out with the National Curriculum. An Introduction to the National Curriculum and Religious Education* York, NCC.

National Curriculum Council (1989) *Curriculum Guidance One: A Framework for the Primary Curriculum,* York, NCC.

National Curriculum Council (1989) *Curriculum Guidance Three: The Whole Curriculum,* York, NCC.

National Curriculum Council (1989) *Curriculum Guidance Four: Economic and Industrial Understanding,* York, NCC.

National Curriculum (1989) *Curriculum Guidance Five. Health Education* York., NCC.

National Curriculum Council (1989) *Curriculum Guidance Six: Careers Education and Guidance,* York, NCC.

National Curriculum Council (1989) *Curriculum Guidance Seven: Environmental Education* York.

National Curriculum Council (1989) *Curriculum Guidance Eight: Citizenship* York., NCC>

Primary Association (1992) *The National Curriculum Making it Work at Key Stage Two* Derby, PA.

Research in Education

Burgess, R. (1984) *In the Field: an Introduction to Field Research.* London: Allen and Unwin.

Cohen, L. and Mannion, L. (1981) *Research Methods in Education* London: Croom Helm.

Elliott, J. and Adelman, C. (eds.) (1982) *Eliciting Pupils Accounts in the Classroom* University of East Anglia: Ford Teaching Project.

Harding, S. (ed.) (1986) *Feminism and Methodology* Open University Press and Indiana University Press.

Nias, J. (1989) *Primary Teachers Talking. A study of teaching as work.* Routledge.

Walford, G. (ed.) (1991) *Doing Educational Research* Routledge.

Wilson, J., Sugarman, B. and Williams, N. (1968) *Problems of Research in Moral Education* Farmington Trust

Research in Global Education

Dorion, C. (1990) 'Environmental Education in the Primary School Curriculum: an investigation into teachers' perceptions and practice in Herts., Berks. and Avon'. PhD University of Reading.

Greig, S., Pike, G. and Selby, D. (1986) *Global Impact Survey* C.G.E. York/WWF.

Jungkunz, T. (1987) *How School Children View Third World Countries. A Preliminary Investigation into research methodologies* Oxford Development Education Unit.

MacKenzie, A. (1991) Research into the theory and practice of development education in the current social political and economic climate, PhD Research, Faculty of Education, Goldmiths College. London University and WWF.

Mares, C. and Harris, R. (1987) *School Links International: interim report on the evaluation of pupils' attitudes* Schools Research Project, Brighton Polytechnic. Avon County Council and the Tidy Britain Group.

Minnesota Department of Education (1991) *Model Learner Outcomes for International Education,* Minnesota Department of Education.

Price, G. (1984) 'Classroom techniques for demonstrating and assessing change in pupils' attitudes and values; with special reference to development education'. Diploma in Curriculum Development, Oxford Polytechnic.

Steiner, M. (1992) *World Studies 8-13; Evaluating Active Learning,* Manchester Metropolitan University Press

Thomas, O.G. and Chapman, J. (1991) 14 Year Olds' Images of 'Third World' Countries: a comparison of 2 research methodologies, Oxford Development Education Unit.

Unesco (1965) *International Understanding at School: Report on Associated Schools Project in Education for International Understanding and Cooperation.* Paris Unesco

Art

Afro-Caribbean Education Resources Project (1981)*Words and Faces,* London: ACER

Butler, J. (l990) *Art against Apartheid: art and cross- curricular activities for KS2 & KS3* Oxford: Oxfam Education

Mason, R. (1988) *Art Education and Multiculturalism* London: Croom Helm

English Language and Oracy

Baddeley, G. et al. (1991) *Teaching Talking and Learning in Key Stage two* NCC./NOP

Barrs, M . et al. (1990) *Patterns of Learning: the primary language record and the National Curriculum* London: Centre for Language in Primary Education

Brown et al (1984) *Teaching Talk* Cambridge University Press

Centre for Language in Primary Education (1988) *The Primary Language Record* London: I.L.E.A

Corson, D. (1988) *Oral Language across the Curriculum,* Clevedon, Multilingual Matters

Cox, B.(1991) *Cox on Cox: an English curriculum for the 1990s.* London: Hodder and Stoughton

Gorman, T. et al. (1988) *Assessment Matters. No.4 - Language for Learning* SEAC.

MacLure, M. and Hargreaves, M . (1986) *Speaking and Listening: Assessment at Age 11* NFERI/Nelson

Myers, K. (1992) Genderwatch! after the ERA Cambridge, University Press.

Naidoo, B. (1992) *Through Whose Eyes? exploring racism —reader, text, and context.* Stoke on Trent: Trentham Books

National Curriculum Council (1991) *Assessing Talk in Key Stages one and two* NCC and NOP.

Norman,K.(1991) *Teaching Talking and Learning in Key Stages one and two,* NCC and NOP.

Norman, K. (1991) *Teaching Talking and Leaming at Key Stage three* NCC and NOP.

Wray, D. (ed.) (1990) *Teachers Handbooks: Talking and Listening,* Scholastic Publications.

Geography

Bale, J. (1987) *Geography in the Primary School* London: Routledge and Kegan Paul.

Catling, C. (1992) *Placing Places,* Sheffield: the Geographical Association.

Drake, M. (1992) *Development Education and the National Curriculum.* Sheffield: Geographical Association

Wassell-Smith, R. (1990)*Hunger, myths, causes and no easy answers* Pictorial Charts Educational Trust

The Map of the World (1992) London: Pictorial Charts Educational Trust

The Changing Map of Europe (1993) London: Pictorial Charts Educational Trust

Wiegand, P. (1992) *Places in the Primary School* Falmer.

History

Cox, K. and Hughes, P. (1990) *Early Years History: an approach through story* Liverpool: Liverpool Institute of Higher Education.

Geographical Association (1992) *History and Geography through Story* Sheffield: GA.

Shah, S. et al (1992) *Today's History for Tomorrow, Teaching History 4-14. A Development Education Perspective in the National Curriculum ,* Inter agency Committee for Development Education (extensive bibliography).

Humanities

Campbell, J. and Little, V. (eds.) (1989) *Humanities in the Primary School,* Falmer.

Dufour, B. (ed.) (1990) *The New Social Curriculum: A guide to cross-curricular issues,* Cambridge University Press

Mathematics

Ross, A. (1984) *The Story of Mathematics,* A+C Black

Shan, S.J. and Bailey, P. (1991) *Multiple Factors, Classroom mathematics for equality and justice* Stoke-on-Trent: Trentham Books.

Personal and Social Education

Lang, P. (ed.) (1988)*Thinking About... Personal and Social Education in the Primary School* Oxford: Basil Blackwell.

Religious Education

Barratt, M. et al. (1989) *Attainment In R.E.: A handbook for teachers,* Westhill College, the Regional R.E. Centre (Midlands).

CAFOD (1992) *'Here I am ': adding a global dimension to the national R.E. programme* London: CAFOD.

Hammond, J. et al. (1990) *New methods in R.E. Teaching: an experiential approach* Harlow: Oliver and Boyd

Lamont, G. (1993) *Initial Guidelines for Values and Visions* Manchester Development Education Project.

Religious Education Council (1991) *R.E., Attainment and the National Curriculum. Report of the working party of the R E. Council of England and Wales* Religious Education Council.

Rudge, J. (1991) *Assessing, Recording and Reporting RE: a Handbook for Teachers* Westhill College, Regional RE Centre (Midlands).

Stone, M. (1992) *Don't Just Do Something, Sit There! Developing Children's Spiritual Awareness,* Lancaster: St. Martin's College.

Wood, A. & Richardson, R. (1993) *Inside Stories: wisdom and hope for changing worlds* Stoke on Trent: Trentham Books.

Science

Barnfield, M. et al (1991) *Why on Earth? an approach to science with a global dimension at key stage 2,* Birmingham: Development Education Centre.

Peacock, A. (ed.) (1991) *Science in Primary Schools: The multicultural Dimension* London: MacMillan Educational Ltd.

Thorp, S. ed. (1991) *Race, Equality and Science Teaching,* Association for Science Education.

Topic Work

Antonouris, G. and Wilson, J (1989) *Equal Opportunities in Schools. new Dimensions in Topic Work,* London: Cassell

Arnold, R. (ed.) (1991) *Topic Planning and the National Curriculum,* Harlow: Longman

Durie, D. et al (1992)*'Fitting it all together',* Topic Work and the Primary Curriculum Sheffield City Council Education Department

World Studies/Global Education Issues

Carrington, B. and Troyna, B. (eds.) (1988) *Children and Controversial Issues,* Falmer.

CEWC, (1992) *World Dimensions in the National Curriculum* Council for Education in World Citizenship, London

Claire, H. Maybin, J. and Swann, J. (eds). (1993) *Equality Matters: case studies in the primary school.* Clevedon, Multilingual Matters.

Fien, J. (1992) *Overcoming the Fear of Indoctrination in Environmental Education* Perth: Australian Association for Environmental Education Conference.

Education for the Environment: Critical Curriculum Theorising and Environmental Education, (1993) Victoria: Deakin University and Griffith University

Grieg, S. Pike, G. and Selby, D. (1987) *Earthrights,* WWF/Kogan Page

Hampson, T. and Whalen, L. (1991) *Tales of the Heart: affective approaches to global education* New York: Friendship Press.

Lynch, J. (1992) *Education for Citizenship in a Multicultural Society* London: Cassell.

Oscarsson, V. (1992) *Teaching about International Relations* Swedish National School Agency

Oxfam Activities (with some school children) (1992) *A Million Ways to a Fairer World,* London: Puffin.

Richardson, R. (1990) *Daring to be a Teacher* Stoke-on-Trent: Trentham Books.

Runnymede Trust (1993) Equality Assurance in Schools: quality, identity, society. Stoke-on-Trent: Trentham Books.

Starkey, H, (ed.) *The Challenge of Human Rights Education,* London: Cassell.

Stradling, R. Noctor, M. and Baines, B. (1984) *Teaching Controversial Issues,* Edward Arnold.

Wren. B. (1986) *Education for Justice* SCM Press.

General Index

Sources for Development Education Materials

ActionAid, The Old Church House, Church Steps, Frome, Somerset BA11 1PL.

Birmingham Development Education Centre, Gillet Centre, 998 Bristol Road, Selly Oak B29 2LE.

Catholic Action For Overseas Development (Cafod), 2 Romero Close, Stockwell Road, London SW9 9TY.

Christian Aid, PO Box 100, London SE1 7RT.

Manchester Development Education Project, 801 Wilmslow Road, Didsbury, Mancbester.

Oxfam Education, 274 Banbury Road, Oxford OX2 7DZ.

Geographical Association, 343 Fulwood Road, Sheffield S10 3BP.

Save the Children, 17 Grove Lane, London SE5 8RD.

Unicef UK, 55 Lincoln's Inn Fields, London WC2A 3NB.

Worldaware, 1 Catton Street, London WC14 4AB.

Worldaware and **Leeds Development Education Dispatch Unit**, 153 Cardigan Road, Leeds LS6 1 LJ, collate and distribute materials from a wide range of sources.

Most local development education centres stock a range of publications. There are now around 50 Centres: the **National Association of Development Education Centres**, 29-31 Cowpere Street, London EC2A 4AP, will provide details of your nearest Centre.

Activities Index

Index of photocopiable planners, evaluation and work sheets